SEEDS OF A NEW CHURCH

'... Our task is not merely to hoard this precious treasure, as though obsessed with the past, but to give ourselves eagerly and without fear to the task that the present age demands of us – and in so doing we will be faithful to what the church has done in the last twenty centuries. ... Christians and Catholics of apostolic spirit all the world over expect a leap forwards in doctrinal insight and the education of consciences in ever greater fidelity to authentic teaching. But this authentic doctrine has to be studied and expounded in the light of the research methods and the language of modern thought. For the substance of the ancient deposit of faith is one thing, and the way in which it is presented is another.'

From *Gaudet Mater Ecclesia*, Pope John XXIII's opening address to the Second Vatican Council on 11 October 1962.

John O'Brien CSSp

Seeds of a
New Church

the columba press

First edition, 1994, published by
the columba press
93 The Rise, Mount Merrion, Blackrock, Co Dublin

Cover by Bill Bolger
Origination by The Columba Press
Printed in Ireland by
Colour Books Ltd, Dublin

ISBN 1 85607 089 1

Conter

PART THREE: READING THE SIGNS

Introduction

The idea of writing this book grew out of the realisation that, even as the familiar model of church in this country was in serious decline, a new model of church was coming to birth in the lives and creative pastoral initiatives of a significant number of groups. Rather than simply lament the lack of will for serious renewal in the wider church, I thought of trying to affirm what these groups were attempting as well as seeking to theologically focus how the seedbed of a renewed church could be found in their faith and struggle. Of the many groups seeking to bring about renewal in their own way, some twenty-one such groups have contributed directly to this book.

To these contributors, I express my sincere appreciation of their willingness to participate in this project. In a sense, this is their book since it is about the church that is coming into being in what they seek to live out. It is written primarily in a spirit of solidarity with them. It is also written for those actively participating in the life of the church, especially if they are exercising ministry or leadership. For I am quite sure that many of them are grappling with the same issues I am trying to deal with here and perhaps struggling with the implications of the realisation that led me to begin this project in the first place. Lastly, it is written for the growing number of people who, although open to spirituality and the works of reconciliation and justice, feel increasingly distant from what they perceive the church to be. My hope is that in these pages, some of them at least, may see more clearly the fundamental link between their own hopes and searching, and the life of the community of faith inaugurated by the death and resurrection of Jesus.

From a theological point of view, this book is intended to be a kind of practical ecclesiology. It seeks to say not just what the church is, in terms of a set of principles and a list of quotations, but what the church is by seeking to say, 'how we may be the church' in the here and now, in a manner faithful both to 'the trad-

ition' of the apostles and to the struggles and hopes of people in
the real world of to-day. Elsewhere, I have sought to argue that
theology, even with its mystical and transcendent referents and
the necessity of theoretical rigour, is an essentially practical un-
dertaking. Here, I am seeking to illustrate this in relation to the
community of faith called the church.

If some readers find this an anecdotal rather than a systematic theology, I can only reply in part, that at its heart, Christian theology
is always the narrative theology of an event – the event of Jesus.
Ecclesiology too has a narrative structure, because it is concerned
above all, with how the living community of faith can incarnate in
its history the sacred and subversive memory of the event of
Jesus. Needless to say, the picture painted here, while having the
merit of being practical and rooted, will thereby be somewhat
partial and limited. But that in turn, may indicate how the church,
far from being 'a perfect society' fully formed, is always in the
process of self-constitution. Besides, I have no wish to take refuge
in generalities and avoid the socio-political rootedness and implications of all theological reflection. In this way, the book is an invitation to further dialogue and deeper conversation and welcomes constructive criticism and amplification.

The first part of the book attempts to describe why the present
situation of the church in this country, for reasons theological,
pastoral and organisational, simply cannot continue. The second
part contains the contributions of some of the creative pastoral initiatives in which a renewed church is coming into being. Rather
than interpret or comment on them at this stage, I was anxious
that each group would speak its own word. For I believe that this
must be a feature of any model of church adequately expressing
the foundational reality of communion in the Holy Spirit – many
gifts; one Lord! The third part seeks to theologically evaluate the
preceding parts: firstly, by highlighting the ecclesiology, or notion
of church, implicit in them; secondly, by examining the main
theological assumptions of this notion of church; and thirdly, by
seeking to point the way to action to concretise this vision. In this
way, a see-judge-act methodology is being attempted. While intended as a serious theological reflection, a deliberate effort has
been made to avoid being unecessarily academic and technical.

I am grateful to confreres and friends who supported me during
the writing of this book at a time of loss in my own life. From the

beginning, Seán O Boyle was enthusistic about this project. Ciarán Earley and Katherine Sheehan read parts of the early draft and Tom Whelan the whole manuscript. The book has benefited from their comments. The Theologate community at Kimmage Manor was always welcoming and my particular thanks go to Peter Conaty, Jim McDonnell and Paul Leyden.

I can only hope that in the places where this book seems critical of aspects of the church, it is a critique born of love and solidarity. For it has been written out of commitment to the church and in the belief that its purpose is to be the sacred and subversive sign of Christ's presence in the world. In the words of the century's greatest ecclesiologist, the church written about in these pages remains 'Cette Eglise que j'aime'.

PART ONE

Signs of death and signs of life

Decline and death

By almost any reckoning, the familiar form of the church in this country is in a period of decline and may even be dying. When I say 'the church', I am speaking more of its institutional profile than of its spiritual reality, more of its socio-cultural shape than of its evangelical mission and more of its organisational influence than of its mystical permanence. Yet, what has characterised Catholic ecclesiology, or reflection on the church, throughout the ages is precisely the conviction that the community inaugurated by the life, death and resurrection of Jesus is something which portrays and effects its inner mystical and divine reality through being visible, organised and effective in human history and culture. Whether it is Bellarmine's 'as visible as the Republic of Venice' or Vatican II's 'light of the nations', the point is the same: the church is something mystical made concrete. It is this concrete reality, in its present institutional form, which is dying.

This situation has been brought about by a series of massive shifts in human consciousness to which the church, with its structures and discourse still largely rooted in medieval European culture, has great difficulty in responding.The indications of this decline and death are everywhere visible. They are clearly evident in the two areas of life which, whatever about their true and real theological importance, have been long perceived as the two key areas of Christian identity and influence: Mass attendance and sexual morality. All informed observers agree that even the increasingly modest statistics for Mass attendance are highly optimistic. There are now numerous working-class suburbs in Dublin where regular participation in the eucharist is down to little more than 10%. Whether in such situations, or even in the most traditional rural parish, a breakdown of participants in the eucharist by gender, age and occupation – or by the lack of it – makes for disturbing reflection.

In the area of sexual morality the indications are equally clear. For some years – sometimes almost without differentiation – the church, or at the very least its official leadership, has hung its colours on the mast of preventing the legalisation of contraception, divorce and abortion and, in an essentially rearguard action, has secured a series of Pyrrhic victories. Effectively, the battle has been lost in all three areas. However regrettably, it can only be a matter of time before this *de facto* situation is enshrined in legislation.

As a result, for the first time since the foundation of the State, the church will have to come to terms with the fact that the gospel of Jesus Christ forms no significant part of the ideology of the State. Of course, to anyone observing and reflecting on the realities of unemployment, emigration, inequality and ghettoisation, as well as the hypocrisy in public life, long acceptable to and even taken for granted by the powers-that-be in this country, the divergence between gospel and national ideology has long been abundantly clear. The narrowing of social ethics to sexual morality has, regrettably, heretofore prevented the church leadership from grasping this.

The ending of its fairly cosy relationship with the powers of this world points to a new and exciting era in the history of the church in this country. The church can cease from being effectively the spiritual legitimation mechanism for the national ideology – whereby various kinds of exploitation and inequality remain socially acceptable – and assume its original evangelical role in relation to the injustices and materialism of society. It is part of the thesis of this book that this is an opportunity to be welcomed.

Before this kind of sea change is possible in the consciousness and priorities of the church, there has to be a real internalisation of the fact that the old way has changed and cannot be restored. Reflection on diminishing resources, especially in the area of personnel, will be instructive in this regard. There was an abundance of vocations to the ministerial priesthood, the religious life and the missionary movement in the recent past. Clearly, this was linked to socio-historic as much as to religious factors. It would however, be oversimplistic to accept the reading of the school of thought which tries to explain all this away in solely sociological terms, without reference to the deep piety and genuine Christian commitment of a very large section of the population.

The socio-cultural form of this piety was however rooted in a traditional way of life which under the onslaught of market forces in an economy governed by the structures of an advanced form of transnational capitalism, is rapidly disappearing. In the meantime, a piety – or in other words a generally shared expression of faith and devotion – adequate to the complexities of a secularised society and elaborated in such a way as to address the common conscience of the nation, has not yet been developed. Moreover, the great fear is that the officially-appointed leaders in these areas are by age, inclination and training incapable of facilitating such a development.

The end of an era

But even apart from these deeper issues concerning the kind of church life that can adequately communicate the power of the gospel in a secularised society, a cold look at the numbers will make the point. The fact is that vocations in the traditional sense are in rapid decline. This is so even in the case of the diocesan priesthood. Here, it is principally due to the fact that there is an unrepresentatively large number of priests of the previous generation still in active ministry, as well as the return to this country of priests of the same generation previously involved in missionary work overseas, that masks the grave crisis in ministry. In a short few years, a huge proportion of the clergy will reach retirement age. It is an inescapable fact that most of them will not be replaced.

In the case of religious Sisters and Brothers, the landscape is even more bleak. Vocations to the religious life as such, are now down to a trickle. A greater emphasis on individual freedom and opportunity, the emancipation of women, a re-evaluation of and emphasis on the dignity of marriage, a sexual ethic that emphasises personal responsibility, multiple career choice for qualified creative people, the increasingly provisional nature of decisions of whatever kind and the possibility of temporary commitment in a variety of apostolic endeavours, may well make a permanent option for poverty, chastity and obedience seem less and less attractive or important.

Moreover, the inevitable internalisation of the prevailing ethic in a consumerist society hardly promotes the values of dedication and self-sacrifice. In addition to this, however, it was the experience of many young religious that the institutes in which they sought to dedicate themselves fell far short of the creativity and commitment they proposed to their members. Many, in order to remain faithful to the very idealism which brought them to religious life in the first place, left that way of life in order to express that idealism.

Quite clearly, the passing of one way of being the church with the losses that may entail, is not without its positive aspects. In the view of the writer, it will make possible a variety of ministries and responsibilities which, if adequately developed, can only enrich the life of the church and give greater thrust to its transformational task in society. But for the moment, that is looking ahead. We must first accept that the old is passing away. Nowhere is this more evident than in the field of education. Different lobbies in this field have, in recent years, been too busy securing their own rights and interests to give adequate recognition to the truly extraordinary commitment of religious Sisters and Brothers to education and development in this country. In the habitual manner, we will wait until people are gone to give them the recognition they deserve. But the day is coming sooner than many realise. The involvement of religious in education is in its last phase. First was the shift from teaching to administration; now comes the phase of setting up Boards of Management or, in the case of elitist schools, Boards of Governors.

With this will come the passing of a whole tradition. It should however, be recognised that, for some time now, Christian education has been an aspiration rather than a reality. Most Catholic schools simply fitted into the State's view of what the school and the curriculum should be. Increasingly, that view is defined by technological goals defined in function of the economic structures of an advanced capitalist economy, without reference to moral principles, social justice or the spiritual dimension of the human person. Points of tension and conflict, when these arose, concerned control of positions of power, physical plants and institutions, often with little enough regard to the value system being transmitted in them. The hours for Christian doctrine or religion were always pencilled into the timetable, though there could be a huge variation in how seriously they were used. When it came to the real agenda, the values of the market, competitiveness, individual advancement, material success and class distinction were tacitly accepted and solidly reinforced, almost without reference to any gospel-based ethic.

As religious themselves have recognised with increasing clarity, the traditional involvement of the official church in education, while in the beginning strictly necessary and even heroic, became increasingly ambiguous, not only, one must stress, as a result of the secularisation of the school system but, just as importantly, in terms of the refocusing of the vocation of religious themselves to be visibly identified with the oppressed and marginalised of society. This has been most obviously so in the case of the fee-paying schools. Behind the pretence of a 'Catholic ethos', their real priority has been protecting the privileges of class. When, in such institutions, religious are replaced on the Boards of Governors by successful individuals drawn from the world of business and finance, what will prevent the elitism becoming more naked and the exploitation of Catholicism more cynical?

It is true of course, as was continually pointed out, that the parents wanted the religious running the schools. They did, but in most cases, to ensure the career prospects of their children and not at all because of any commitment to the gospel of Jesus or because of any wish that the values of this gospel would be so deeply communicated that their children might make radical options in life. This is now so, even in the case of vocations in the traditional sense. A generation ago, parents prayed that a daughter or a son might become a religious or a priest; nowadays, vocation directors will tell you, that if a young person shows interest in a religious vocation, parents will be often less than sympathetic and will sometimes be quite opposed.

What is true of education is also true of hospitals and social services. Hospitals run by religious will be fewer and the number of religious in them will be fewer. Even when a limited number of professionally trained religious will be available for such positions, the complicated problem of the involvement of religious in private medicine will make many such religious wonder if this is the right place for them to be.

As the health service becomes an increasingly two-tiered edifice, with less ready access to expertise in the lower tier, religious will be increasingly obliged to ask themselves about their role in facilitating consultants in private hospitals, when thereby, the poor have even less access to these consultants' skills. That the majority of these consultants are themselves professed Christians and the products of 'Catholic schools', yet apparently not particularly upset by the glaring differences in health care for different social classes, is itself something that gives rise to some deep questions.

Obviously, lay people have been involved in all these different kinds of works and institutions for a very long time. But theirs has always been an auxiliary, if not to say subservient role. They were expected to contribute, to support and, implicitly at least, to obey. Loyalty was prized far above creativity. In short, they were told they were the church, but on the church's terms. With rare exceptions, lay people were not allowed a significant role in shaping the orientation and priorities of these institutions. In many cases, church authorities were perceived as blocking the emergence of a system enshrining partnership, accountability, purposefulness and self-evaluation. While the church's stated values were those of the kingdom of God, its perceived value system seemed to refer more to control, respectability and a desire to perpetuate the past.

Need for something new

A large number of people today, whether inside or outside the visible church, or just on the margins, have a strongly developed sense of their own dignity and responsibility; they have the experience of professional competence in a wide variety of demanding situations; they are more educated and have replaced the authority of tradition with the authority of their own experience. Their listening extends beyond politeness only to what speaks to their reality in an informed way.

It is of course, also true that there is massive alienation in present-day Ireland as well as widespread mind-control, particularly on the part of the electronic mass media. People are not nearly as free as they imagine themselves to be. Yet, by and large, those who are alienated from the ordinary patterns of life and social intercourse, are also alienated from the church.

The implicit value system communicated by multi-channel television viewing is not that of the kingdom of God. There will be increasingly less and less public affirmation and support for a spiritual world-view and active church membership. It will become increasingly a matter of personal choice and probably of counter-cultural choice. The problem is that personal counter-cultural choice is the one thing that official Christianity in this country has rarely proposed as a value, to the extent that in matters religious, personal choice has, in the recent past, been more associated with abandoning religious practice than in committing oneself more wholeheartedly to it.

What is emerging is a situation that, theologically speaking, calls for re-evangelisation. But too sudden a jump into theological terminology risks clouding the issues and missing the point. The point is that a certain way of being the church is becoming increasingly incapable of communicating with larger and larger numbers of people and seriously risks becoming irrelevant. Moreover, even when it does communicate, it is not always communicating the gospel. The issues, if this is to be addressed, are realism, honest communication and a definable identity.

Realism means accepting that things have changed and changed utterly; accepting that something needs to be allowed to die and something else needs to be allowed to be born. It means taking a good look at the alienation of the unemployed and the working class from an increasingly middle-class church. It means taking a good look at the alienation of reflective women from patriarchal structures that brook no criticism. It means taking a good look at the pain of all those groups of people who, for whatever reason, cannot fit their lives into the officially sanctioned patterns of sexual behaviour. It means looking at how ineffectual organised Christianity is in addressing the scientific and artistic communities. It means reflecting on the yawning gulf there is between the youth pop culture and the experience of boredom in Christian worship. It means taking a long look at the undefined middle group – increasingly middle-class and middle-aged – who continue to participate and asking why they come, what they receive and how are they empowered.

Honest communication means saying to the world who we are and what it is we propose. That in turn, means abandoning the pretence of being some kind of 'perfect society' – a pseudo-theological term used frequently in the recent past to pretend that the church was somehow self-contained and above the ambiguities of history – and joining with our fellow women and men of all persuasions with modesty and purposefulness in the struggles of daily life. This means the church entering the public forum of debate, criticism, communication and advocacy as one participant among many, making its case on the moral authority of its praxis and not on the basis of institutional privilege. The time was when that was an option; the church was influential enough to do so or not do so. Now the option is to communicate and convince on the same basis as everybody else or not to communicate at all.

This in turn, implies the courage to reformulate the gospel in a manner that is faithful to that gospel's own inner truth and yet intelligible to self-directed people in a secularised society. It means the courage to propose that gospel as the basis of a true humanism, risking, on the one hand, rejection and, on the other, having its institutions and customs critiqued and reconstructed in the light of that reformulation of the gospel.

The civil socio-cultural search for a new Irish identity necessarily implies for the church a search for a new expression of Christian

identity. For its task will be to embody itself as a leaven for transformation in a new kind of society. There is not now – and probably never was – any such thing as a Christian society. To be Irish is
not necessarily to be Christian; and to be Christian is not necessarily to be Irish. Once and for all we must part company with the
'here comes everybody' brand of Irish Catholicism. In a society
which values human freedom, one must freely choose to be a
Christian and this follows not only from a theory of human emancipation but from the nature of Christian discipleship itself. If we
want a church come of age, we must accept the consequences, one
of which is that not everybody may want to be part of it.

To try to hold everybody, which seems to be the tacit real agenda
of the church leadership even now, will have disastrous consequences. On the one hand, 'everybody' will simply be an ever-
shrinking middle ground lacking definition, incapable of articulating a transformational pastoral plan and condemned to ineffect-
ually seeking to restore the past as an expression of Christian
identity and witness in the world. On the other hand, such a
church will be incapable of creative interaction with the issues of
contemporary society and will be reduced to being a religious
legitimation of the concerns of the bourgeois individual, as is
already the case in so many mainland European countries.

Malaise in ministry

Because of the expectations of the institution itself, of traditional
believers as well as the expectations internalised in their training
by pastoral agents, this situation of rapid change and disintegration has given rise to a serious malaise and loss of confidence,
especially among the clergy.

This malaise and loss of confidence has its roots partly in the
Tridentine notion of the priesthood, especially as traditionally exercised in this country. In order to counteract what it perceived to
be a Lutheran denial of the priesthood of the presbyterate, Trent
effectively spoke of ministry as if it were restricted to ordained
ministry. As the Irish people emerged from the indignity and
oppression of the Penal Laws and then from the virtual genocide
of the Great Hunger, nearly all the leaders at local level were the
priests. How they fulfilled this role depends on one's point of
view, but, in all likelihood, the detractors are just as far off the
mark as the hagiographers.

What is clear is that they were the leaders and in most cases equal to the task. In a still traditional society composed mostly of poor people, they were educated, part of a well organised network, had clear goals and, most importantly, the vast majority of the people identified with them most of the time. As society became more educated and complex, so did this leadership role. As time passed, such traditional leadership could continue only if one and the same man could be a financial planner, a builder, an educational administrator, a homilist, a liturgist, a spiritual guide, a counsellor, a social worker, an athletics coach and dispenser of charity, all rolled into one. The amazing thing is that so many managed to fill such a role for so long. But as each area of leadership became more specialised and compartmentalised, and as all kinds of women and men became more qualified, clinging to the traditional leadership role was perceived as clinging to power.

Inexorably, priests became involved in a series of contemporaneous power struggles with a wide variety of interest groups; struggles they were bound to lose, given the kind of society which had emerged. With the consequent loss of influence, the moral and spiritual quality of society may well seem to be somewhat diminished in the intermediate term. But, more profoundly, this loss of power gives the church its first opportunity for over a century to rediscover its Christological heart, to identify itself with the oppressed and abandoned of society and to readdress that society, not so much in its own institutional interests, as by the power of the gospel.

In the meantime, there is a sense of diminution and disorientation. The traditional role has become impossible. To the generous and committed – probably the majority – who at great cost simply tried harder, ministry, in too many cases, has become a burden heavy to bear; exhaustion, depression and burn-out are not uncommon. Some, perhaps less sensitive to the shifting parameters, still attempt to function as if little has changed; for the strong, this results in semi-permanent conflict and, for the not so strong, increasing irrelevance. For still others, consciously or unconsciously looking for the line of least resistance, there is what more and more people describe as 'just going through the motions'. They keep the head down, do the minimum and do it in an increasingly empty way. A question like 'Just what do you do all day?' might not be easy to answer.

The malaise is evident when priests gather to talk. We might distinguish three kinds of conversation. There are those who will talk about anything under the sun except theology and the faith itself. In some cases, this is because of a fear of what it might open up; in others, it is because of an apparently rock-like certainty that the faith and the church are so permanent and unchanging that exploration of any kind is irrelevant.

For a second group, there is talk of the church and things theological, but all with a somewhat painful air of negativity. Whether it is nostalgia for the past, anger at powerlessness, confusion about where to turn or criticism that will never lead to action, these conversations, far from focusing and empowering the participants, send them away even more depressed.

A third group wants change, eagerly discusses pastoral initiatives as well as their theological premises, but for the most part experiences a solid wall of incomprehension and opposition from those with the power to make decisions. Some just get on with the job, free themselves from dependence on approval and try to be creative. For others, the predominant experience is that of observing the disorientation of the church being compounded by the refusal to change. For a minority, there is the good fortune of actually obtaining permission and sometimes even support for their initiatives.

Apart from those individuals blessed with a positive disposition, and a minority fortunate enough to be involved in various kinds of specialised ministry for which they have a special aptitude or training, the priesthood itself is passing through a difficult period. Behind the statistics, the patterns and the prognoses, hangs a tale of human dislocation and suffering. Long endured silently, spiritually sublimated, politely unacknowledged or conveniently overlooked, this is now being admitted and owned. The pastoral and theological journals make increasingly explicit reference to it. Fictional writing, which almost everybody recognises, develops it and, whether violently or gently, lays it bare for everyone to see. Caught in a limbo between an authority-based ministry that is no longer acceptable and a skills-based ministry for which they were never trained, a whole generation of clergy is hurting.

But the laity is hurting too, because this sense of dislocation and creeping irrelevance produces a lack of leadership and an uncertain, if not to say non-existent, pastoral strategy. The result is a perfunctory pastoral performance, trite homilies, boring liturgies, minimal visitation and the absense of a social project. In the search for relevance, the conventional is canonised. Soon we are merely repeating what the world has already said sooner and – on its own terms at least – more effectively.

Lost opportunities

Inevitably, the question will be asked as to whether this situation could have been avoided. In a sense, it is a useless question and worth exploring only if it brings home the urgent need for renewal and reconstruction. Like many powerful institutions, the church has become the victim of its own success. The church that re-emerged with Catholic Emancipation was enthusiastic, clear about its priorities and, considering what it had come through, extraordinarily well organised. It set about its perceived pastoral task with fearsome energy and eventually succeeded in putting in place most of the institutional and legal supports it considered necessary for its pastoral mission.

But power tends to corrupt. From then on, the priority imperceptibly became a matter of protecting what had been achieved and that, in turn, a matter of defending institutions. But the world keeps on turning and what is an institution of emancipation and service in one era can become an institution of conservatism and domination in another.

The Irish bishops at Vatican I had passionate – and differing – views on the burning issues of the Council. The Irish bishops at Vatican II had almost nothing at all to say on anything. Understandably perhaps, it did not dawn on them that the problematic of mainland Europe was soon to become their own. Ireland was another time, another place. Their message on returning from the Council, seemed to be that nothing should disturb the even tenor of our lives. Apart from the translation of the Mass into the vernacular and a somewhat more relaxed – though for many people, confused – position on sin and eschatology, Vatican II, in the sense in which the Council Fathers intended it, had little or no impact upon the Irish church.

The Irish church leadership acquired a reputation for conservatism which it has never lost. On only three occasions in the meantime has it figured in international theological debate. Once was to short-circuit the debate on priestly celibacy at the 1971 synod and another was to defend the non-admission of women to priestly ordination. The honourable odd man out was Cardinal Ó Fiaich's defence of the status of the Secretariat for Christian Unity in 1985. It is true that Vatican II was somewhat Eurocentric and irenic in its analysis and understanding of the 'modern world' but in fairness, it did not so much accept this modern world's value system as the fact that its values and problematic were an inescapable social reality. Church leadership in Ireland did not want this 'modern world' and saw its role as keeping it at bay. But, with honourable exceptions, it did want the economic structures, monetary policies and political alliances that would inevitably give rise to it.[1]

Vatican II was a lost opportunity and the visit of Pope John Paul II was another. Hastily arranged and, in pastoral terms, poorly planned, it compounded a misreading of the real situation with the absence of a pastoral strategy. It could have been so different; not as a dramatic spectacle which it certainly was, but as a springboard for spiritual and pastoral renewal, which it certainly was not. It might have been conceived as the culmination and celebration of a prolonged period of animation and renewal of two to three years. Beginning with programmes of personal renewal, moving on to parish renewal through the creation, animation and interlinking of different kinds of groups, moving on through the phase of diocesan renewal to that of the local church, the visit could have been the focus and endorsement of this: a local church on the path of renewal, celebrating its conversion, its faith and its communion with the church universal.

But that would have presupposed a forward-looking pastoral plan based on an analysis of the emerging social reality and developed after wide consultation. It would also have meant allowing a new kind of animator or leader to emerge with the requisite pastoral vision and skills. It would have meant endorsing this leadership and what it gave rise to and seeing it as a gift rather than as a threat.

Such a pastoral strategy, based on an analysis of the social reality and involving priorities and options and risking losses and gains, was the one thing the bishops did not have. Insofar as they had one at all, it was the unarticulated hope of restoring what they perceived to be the fervour and the order of the recent past. When a last-minute plan was hastily knocked together to prepare for the visit, it was based almost entirely on re-vamping the devotional practices of the previous generation. This writer remembers well his feelings at the time. Firstly, the attempt to lay aside all reservations and wholeheartedly enter into the event with devotion and expectation. Secondly, the sense of disappointment and depression when it was over; the feeling that it had been a quick fix with no substance. The visit was not only a lost opportunity; it was a step backwards, because it created the illusion of vitality. A triumph of image-creation, it mistook the image for the reality. It was the 'last hurrah' of the triumphalistic church.

There have been other lost opportunities too; less dramatic perhaps but no less significant. The unwillingness to take creative lay people seriously; the marginalisation of prophetic religious; the facile assumption that the experience of missionaries in relation to base communities, dialogue with other ideologies or the inculturation of the gospel, were not relevant to Ireland. Documents were indeed written and statements were made but the followthrough was haphazard. Moreover, whether it was justice, reconciliation, or the dignity of women that was written about, somehow the principles never seemed to be applicable to the structures, priorities and exercise of authority of the church itself.

Then there was the *'affaire* Casey'. It stunned the church and exposed a credibility gap. It was an invitation to honesty and repentance but produced only fear and paralysis; an invitation to humility whose response was embarrassment. Above all, it was an lost opportunity to listen.

Reformation

The synoptic gospels are filled with a sense of apocalyptic urgency. Jesus comes across as urging a change of mentality and a new praxis. There is a coming catastrophe and it cannot be avoided if things continue as they are. Jesus does not address an irreligious people in order to make them religious, but rather subverts the manner in which an institutionalised religion enslaves peoples' consciousness and legitimates injustice through promoting a caricatured notion of God. He does this by revealing the true God in his own person and praxis. The present situation of the church in Ireland offers it a unique opportunity to be addressed and renewed by the freshness, the challenge and the urgency of the original gospel message.

From one point of view, it may be a tragedy that organised Christianity in this country is rapidly declining in influence, but the real catastrophe would be the failure to recognise this as a call to conversion and reformation. The term 'reformation' is used here deliberately. 'Renewal' while essential, can be too easily spiritualised and domesticated. For we are speaking of a call to re-form the church in its spirituality, its structures, and its priorities; no longer on the basis of consolidating its former institutional aspirations, but from the standpoint of the marginalised and excluded and the poor in spirit who live in solidarity with them.

Humanly speaking, the conditions for hope are exactly the same as the conditions for despair. It is the orientation of the human spirit that makes the difference and, for those who seek in faith, to know and love God – however haltingly – all things work together unto good. Paradoxically, to recognise that the institutional form of the church is dying is itself an act of faith in Christ's fidelity to his church. Theologically, it derives from the ability to see the difference between the historical community of faith, which lives to celebrate the sacred and subversive memory of Jesus and is enlivened by his Holy Spirit, and those aspects of its institutional form that are culturally adaptable and essentially relative. While theologians seek to discourse learnedly about this, thousands of lay people instinctively recognise the distinction and live it out in their daily lives. They know the difference between the gift and the parcel in which it is wrapped.

The true church

For the believer, however scandalous it may appear to say so in a pluralist world, the church, in its foundational reality as the body of Christ, is the continuation of the enfleshment of the Word of God and is an essential and irreplaceable element in God's will for the salvation of the world. This true church does not fear death to self because it is forever dying and rising with Christ. This true church is always focused on its crucified Lord and not on its worldly status. This church's guiding principle is firstly the Holy Spirit who moves with divine sovereignty over the whole creation and in every human heart and not the canons it enacts for a more ordered administration.

This church's celebration of baptism is a daily entry into the vulnerability of a world threatened with death, to be one with Christ who reveals his divine glory in the emptiness of his cross; and not an insurance policy for individual salvation. The bread it breaks in the eucharist, is broken in solidarity with the brokenness of the world and the brokenness of our own hearts; and not as the formal ritual of official religion. The reconciliation and forgiveness it celebrates is firstly for itself, because being the community which recognises the truth of human existence, it is a community which, far from possessing any sense of moral superiority, is most keenly aware of its need of divine mercy.

The community which it seeks to embody is the sign and the servant of that quality of human emancipation and solidarity for which people struggle, and not the last refuge of a feudal order. Its structures are those of communion and participation and interdependence and only in a very secondary sense a hierarchy. When it ordains for ministry it does so for animation, empowerment and service and not just for office, much less domination. It is a church which exists, not for itself but for the transformation – both historical and eschatological – of the world. This church, having already hung with Christ upon the cross, does not fear institutional death, but welcomes the opportunity to be reborn in the likeness of Christ.

While always referring itself to its inner mystical reality, this church seeks to be enfleshed in human history and culture. It does not seek to be less incarnate than its crucified Lord and so it does not shy away from the issues of structures and organisation. But there are different degrees of permanence and validity in these structures. For on the one hand, there is scripture, the sacraments of the liturgy, ordained ministry, an episcopacy in communion with Peter, and, on the other, there are the various ways in which these things can be caricatured and their meaning virtually lost: in fundamentalism, in formalism, in restorationism, in authoritarianism.

A truly Catholic theology will speak of a concrete, visible, historical church, but it will distinguish what is of divine origin and dominical institution from their cultural unfolding and will recognise a hierarchy of truths. It will distinguish the authority of 'The Tradition', canonically expressed in scripture, from the various 'traditions' that spring up for whatever reasons. It will trace the necessary development of doctrine in ecumenical councils, but distinguish this from the non-binding pronouncements of Vatican congregations. It rejoices in the fact that there is a legitimate plurality of theologies in the church today just as there always has been throughout its history and even in the New Testament itself and it will refrain from imposing a simplistic uniformity.

It will recognise that, in addition to legitimate developments that essentially expound and clarify fundamental doctrines, there are all kinds of ideological and cultural accretions whose value is relative and can easily be discarded. It is not afraid to point out that in addition to cultural accretions there are also exaggerations, distortions and abuses. If there is a hierarchy of truths there is a hierarchy of structures. Sadly, the propensity towards institutionalisation often means that it is the less important that gets more emphasis than the fundamental. The law of clerical celibacy is, in practice, considered more important than the right of the people of God to the eucharist. A theologian's fairly arbitrary and subjective speculations on the Holy Spirit and the Virgin Mary pass unnoticed: the same theologian's analysis of how the church operates in a capitalist society results in his being silenced and eventually hounded out of the ministry. To elevate the kind of structures that come into being through cultural accretion and the consolidation of power into something permanent to which the sanction of God's will is attached, would be idolatry. To direct the energy of the institution, its ministers and its theologians more to justifying and consolidating these structures than to proclaiming the gospel, is practical apostasy. For then, our faith is in our power structures and not in God.

What not to do

It is time then to look for the signs of life and hope; to the places and the people where the renewed church is living, working and communicating. At the risk of repetition, let me say once again; there is a crucial and all-important distinction between the church and the secondary structures employed to consolidate a given historically conditioned and, hence, essentially relative model of church. We are witnessing the irreversible decline of one such model. We have to realise that our mission is to be the midwife to something new, whether or not we will be around to see it in full bloom. This means resisting the temptation to restorationism. For that is what it is: a temptation!

Despite its attractiveness to various interest groups, the restoration of the past as a recipe for renewal, can only spell disaster. It is not what the people of God want and therefore it can only be imposed and subsequently enforced. Such imposition can only be effective if ideologically legitimated and that, in turn, can only be achieved by a dehumanising return to preaching a caricature of a god who rewards and punishes according to the logic of the successful.

When one adds reflection on the psychoanalytic roots of such religion, as well as the internalised pathologies it can give rise to, one suspects one is no longer dealing with the gospel of Jesus. If pursued, it will result in a scenario not altogether unfamiliar to those who have experience of the church in other European countries: an ecclesiastical power structure existing primarily for its own functionaries; the growing irrelevance of the institution to daily life; the alienation and loss of the energies of creative and generous people.

A second temptation is to do nothing: to sit tight and wait for the storm to blow itself out and the flood waters to subside. While this may have some appeal to those who simply cannot come up with any way forward at all, it fails to grasp that what has occurred is not a passing phase but an irreversible cultural revolution. This writer is no less saddened than the most conservative bishop by some of the things this new matrix of values will bring in its wake, but like *Gaudium et Spes*, it is not a matter of uncritically endorsing everything about the 'modern world', but rather of accepting that it is the social reality in which we live.

For the church leadership, Vatican II still represents the shape of the future, but the council was over before more than half the population of the country was even born. This population does not look back with nostalgia to the order of the past; it never knew it. The only Ireland it knows is the Ireland of the Northern troubles, E.C. dependency, monetarist economics, hegemony of the media, pop culture, individual freedom and self-expression, unrealisable expectations, endemic unemployment, substance abuse, semi-permanent entertainment, corruption in high places and flaunted privilege. The church it knows is one which is somehow vaguely there in the background; it is a church which has little enough to say about many of these structures and apparently no means of re-shaping them.

The emerging culture is strongly youth-oriented, while the church leadership is middle-aged, if not elderly; it is a culture where women are progressively emancipating themselves, while

the church leadership remains a patriarchy; it is a culture of experience, while the church seeks to uphold the authority of culturally
unintelligible traditions; it is a culture of images and instant news,
of changing language and multiple choice, while the church is
perceived as clinging to the past and extolling it in categories intelligible only to itself and taking years to decide on issues which
women must deal with every night.

It is a culture not without its contradictions, its dishonesty, its systematic violence and its marginalisation of the poor, but the
church is not perceived, in practice at least, to be unambiguously
on the side of its victims. It is an overeroticised culture which pays
for its obsession with sex in dreadful instability and rampant disease, but as long as the church is perceived as being suspicious of
sexuality, its voice cannot be heard on these issues. It is a culture
where people imagine themselves to be free, but hold opinions
manufactured for them by the media, which prosper by legitimating the system. The church perceives the media as hostile and the
media perceive the church as suspicious and secretive. The result,
in short, is a value system progressively more materialistic into
which the church has less and less input.

The metaphysician will, perhaps, note that what is perceived may
be different from what is real, but in an image-centred culture,
perception is the reality which shapes consciousness and action.
These are not passing trends. They are the virtually inevitable
socio-cultural repercussions of the economic and political options
which the Irish people have allowed their political representatives to make for them and repeatedly endorse. The mainstream
church leadership has for the most part up until now, failed to
grasp that one cannot have the supposed economic benefits of advanced capitalism without also buying into the value system and
cultural forms it brings with it, in order to legitimate itself. It is
this value system and not the gospel of Jesus, which is becoming
the principal pivot around which the emerging culture revolves.
It is not here in passing but will stay as long as the preferred economic system can legitimate itself. To lie low and wait for this to
change – when for 'change' one should read 'change back' –
would be the height of folly.

There is also the temptation, once again attractive in high places,
to see the engine and model of renewal in trusting in one or some
combination of the various neo-conservative church movements

which have gained in power and influence especially during the present pontificate. Obviously the favoured front-line troops of the restorationist movements, their considerable financial resources, political connections and undoubted ability to attract able people of a certain disposition and orientation, mean that they will be a force to be reckoned with in ecclesiastical politics for some time to come. In fact, their influence and perhaps even control, over the ecclesiastical power structure is probably growing. But because of their orientations, methods and apparent goals, it would seem to be shortsighted and ultimately self-defeating to see in them the seeds of a church capable of transforming the post-modern world in the name of the gospel.

Their links with and possibly even origins in far-right political thinking, give them little empathy with and rootedness in the Irish experience. At a time when the church needs to be less concerned with itself and more with the transformation of society, it hardly needs the kind of movement whose first and final loyalty is to itself, which often appears to seek to be a church within the church and whose attitude to local bishops seems to be either to manipulate them or seek to render them ineffective. While the church in this country struggles to become an open communicating community, these groups are virtually secret societies. While the church struggles with the evangelical imperative to make an option for the poor, these groups blatantly court the rich. While the church struggles with the call to become less authoritarian and rediscover an evangelical simplicity, these movements play power politics within the church in order to refashion a travesty of the church that would play power politics in the world.

Where to look

It has often been remarked – and in fairness, it was usually clergymen who said it – that the surest proof of the divine origin of the church was that the clergy had not succeeded in destroying it: an oversimplistic statement perhaps, but with an unmistakeable ring of truth. Over a century ago, Newman wrote a small but profound book on consulting the laity in matters of doctrine. It reminded the – hierarchical – church of the constitutive role of the laity in shaping the very identity of the church: of protecting its faith and praxis and handing these on, even – or perhaps especially – in situations where the hierarchy was failing to do so.

The church, Vatican II taught – in a phrase that many in positions of power would like to see fall into disuse – is the people of God. As baptised Christians, the ordained are part of this holy people. As ordained presbyters and bishops, they constitute a ministry of service to it. This ministry includes the exercise of spiritual authority. But that in turn, is subject to the word of God, alive and active in the priestly people as a whole and not exclusively in the hierarchy.

The sacred sign (mysterium) which is the church then, is all the people of God together; and the laity is its unacknowledged spiritual wealth. Most of the people who pray, worship, do innumerable acts of kindness, hear the word of God, support the weak, struggle for the oppressed, pass on the faith, comfort the sick and dying, care for the earth, forgive their enemies, ensure the continuity of the parish, start again in the face of failure and shape and transmit the spirituality which empowers people in the ups and downs of the everyday, are lay people – and a majority of them are probably women. Certainly, they do so with different degrees of interest, devotion and continuity. But then, so do clergy and religious. They do not have either the support or the debilitation of approved clerico-religious spirituality but they are the people in whose daily lives of struggle, celebration and ordinariness, the gospel of Jesus takes on reality.

Church leaders are forever telling such people that they are the church, but with a terrible double-think. They are the church, they are told, but they are not allowed to contribute to establishing the church's structures and priorities; they can work for it and even minister in it, but only within pre-determined parameters. They can support it, defend it, pay for it, but not participate in shaping its doctrines, moral positions or organisational structures.

Administratively, this may appear to be a neat solution, at least from the standpoint of the present administrators, but theologically, it is an absurdity. It is a practical denial of the grace of baptism and confuses ministerial office with bureaucratic power. As the laity become more qualified, professionally, pastorally and even theologically and – dare one suggest it? – the clergy less so, the situation becomes not only theologically unsupportable but organisationally preposterous.

There is, however, a deeper issue. It is the issue of faith and spiritual search. As faith becomes less a matter of convention and culture, it becomes more a matter of personal search and conviction.

If we live in an age of changing values, then it is also an age of
spiritual searching. Even as one model of church declines, another
grows; as one way of doing things collapses, another takes on life.
As disillusionment grows with the institutionalisation of the
church, some may give up on it but others search and struggle for
other ways to be Christian community and to challenge the wider
church to renew itself by forming communities, more real, more
living and more relevant.

Vocations to the priesthood may be declining, but vocations to a
responsible living out of baptism are on the increase. There are
really so many individuals and groups, certain in a very basic and
existential way, of the relevance of their faith and hope to the
issues facing people in contemporary society. Many of these in
turn, have embarked on a genuinely spiritual search for ways and
means of becoming the presence of Christ in this world. Most of
them are lay people but some are religious and priests who have
recognised that it is here, and not in redundant attempts to recon-
stitute the past, that the Holy Spirit is speaking to the church.

Some make a very personal journey, often unguided and unaccom-
panied by those whose vocation and training it is to accompany
them. On this journey, some may appear to get nowhere but
others arrive at a point of authenticity which gives them a spiritual authority of their own and sometimes an attitude of compassion mixed with regret at the official purveyors of spiritual experience. Others form groups, sometimes in a very simple way, to talk
about shared problems and struggles, to read scripture, or to
pray. Some of the groups limp along and learn to acknowledge
the fragility of human existence. Others grow more strong and
focused, but through them both, people develop a new sense of
what it is to be the church.

There are groups which form for a more socially defined purpose:
to deal with problems in the neighbourhood; to campaign for an
issue; to vindicate the rights of the marginalised; to learn new
methods of confronting the oppression that is everywhere around
them or to live more in harmony with the rest of creation. Sometimes, people come into such groups because of their Christian
faith: they just as often come into them because their natural
human faith impels them to be concerned about something that
cannot be ignored even though their official church faith often
seems to have little enough to say to a situation that sorely demands a response.

For those who get involved because of their Christian faith, and even for a small minority of the others, that faith sometimes becomes the engine that powers their commitment. Because of the issues and questions that arise through their involvement, and the way the groups evolve to deal with these issues, that faith is in turn, questioned, refocused and reappropriated. For others, although motivated by faith in the first place, the gap between the official version of this faith – or at least what they have been conditioned to believe that to be – and the vision and ideas they need to sustain their commitment, grows even wider. Denied the kind of accompaniment that might facilitate the bridging of that gap, some feel obliged either to choose between a pre-critical faith or a commitment to social transformation devoid of any explicitly religious motivation. In neither case is there a process of reconstructing that faith and making it more adult.

Christ's fidelity to the church

This book would wish to be an act of faith and hope in the future of the church and therefore an act of love for the church. It follows from a belief in Christ's fidelity to that church, which is his own body, and the action of the Holy Spirit among the members of that body. Vatican II, in the *Dogmatic Constitution on the Church*, stated something already clear from scripture and tradition: that the Holy Spirit does not work only through the hierarchy. It is time to give concrete recognition to this. In Ireland today, there is a renewed church struggling to be born and this book is, to a great extent, about this church. First, it was necessary to show – for those to whom it is not yet obvious – that the familiar model of church was dying, for until that is accepted, the groups whose faith and praxis one wishes to discuss here can always be dismissed as peripheral.

Yet more and more, it is outside the familiar way of doing things that one finds life and commitment. This is church life; it is Christian commitment. The second part of this book will present the life and action of several such groups – and there are certainly others. Together, they represent the beginning of the renewed and reformed church, for it is in and through them that the gospel of Jesus is addressing the social reality in which we live.

If the service of authority in the church is a living ministry, then its first task is to discern the action of the Holy Spirit among the people of God – since it will hardly make the mistake of assuming itself to possess a monopoly of that Spirit. Having discerned this action, it will affirm it without dominating it. It will help to clarify it without controlling it and in dialoguing with it, will be just as ready to learn as it is to teach.

After working for several years in various pastoral initiatives in Ireland, I returned to Pakistan in 1989. Three years later I came home on leave. Throughout that time at home, two things became clear to me, one of which filled me with sadness and the other, with hope. The first was that the church, in its tried and trusted institutional form, was dying through lack of a sustained will for renewal; and the second was that it was being reborn in a different form in the lives and actions of creative and committed people. Rather than simply lament the passing of the old, one wanted to somehow contribute to supporting the new, by allowing it to speak for itself and initiating a process of affirming and evaluating it theologically so that it might address the wider church in a communion of critical solidarity. The argument is that in what these and similar groups are striving to do there is the seedbed of a new model of church.

Seedbed of a renewed church

Obviously, it is not possible to say something about everything, so some selection process is necessary in the choice of groups; but according to what criteria? Firstly, I limited myself to groups of which I had first-hand knowledge as well as groups I knew about from people whose insight and commitment I valued and trusted. In particular, I was looking for groups whose emphasis was on lay people developing their own structures of participation and who would be ready to speak for themselves. This means that this study is necessarily limited and partial though it does have the merit of being concrete and rooted. I will welcome criticism and amplification.

Secondly, I sought out groups who were actually doing something, for it is not enough to know what one is against, one needs to know what one is for and be active in making it come about. What this means is affirming the primacy of orthopraxis over orthodoxy; faith being, firstly, an existential or practical commitment to the transformation of the world through Christian discipleship and, only secondly, albeit necessarily, the task of clarifying and transmitting in terms of a common tradition, what that discipleship is.

Thirdly, one looked for groups where the 'reception' of Vatican II was a reality. For the nature of Christian community and tradition is such that 'a text' has meaning and is real only when it is received by people active in living out what the text sought to grapple with and communicate in the first place. It is not that these people spend hours wondering what a particular text of Vatican II may mean: far from it! They are, rather, people who have made the joys and hopes and struggles and griefs of the people of today their own. They instinctively recognise that the divine graciousness at work among themselves is also at work in all people. For them to be the church is to be at the service of the transformation of the world. In this way, they grasp Vatican II far more profoundly than those who wrestle with the words of the text only in order to ideologise it.

Not all the groups chosen necessarily represent the writer's favoured options. Some work for radical alternatives; some seek to bring out the best in what used to be; some depend entirely on their own spiritual resources. Some are committed to social transformation; some to inclusiveness; some to liturgical renewal; some to prayer. Some reach out to the weak; some unmask the structures which marginalise the weak. Some have a clearly defined link to the church as was; some have not. Some are strongly focused; some struggle on in fragility.

While the list is limited and partial, it has sought to be wideranging and inclusive. Some kinds of groups have not been included and this does not necessarily imply a lack of respect or appreciation of the dedication of the individuals involved in them. But groups which were intended to be the concrete outreach of a previous model of church cannot, without reconstruction and despite the generosity of their members, be the basis of a new model of church. Religious are included in the survey only when their praxis is linked to renewal and represents a departure from or development of the traditional ministries of their orders.

Reverse mission

For some people there may be misgivings about a missionary writing about the death and rebirth of a church where he is no longer working. Yet it remains the church from which he received his Christian and missionary vocation. One does find a certain resistance in Irish church circles to hearing the reflections of missionaries. Among both conservatives and liberals, it often comes from a simplistic, and sometimes incorrect, understanding of what missionaries actually do. While it can also be the result of missionaries being a little over-enthusiastic about the local church in which they minister, it is more often a case of an unwillingness to be disturbed. Yet if First World theologians may write tomes about missionary situations and local churches in the South, then why can't missionaries reflect on the situation of the church in the First World?

In any event, mission today is reciprocal and is going on in all six continents. The notion of a Eurocentric church evangelising a pagan world is an anachronism, though still peripherally present in the theological imagination of those who won't realise that christendom is ended. Churches willing to send and teach, but unwilling to receive and learn, are still living out of a mentality of spiritual colonialism. There are many aspects of contemporary missionary experience that are supremely relevant to the renewal and reformation of the church in this country.

Missionaries live in a 'foreign' culture. They have to learn its language, its values and its hidden assumptions before they can hope to address it. This means that they have to listen to it with openness, attentively and respectfully. In terms of the background, training and sentient base of the church leadership in this country, Ireland today is a 'foreign' culture. Like 'the past', they do things differently there! Before it can be addressed, it has to be listened to and understood.

The missionary experiences the church as being different from society as a whole. 'Everybody' is not a Christian. The Christian community is one part of society, sometimes significant, sometimes a minority, indeed sometimes significant because it is a minority. It is an experience which demands encounter and dialogue with other religions and ideologies. In this encounter, there is the experience of how others search for the truth and for God and struggle for a more human society. In turn, both the uniqueness of the Christian gospel as well as the basic human vocation to join with others in the common search for a genuine experience of God and the struggle for a just society are re-emphasised. Organised Christianity in this country today needs to recognise that it has not got a monopoly of human authenticity; that outside its visible parameters there can also be spirituality and a commitment to a just society. Christians are joined with such groups in a common search for the good in which, almost as a by-product, their Christian identity is refocused.

Missionaries quickly learn that women hold up 'more than half of the sky' and that they do so in Ireland too. The poverty of the Third World and the intensification of that poverty through structures of oppression, emphasises for missionaries that the gospel is not socio-politically neutral and that it favours the poor. There are increasing signs that the church leadership in this country has, at last, recognised the structural causes of poverty in this part of the world – as well as their links to world poverty – but are not yet clear that acting on this realisation means a reshaping of the church. Many of the groups on whose praxis we will be reflecting, realised it long ago.

Those sent on mission live in a situation of liminality and unpredictability. Permanent strangers in their Father's house, they are forced to seek to find their identity in Jesus Christ and in him alone. Perhaps an over-familiarity with an image of Christ, in a culture too easily and for too long presumed to be Christian, can actually de-sensitise us to him. Perhaps our church needs an experience of defamiliarisation; in order to discover him anew and be empowered by the discovery.

Theological orientation

Like any theological reflection, this present one is not neutral. The standpoint that is beyond any standpoint is a pure illusion. Every argument comes with assumptions and presuppositions. The only real prejudice, as Gadamer has shown, is the prejudice against prejudice. The nearest one can come to objectivity is to be up front in a self-critical way, about one's own presuppositions. For there is no such thing as a presuppositionless inquiry. This present work – no more or no less that any other work – is written from a certain standpoint. It desires far-reaching change in the church and openly proposes it.

The broad lines of the change that it works for lie, it will argue, in the direction of a rediscovery of the contemplative spirit; an unambiguous option for the poor and for justice; the reintegration of the feminine into church life and reflection; and the installation of structures of genuine participation and inclusiveness. The method being followed here attaches considerable importance to allowing creative and committed groups to speak for themselves – the very thing they have been denied for generations. We will conclude this part by summing up the main theological assumptions that we bring to this investigation.

- God has personally addressed the world in a unique, irrevocable and unsurpassable way in the event of Jesus of Nazareth.

- The enfleshment of the word of God in Jesus continues in the community and praxis of the people of God who, by living out of the sacred and subversive memory of Jesus, constitute the church.

- The church, as the community which celebrates God's limitless compassion for all creatures, irrespective of their supposed moral situation, exists not for itself but in the service of humanity.

- The fundamental principle of life, authority and organisation in the church is the Holy Spirit who is poured out with divine graciousness over all creation and into every human heart. This life in the Spirit is celebrated through visible signs and actions called sacraments.

- The praxis of the true church and all theological reflection aimed at defining, clarifying, communicating and protecting its identity, proceed from a preferential option for the oppressed.

- All the baptised are equal in dignity as disciples. While there is an ordained ministry as well as a ministry of authority in the church, they are not necessarily co-terminus and structurally immutable and must never be allowed to degenerate into authoritarianism.

- The people of God are called to be a community of holiness and historical responsibility. Christians follow their vocation to holiness through a commitment to history and read history in the light of the infinite compassion which is God's holiness.

- As a community subject to the word of God, the church recognises its permanent need for reformation. In our day and in this situation, it is called by the gospel to pay particular attention to the issues of poverty, justice, gender, participation and accountability.

- As a prophetic, witnessing community, the church discloses the glory of the triune God, the source of all life and liberation. Today it is called to witness to the unoriginatedness of the Mother-Father through a rediscovery of its contemplative life: to the enfleshment of the word through an unambiguous commitment to justice; to the outpouring of the Spirit through creating structures of inclusion, equality and participation.

Footnote

1. The term 'modern world' is being used here in a non-technical sense for, quite clearly, we now live in a post-modern world characterised by multiple deconstructionist movements where the pretensions of modernity have given way to a growing disillusionment. The term 'modern' is being used here simply to indicate that, in Ireland, the structures and value-systems of the recent past have been surpassed and cannot be restored and that religion in particular does not provide an all-pervasive foundation for the emerging culture.

PART II

The seeds of a new Church

THE STRUGGLE FOR JUSTICE
Written by Brigid Reynolds and Sean Healy
on behalf of the Justice Commission of CMRS

The world in which we live today is composed of many complex institutions and structures. There are many possibilities and opportunities. However, there are also many problems and areas of injustice. Before we can make a judgement on any of these areas of concern, we need to analyse the reality in a structured way. It is in determining the economic, political, cultural and social structures that we can begin to see the causes of problems. Problems can only be solved when the causes are addressed in coherent and systematic ways.

Developing alternatives from a gospel perspective

The values base from which the CMRS Justice Commission works plays a central role. The struggle is to hear the gospel, to respond to its call and challenge in a way that brings good news to our world in the 1990s. The commission believes that there is no value free economics or sociology. In doing its analysis and in interpreting the findings the commission acknowledges that its goal is to operate from the values of the Christian scriptures.

While it is critically important to do a vigorous social analysis if real change is to happen, it is equally necessary to envisage alternatives to the present structures. Part of the resources of the commission is allocated to research into alternative models of political, economic, cultural and social structures and evaluation of them from the values perspective of the gospel.

Policy development

The social analysis, reflection from a gospel perspective and research into possible alternatives is a prerequisite for public policy development. Each year when Government is preparing the national budget the commission publishes its socio-economic review which looks at the choices that have been made, especially about the distribution of resources and how these decisions affect various groups in society. Recommendations are made outlining what is possible within the fiscal constraints of the forthcoming budget. When the budget is announced, a comprehensive critique is published from the perspective of the pre-budget submission.

The commission regularly organises a social policy conference. In each of these, one issue of public policy is researched and discussed in depth. The papers which are published at the conference provide policy makers and others with an analysis of the present situation, a critique from a values perspective and some options for the way forward. Among the issues discussed to date were family income policy; taxation; work, unemployment and job creation; rural development policy; power, participation and exclusion.

The stance of the commission and the policy areas examined are influenced greatly by the experience of people who are excluded from the benefits of decision-making and by those who work with these groups.

Advocacy, enabling, communications

The commission aims to study the effects of public policy decisions from the perspective of people who are poor or excluded. It tries to be a true voice for those who are voiceless while simultaneously providing support and encouragement to groups to develop their own voice.

Through workshops, seminars, talks and extensive consultancy work, the commission tries to educate, conscientise and motivate people to become involved in action for transformation. It also provides skills of analysis, leadership, development of common vision, planning and evaluation. Groups who become active are guaranteed support and ongoing consideration in so far as the resources allow. Groups are encouraged and helped to network with each other.

The commission encourages two-way communication with its own members and other groups concerned with similar issues. In so far as it is practicable, it publishes its research and reflections so as to stimulate debate on the issues of concern. When it is considered appropriate, media coverage is sought to highlight issues and encourage a national debate.

These activities are guided by a simple framework. Firstly it is important for the group to establish where they are (analysis of the present), secondly they need to agree on where they wish to go, their destination (vision of the future), thirdly strategies are needed to move from the present to the desired future (these involve policy development, planning, implementation and evaluation).

Ireland today

The commission sees its policy as answering the gospel call to transform society. When we look at Ireland today – north and south – we see a society which ranks among the top twenty per cent of the world's richest societies. We see people who have gained a great deal, materially, in the four decades since the end of the Second World War. We see a world of possibilities and op-portunities open before many members of this society. At the same time, we see great divisions and marginalisation in this soci-ety. One in every three people is below the poverty line. About one in five of the labour force is unemployed. There is a major scandal of rural poverty. Many urban dwellers live in degrading conditions.

When we look at power structures in Ireland, we find that the pro-cess of decision-making involves the direct participation of a small elite who lead the major interest groups representing the powerful in Irish society. Those who can lobby, persuade, manip-ulate, even threaten the society, ensure their voices are heard. This network of consultation and decision-making excludes all those sectors of Irish society which are not powerful or sufficiently organised to ensure they are heard. Among the excluded groups are poor people, unemployed people, small farmers, low-paid workers. Power in Ireland – north and south – is in the hands of a small elite.

While maintaining many traditional values, Ireland is undergoing profound change. In the past few decades, the values of the con-sumer society have become dominant. People assume that every-thing is replaceable. Priority is given to using human ingenuity and cheaper production methods regardless of quality or conse-quences for the environment. 'Success' and profit are the object-ives and they are sought in the shortest possible timeframe. With-in this materialist and consumer society, the religious practice rate is very high by any standard. Many church people, however, question the division between the religious ideals pronounced by various churches and the values that guide the day-to-day lives of a great many church members.

There are sharp class divisions in Ireland. The potential for mobil-ity out of the more marginal and disadvantaged categories will be slight in the future if we continue to follow the present develop-ment model. There are other major divisions in Ireland between rich and poor, between young and old, between men and women, between north and south, between the various groups involved in the conflict in the North of Ireland, between urban and rural dwellers, between the employed and all others in society, and so on. The more we look at our society the more we realise that there are groups who benefit from its economic, political, cultural and social structures and others who do not. The number who do not benefit from the present situation is growing and the gap between them and the rest of society is widening. This is not due to some relentless law of nature. Rather it is the result of decisions taken by people to organise society in this particular way.

An alternative future

Is this the way God wishes our society to be organised? What kind of alternative future do we have to offer and what are we doing to articulate and make concrete this alternative? These questions become especially important given the changing European context in which Ireland is situated. When the politically and economically powerful in our society address the future, they offer us today only one vision – that of a society with expanding production (using more technology), fewer people employed and with the remainder engaged in a life of leisure. They see power as being in the hands of an even smaller elite. The majority would have no say in the shaping of such a society and would not participate in its operation to any great extent. The very meaning of life would be radically altered, human rights would be eroded, human dignity would not be respected, human development would not he facilitated and the environment would be exploited.

We believe this vision needs to be seriously challenged. Our Christian values state clearly that we should not accept the present growing divisions in our society but should, instead seek to eliminate them. We need to search for and strive to achieve balance in our values, goals and priorities. We need to move from quantitative to qualitative values and goals, from organisational to personal and interpersonal values and goals. We need to move from values that are economically based towards values that put far more emphasis on the real needs and aspirations of people. We need to move from mechanistic to organic values, from masculine towards feminine priorities. We need as a society to change direction, to find and maintain balance in all our relationships – with ourselves and God, with people we are close to and people in the wider world and in our relationship with the environment.

A society moving along these balanced lines would be a just society based on the biblical understanding of justice as a harmony which comes from fidelity to right relationships with God, with our neighbour and with the environment.

We stand at a moment of great change in human history. Ireland, in strengthening its commitment as a European partner, is embarking on an uncharted journey where many choices about our future will be made. We believe that Irish religious should be involved with all Irish people in making these choices. We should not be afraid of this. We should not consider such a role as arrogant or unrealistic. The gospel calls us to be involved in shaping a future which is closer to the values of Jesus Christ.

Christian faith and action for transformation

The commission sees its mission as answering the call to transform society as expressed in scripture and the social teaching of the Catholic Church. 'Transformation' is understood as a process which moves people and society generally, from where they are towards where God wishes them to be.

This process is rooted in the biblical call to every person to become involved in the process of building the reign of God. It responds to the challenge to continually 'cast off the old' and 'put on the new' (Eph 4:22 ff). This call is not just an invitation to individuals to conversion, but is addressed to the whole of creation. (Romans 8:22). All the structures and systems of our society need transformation so that God may reign and all may be free.

The social teaching of the Catholic Church echoes the call of the gospel and its response involves analysis, reflection and action. Pope Paul VI put this very succinctly in *Octogesima Adveniens* when he said 'It is up to the Christian communities to analyse with objectivity the situation which is proper to their own country, to shed on it the light of the gospel's unalterable words and to draw principles of reflection, norms of judgement and directives for action from the social teaching of the church' (4). In 1971 the Synod of Bishops emphasised the central role that action to transform the world must play in the life of anyone who wishes to follow the Christian life. It said: 'Action on behalf of justice and participation in the transformation of the world fully appear to us as a constitutive dimension of the preaching of the gospel' (*Justice in the World* No. 6).

Pope John Paul II articulates his concern not only about just structures within countries; he also raises issues around the interdependence of nations. The recent encyclical *Centesimus Annus* says poor people 'need to be provided with realistic opportunities. Creating such conditions calls for a concerted worldwide effort to promote development, an effort which also involves sacrificing the positions of income and of power enjoyed by the more developed economies. This may mean making important changes in established life-styles, in order to limit the waste of environmental and human resources, thus enabling every individual and all peoples of the earth to have a sufficient share of those resources' (No.52).

Spirituality

Active participation in the transformation of the world requires a spirituality that nourishes and supports the person or group. The commission subscribes to a very wide definition of spirituality as that which moves and shapes us and influences how we relate to ourselves, God, people and the environment. Occasionally the commission gives time to the discussion of spirituality. It explores questions around the issues of faith and service; values which support the status quo and values which challenge it; what motivates the prophet; spirituality and spiritualities; spirituality of the mysteries of Christian faith, etc. The commission is particularly concerned that more people would get involved in discussions on spirituality. It believes every person has a spirituality and therefore has an important contribution to make. The commission is particularly interested in supporting people who are involved in the work of justice in reflecting on their spirituality. The commission believes that the insights and experiences of this group have a major role in shaping the future of Christian spirituality.

OPTING FOR THE POOR
Written by Fr Peter McVerry and the Arrupe Society,
Upper Sherrard Street, Dublin

Our work began in the late Seventies when, working with young people in the inner city, we became aware of a small number who were then homeless. We sought funding from the Eastern Health Board to set up a small residential hostel for homeless boys from the inner city. Politically, it was a good time to seek funding as the inner city had gained considerable notoriety for handbag snatching and joyriding. In response, the Department of Justice planned to open a juvenile prison in Co Cavan which provoked a storm of protest from child care agencies as being a totally inappropriate and inadequate response. In order to be seen to be doing something more constructive, instructions were given from the Minister of Health to a reluctant Eastern Health Board to get three neighbourhood youth projects, including ours, off the ground in the inner city as rapidly as possible.

Our first hostel then opened in 1979 in the inner city for homeless boys aged 12-16. Subsequently, it became clear that an aftercare project was needed for boys leaving this hostel who had nowhere else to go. At that time, I was living in Ballymun and we applied to Dublin Corporation for a flat to be used as a temporary solution to the problem of older homeless boys. This flat quickly became a resource for local Ballymun children who left home and it eventually lost its link with the inner city project. When finally we got a house to replace the flat, the numbers who were seeking accommodation had grown so great that we had to keep both running and subsequently another house had to be provided to accommodate the overflow. The flat in Ballymun remains hopelessly overcrowded.

We are now a community-based project for homeless boys in Ballymun. Most of the young people who come to us refer themselves by simply turning up at the door or are referred by their parents. Our policy is not to turn anyone away and, if they cannot return home and we cannot get a place for them in another hostel, then we feel an obligation to keep them – hence the overcrowding. We also, and deliberately, do not have any admission criteria apart from the fact of being unable to return home, as we are aware that the more damaged and therefore more disruptive young people find it more difficult to get places in existing hostels as the hostels do not have the resources or often the training to deal with their problems. As every young person has a right to a place to live, we try to accommodate the more difficult young people, while very aware of the inadequacies of our hopelessly overcrowded and underfunded service in meeting their needs.

We also see the neglect of young homeless people as a denial of their fundamental rights, their right to food, shelter and care. We do not believe that the provision of fundamental rights in any society should be left to charity and fund-raisers! Nor should it be the responsibility of church bodies or personnel to provide such services. In our case, if our fund-raising committee should suddenly disband or the donations from the public should for some reason dry up, as many as twenty-five young people would find themselves with no place to live, forced to rob or prostitute themselves in order to eat and living a totally meaningless and destructive life on the streets. This is unfair to these young people as we cannot provide the security which they need. Hence, the more important part of our work is awareness-raising amongst the public and lobbying our decision-makers so that the rights of homeless children will become enshrined in law and provided by the structures of our state. This, in practice, means that the Health Boards would have a statutory obligation to homeless children and would take responsibility for the provision, funding and adequacy of services for homeless children, even where they delegate the running of services to voluntary bodies.

We would see the role of the church in this area as being a prophetic role – raising its voice in protest at the neglect of homeless children by a society that claims to be Christian, demanding that change must immediately occur to ensure their rights, and not ceasing to make that demand until it happens. For the church to step in, and through its own personnel and resources, substitute for the neglect of the State would be to perpetuate an unsatisfactory and unjust situation. However, where such a move is seen by the church to be an interim step, a regretful but necessary step, and is therefore accompanied by a loud and persistent demand for the State to take its responsibility for the basic needs of people more seriously, then such a move can be a very positive step – not only does it relieve the suffering of a group which cannot wait for the ponderously slow progress of political involvement or for bureaucracy to get its act together, but it also gives the church a valuable experience and insight which makes its demands in this area more authentic, insistent and credible.

Homeless children are one of the most vulnerable groups in our society and they deserve a priority which few other needy groups could match. They are still children and so society considers them to be still dependents and not expected to take full responsibility for their own lives. Many of them have already been very damaged by their experiences at home. If left on the streets, they are clearly at huge risk: they become inevitably involved in the criminal justice system as they take to petty theft or shoplifting in order simply to eat or clothe themselves; they end up with a criminal record or even a term in prison for no other reason than they were hungry, with all the consequences that that entails for their future, such as jobseeking or emigration; they risk involvement with drink or drugs just to escape from the utter boredom and meaninglessness of life on the streets; they are prey to offers of money in return for prostitution; they become distrustful of adults and their peers and find relationships difficult to sustain. The moral demands made on us by the plight of homeless children have an absoluteness that transcends political barriers.

Every person has the dignity of being a child of God; the gospel is the revelation of a God who is Father and Mother of everyone, with no exceptions. When we leave a homeless child on the streets, we are in practice saying that this child is not worth the effort, or the money, or whatever it takes, to remedy his or her situation; we are prepared to relegate them to the margins of life in our society; they are denied basic rights and prevented from participating in society. We are in practice denying the dignity of that child and so denying that God is his or her Father; we are therefore worshipping a God that does not exist.

For me, the kingdom of God, while it cannot come in its fullness in a world that is human and therefore sinful, is still an ideal that we have to try and establish even here on earth. That kingdom is one of peace and justice, from which no-one is excluded, in which everyone feels loved and respected and cared for and appreciated. To reach out to young homeless people, to show them that they are just as important as anyone else, to show them that they have the same rights as everyone else, to try and include them in one's own life and in society, is to add one little brick to the final building of the kingdom. The basic human virtue of compassion and the gospel imperative to respect the dignity which each one has as a child of God is the primary motivation for our service to homeless children. In practice, the relationships that are established with the young homeless boys in our care also become important motivational forces. As with a parent, the possibility of these boys becoming homeless again if we were to close or be forced to close through lack of finance would be so distressing that we keep going through the rough times and the crises and the sometimes apparently insoluble problems – the thought of giving up does not arise. Nevertheless it would be our hope and indeed our goal that we would cease to exist as soon as possible! When the Health Boards accept their responsibility for the rights of homeless children and put in place the services which are necessary to ensure the provision of those rights, then we will no longer be needed and we can happily and contentedly give up.

In working with homeless young people, we ourselves have been changed. You begin to see the often insurmountable obstacles which face the young people we are dealing with – the irrelevance and disinterest of the educational system, the lack of job opportunities especially for young people with few qualifications or skills, the absence of counselling for young people with problems who cannot afford to pay for it, the absence of drug rehabilitation services, the impossibility of getting housing when they leave home or hostel and as they prepare to start their independent life in contrast to the ready willingness of the criminal justice system to intervene and punish those who rebel or those who cannot cope and its willingness to find vast sums of money to pursue this aim. Very often all of these obstacles simultaneously face each individual young person with whom we are dealing. Seeing Irish society through the eyes of those who are at the bottom of that society raises questions about that society and its values, which may not be at all apparent from a relatively comfortable and middle-class perspective: seeing our own blindness and complicity in the structures which ensure that those who are relegated to the margins of society stay there; seeing Irish spirituality through our on-going failure to meet the basic needs of young homeless children – and others – and the apparent ease with which Irish Christians can live without feeling challenged by such a situation.

Above all it makes us angry: angry at the waste of life and potential which often characterises the plight of the young people we deal with and at the seeming indifference of a society which repeatedly gives the same message to these young people, namely 'We don't care'. We see the importance of anger in a spirituality that does justice – anger and love for the poor are two sides of the one coin: love for those who are unnecessarily suffering must, if it is genuine, involve anger at the cause of that suffering and a determination to remove it. The absence of anger is a failure to love. Yet our traditional spirituality sees anger as something negative, to be avoided. Only people who are angry – an anger born of love and channelled appropriately – will be effective in building the kingdom of justice.

We have come to see the neglect of homeless children as an indi-cator – a litmus test – of the extent to which we are a caring society. The usual excuses do not fit – we don't have the money, they should help themselves and not depend on others to do it for them, they are not worth helping, and so forth. Homeless children reveal to us a society that has failed to care.

THE POOR PERSON IS A PERSON
Written by Katherine Sheehan on behalf of
CentreCare, Cathedral Street, Dublin 1

CentreCare provides a space at the city centre where people in distress can come and speak about their concerns and be listened to. CentreCare grew out of a belief that around the centre of any city there are always a group or groups of people moving about who are either in a crisis situation or who are constantly in dis-tress. Originally the centre was established out of a shared concern between the Catholic Social Service Conference and the adminis-trator of the Pro-Cathedral that there was a need for a 'caring face' of the church at the city centre. In its origins it was not very clear about how the centre would develop.

When the centre began almost 90% of its clientele were homeless men who came mainly because they had no money left, had no-where to stay, or wanted to travel somewhere out of Dublin. Over time relationships were developed with these people which meant that they could call without having an immediate material need which needed to be met. The other development that hap-pened was that a broader range of people began to come to Cen-treCare i.e. people living in flats, houses around the city and from the suburbs. So, over time, the range of issues and people present-ing at CentreCare broadened. What was constant in the change of clientele and issues was the fact that 90% of the people using the service were living on welfare. Another constant has been the bal-ance between men and women. The service has always been availed of by numbers which break down as 2/3 male, 1/3 female in any year. Another thing that is significant is that the clientele of CentreCare are not geographically located within the same area. They come from many areas with their individual issues. This has implications for any possibility of gathering a group of people around an issue of concern to them.

It would be true to say that very many of the people who come to CentreCare are very oppressed in how they see themselves and in how they see their own possibilties of doing anything about their situation. Long-term unemployment is part of the lives of most of those who call to CentreCare. They present at CentreCare with issues in two broad categories.

1) Inadequacy of resources to meet basic needs such as food, shelter, clothing or they may not be able to get their statutory entitlements to these things. Many are illiterate.

2) Human problems – mental health, isolation, family/relationship difficulties, sexuality, depression, suicide etc.

The work

A lot of time is given to being present to people, listening to them. Sometimes it is enough to give people information or access to information so that they can take action themselves. In other cases, a lot more time has to be spent before someone is able to take action on their own behalf. At other times the worker advocates on behalf of a person. The philosophy underlying how we work is based on the belief that people can help themselves if they are given support and the resources to do so.

The range of help offered is from information/advice to support and counselling. Most of this work is done on a one to one basis. We do work with small groups of women and children at the local parish level but this would only take up a small percentage of the time.

As workers, we are very aware of the limitations of one to one work however we also see it as necessary. We see it as necessary to work with individual people and to work at structural change. These two activities are not mutually exclusive although in reality maintaining the balance between the two is very difficult. It probably needs different people to work at the two ends in any agency. We are always aware of the structural roots of many of the symptoms we meet, daily. It is also true that some of the symptoms have their roots in the way people relate or do not relate to each other as fellow human beings. People are very often as oppressed by each other as they are by the system.

Working for change

As mentioned above, CentreCare deals with many symptoms which arise from an unjust system. To date, it has not been possible to gather a group of CentreCare users to act on a social issue. This has been for two reasons: (a) People come from all over the place: (b) Many of the people who use the service do so for a while and then move on. While there is a core of people who regularly use the service, the majority are transient. So CentreCare attempts to advocate to the statutory authorities about issues of welfare, housing etc.

What we are trying to do

We are trying, in a small way, to empower people by making information easily accessible to them and by providing a context in which people can work at their own personal liberation.

CentreCare started, in the first place, out of the concern of two diocesan agencies. CentreCare is a diocesan agency. It is implicitly influenced by a Christian faith perspective. This would be more explicit for some staff members than for others.

Decisions about the work of the agency are made on the whole by a process of reflecting on what we are doing at a staff level. At this stage, I would say there is a shared view by the people working here of what we are about. It has been more difficult to involve the users in a process because of transience etc.

More recently, we have begun talking to people on a regular basis about how they see CentreCare and how it might offer them something else or something different.

Ourselves

To some extent, no direction is given to the agency from the wider diocese or official church leaders. This has left a certain freedom to seek out people who can help us find direction/new ways. So a lot does depend on the vision and values of the people working in the agency. CentreCare staff have been most influenced, I suppose, by people with a creative, liberating view of the church's role. There has been no block to seeking out people like this to support us.

The worker's commitment has been most sustained by calling on people around the place who have a vision of a creative church full of possibilities. The official structure does not seem to be able to offer that kind of support. We have to create something ourselves out of our own beliefs. To some extent, there can be a feeling of working in a vacuum, rather than a feeling of belonging to a wider organisation with a particular ideology. The feeling of being in a vacuum is disabling when spirits are low. On the other hand it does force us to be very critical of ourselves and to continually question what we are about. We have to be our own critics. It comes down to what we believe in ourselves as workers.

The sustenance comes from the people who use the service and from the team spirit that is present in the workers.

Many of the people who call to CentreCare are lighthearted in their attitude despite difficult circumstances. So, that is sustaining for us as workers.

I think that we are probably all challenged to change our view of society by the people we meet. From working in a place like CentreCare, it is very clear that there is a whole group of people who are constantly struggling on the edges of society and who have known nothing else in their lives.

TRAINING FOR TRANSFORMATION
Contributed by Maureen Sheehy on behalf of
Partners in Mission, *c/o DIAE Mountjoy Square, Dublin 1*

'Partners in Mission' is both a movement of people and a series of workshops which brought them together. It has grown from being a two-week annual residential workshop, to being an ongoing process involving thousands of people, mainly in disadvantaged areas throughout Ireland.

The first workshop was organised by the Irish Missionary Union in July 1981. Thirty-six people participated in the workshop. Eighteen of them had worked in either Asia, Africa or South America and several of the others were working in alternative type projects in Ireland.

The twelve-day experience tried to combine work at personal, interpersonal and wider society levels. At the personal level, trust building and listening skills were among the things emphasised. At the interpersonal level, an attempt was made to build the group into a temporary community, and several of those who participated in that original course still keep contact with each other and with the Partners movement. Through social analysis, the participants tried to look at wider society issues and tried to find some glimpses of hope about where they could work together in solidarity, towards a more just and equal society. During the course, the phrase, 'Things can be different', was echoed over and over. The difficulty of working for change and, on the other hand, of understanding how injustice and inequality are built into systems, left participants feeling inadequate and at times even hopeless. The workshop alternated between highs and lows. There were moments when people talked of having nothing to offer but their brokenness. At other times, there was a hope which fuelled people to believe that things could be different. And many of them still believe that today, eleven years later.

One of the basic elements in the Partners in Mission workshop was a hope, based on the promise of Jesus: 'I have come that you may have life, life in its fullness' (Jn 10:10). What did this statement mean? What did working for the kingdom of God mean in Ireland, now? Participants shared their struggle to answer these questions. Then, urged on by a new awareness of the stance Jesus took in the society of his day, they tried to see how they, in turn, could as Christians proclaim the fullness of life in today's Ireland.

Since the first workshop, Partners has tried to call people into a process in which firstly, they glimpse their own unique value and discover the richness of their own dignity and resources; secondly, they try to stand with others, listening, trusting and co-operating to improve the quality of life of the group, or local community, where they find themselves; thirdly, they try to work for change in society, so that justice may be an integral part of daily life. Also, more and more, Partners is aware of ecological issues and the need for all of us to treasure and educate ourselves in conserving our planet for future generations. This work, done at three different levels, is seen by Partners as responding to the challenge of the prophet Micah: 'This is what Yahweh asks of you, only this – to act justly, to love tenderly and to walk humbly with your God' (6:8).

Christian celebration, and particularly the celebration of the eucharist, has been an area of discussion and often struggle, since the beginning of the Partners story. At the first Partners workshop, there was a heated debate on whether or not celebrating the eucharist, should be part of the daily programme. The group ranged from those who believed that since the course was run by the Irish Missionary Union, daily eucharist was non-negotiable. At the other end of the spectrum were participants who felt alienated from and angry with the church. In so far as this latter group wanted to celebrate at all, they wanted to be free to experiment, explore and search for ways of authentic celebration, which might, or might not be, eucharistic. Other workshops have echoed the same struggle. In the process, some participants who hadn't celebrated the eucharist for years, have had a chance, in a small group setting, to understand its meaning anew. Others, who were regular Mass-goers, have for the first time questioned their own mechanical, unquestioning attendance. Between these two poles, there have been many varied and different journeys, hopefully enriched by listening to and sharing in the stories and insights of others.

Since 1981, Partners in Mission has run one or two residential twelve-day workshops annually. No two workshops are exactly the same, and yet there is a basic recognisable pattern in each. The first step is for everyone present to learn each other's names. A lot of emphasis is put on mutual listening, with respect and love. Creating an atmosphere of trust is important. Partners believe that when we trust and pay attention to each other, creativity blossoms and participants begin to 'have room' to use their talents and skills, which hitherto may often have lain dormant or unused. The workshop is constantly balanced between personal, interpersonal and wider society exercises. So a typical day would include time spent on social analysis, learning how groups work and having an opportunity to do work at a personal level. The latter might include trying to name one's own talents and gifts or having the opportunity to share some of one's own story. At the personal level, care is always taken to protect people from 'over exposure' and participants are constantly reminded to only share as much or as little as is comfortable for them. At the communal level, most exercises used in the workshop, can also be used again by participants in their home situation. These exercises would include learning basic facts about how groups work, how different types of personalities in groups affect the dynamics and how, as a facilitator or leader, one can integrate the positive contributions of all participants.

Emphasis is put on the need to keep a balance between 'task and maintenance' in a group. This means balancing the need for members to relate well to each other and, on the other hand, to get their work done. As the emphasis is on experiential learning, the team running the workshop sets up a learning event in which participants can themselves pool their findings on a subject. After a learning experience, the team will then sometimes give an input, summing up what participants have already stated and adding other facts they consider important on the subject. About midway through a workshop, the participants take over the facilitation. They are asked to listen to issues about which the other participants have strong feelings. Then they are helped to plan and facilitate learning events for each other. During the few days during which this is happening, the course is usually bursting with energy. Participants, working in teams, are busily sorting out issues that are generating strong feelings in others and deciding which one they will try to deal with. When the main facilitators reclaim the workshop, participants are much more critically aware of how the workshop is being run and probably learn more as a result. Now they are not only learning together, but observing how they are learning.

One of the outcomes of Partners workshops, is that participants sometimes decide to run similar events themselves when they return home. The Partners central team has responded to many requests to assist former participants to run workshops in their local areas. This sometimes involves one or two facilitators working with a local team. At other times, Partners have simply been involved in helping a local team in planning their sessions from week to week. Partners team consider this extension work a main priority in the use of their time and energy. The guideline for involvement is that they only do what the local people cannot do themselves.

To date over 400 hundred people have taken part in the twelve-day residential summer workshop. However, this type of workshop is not always suitable for many people with families or other commitments. So in the past few years, more workshops have been held over a series of weekends and in people's local areas. Approximately two thousand people have participated in these workshops. During these past two years, and partly as a result of having full time employees, the Partners' programme has been further developed and extended to many different parts of Ireland including the north.

In its work, Partners has two objectives which are being addressed simultaneously. Firstly, it seeks to empower people (individuals and groups) who are alienated by present societal structures, both by working directly with them and by working with those individuals and groups who are in key positions to assist with such empowerment. Secondly, it aims to build a movement for transformation composed of (a) people who are marginalised in society and (b) people who are sympathetic to their cause.

Partners targets its work at three particular groups. The first target group is of men and women from areas suffering from the worst effects of the twin evils of unemployment and poverty. Typically, those taking part are unemployed or from families where unemployment is a key factor; they are welfare recipients; they suffer a lot of deprivation as regards physical and emotional needs; they have lost confidence in themselves and in society; they see little hope of their situation improving in the future. The second target group is that of individuals and groups who work with such marginalised people and/or their families e.g. priests, sisters, health board workers, social workers, community workers etc. Target groups include lay organisations, St Vincent de Paul, welfare rights groups, community information groups, youth organisations, childcare organisations, drop-in centres etc. A third target group is that of individuals and agencies from any walk of life, who are sympathetic to the cause of the marginalised.

There is a strong Christian dimension to the work of Partners in Mission. This dimension is always implicit because Partners is working for a holistic development of people and communities. It is giving priority to the needs of the most disadvantaged sections of society. It seeks to inspire people and to give them hope. It encourages people to strive towards reaching their full potential as human beings. The Christian dimension is explicit in the Partners movement in several ways. Many of the founder members were priests and/or members of religious communities or returned lay missionaries. Other founder members were people with strong Christian commitment. The present management committee, the employees and a wide circle of key people who keep the movement alive are, almost entirely, from that same background and base their work on Christian values. This central group find much of their nourishment from sharing the eucharist together, from days of reflection together, and from formal and non-formal prayer in common. The Partners vision statement has an explicit Christian focus as can be seen from this excerpt: 'Urged on by a new awareness of the stance Jesus took, Partners participants feel called to stand and proclaim the fulness of life – especially where this life is deprived'.

At the first workshops, most participants came alone. In recent years, teams get priority over individuals in the allotment of places. The value of working in teams, rather than as individuals, is a strong part of the Partners' philosophy. It is noteworthy that significantly more women than men have participated in the training programme.

Planning an evaluation is one of the immediate tasks on hand. Then, building on what has been positive in the workshops and movement, and making changes or innovations where necessary, Partners will continue afresh in the work of transformation and in the certainty that things will be different.

THINKING GLOBALLY, ACTING LOCALLY
Written by Sr Scholastica, Moyross, Limerick City.

Moyross in Limerick city, has 1,160 households with a population of 5,500, comprised mainly of young families. With the residential development by the city corporation completed in summer 1987, there were few facilities or resources in the area. Residents were new to each other, seeking to set down roots and to find a way of life in a new situation.

The people had much with which to contend: unemployment rate (1989 survey) was 81%; the locality had no health centre, no community centre, no local job creation initiatives; no shopping centre, chemist or post office. In addition, there was much general apathy, a sense that nobody cared, a lack of cohesiveness and leadership in the area.

One effort which has helped considerably in the development of the area since 1987 actually began that summer when four local people attended a summer workshop on training for transformation. It included some knowledge and experience of adult education as developing critical awareness, human relations training in group work, analysing causes of problems and planning strategies, reflecting on key Christian themes of justice, freedom and fullness of life for all. Our local group found the experience so enlightening that they decided to form a group based on these principles. So in October, a meeting was called of local people active in the area and professionals who were working there as service providers – Moyross Partners was formed.

Five years on, Partners still meet once each month to consider the issues of the area and examine causes, strategies and possible solutions: 'we go around obstacles, not over them'. Those attending any meeting find a sense of welcome, supportiveness, and community interest, all of which encourages a feeling of belonging. Local people speak with freedom and ease to professional workers or representatives of statutory bodies. Mutual respect has developed in this atmosphere, outside the formal business of life situations: they relate as partners.

Growth in the Partnership has been largely a process of growing community consciousness on the part of the people. Adult and community education is a strong feature in this growth, beginning with courses in personal development /home management/ arts and crafts /parenting etc. These were offered first within the Family Resource Centre – a regular four bedroom house rented from the corporation and run by its own management committee. Prospective members for a course meet beforehand with a group from the committee to plan the content – it is a principle of bringing 'adult education to the community rather than community members to adult education at a distance', and this especially in their initial steps. So communication skills, self-confidence, a sense of one's personal worth, a recognition of basic human rights and one's rights as a citizen are imbibed in familiar surroundings. Taking part in courses offers other helps too: participants get to know each other in these small groups, they build up interests, concern, neighbourliness, friendship and many become actively involved in the community.

Issues raised and discussed at Partners meetings are taken on board by the core group and are followed through by liaising with the relevant statutory or voluntary body, by arranging further meetings among the people locally, by getting interviews with management figures and political representatives and by going public on the issue with intent to gain wider support and rectify the situation. Experience has taught that it is more effective 'to work as a group, not as an individual'. As a result of such efforts, Moyross Community Enterprise Centre was opened in summer 1992. It serves as a centre/focus for the community as well as offering facilities for more varied and larger-scale courses and for occasions of coming together. Beside it is the new Health Centre, also secured through much community agitation on the strength of a basic need. The Employment Co-op, commenced by a group of local people (unemployed) in 1989, continues to serve the area through its Jobs Club, while acting as a source of information and of contact with employing agencies.

Community oriented persons would have gained some of these insights from leadership training workshops sponsored by the Partners' group during these years. The courses followed the Training for Transformation model and were opened up to local groups from other areas. In this way, participants' views were broadened and they acquired an understanding of the needs, aspirations, struggles and challenges in areas other than their own. Their horizons were further widened by examining the roots and causes of localised issues in relation to national and international policies. The principle of 'action-reflection-action', emphasised in the methodology, has been adhered to and many committees and groups have an inbuilt pattern of evaluation. So the monthly meeting commences with a theme for reflection to which people are free to respond, and oftentimes concludes with a reflection on the meeting itself. Gradually people come to realise that power is not something that leaders carry about with them; it is a process occurring within a group.

The approach to work-within-the-community is in line with this policy: one helps not by giving things to people but by encouraging self-help; empowering parents to look at their own lives and their children's; securing for them facilities and opportunities to live life with dignity and have a say in discussing, in planning, in the managing of their own futures. And while consensus is aimed at in group decisions, even with time for consideration and repeated talking through, it is not always possible to secure this. But everybody has had scope to voice her/his opinion and if a majority decision is taken it is more fully accepted.

In addition to experience, skills, techniques which community-minded people have gained, they have, more importantly, the will to continue. This 'energy' derives from a belief in the humanity we share, in the human family of which we are part, with Jesus as one of us. While this faith may not often be verbalised in everyday life, it lives on deep in our people. And the knowledge that he experienced poverty and rejection, that he came from a 'backland' in his own country, that he stood with the lowly and deprived, helps make us feel good, feel important to him. It also means that he comes to have more significance in our lives when we give a bit of time to him. And so a few members of a committee or other group will ask: 'When are we having our retreat?' (before Christmas or Easter) and the event will be broadcast locally. This is an occasion for getting outside their own environment for a day or for an evening – a compact-sized group at ease with each other and with the person leading the effort. It is their evening and they are involved in the preparation; sincere participation in the whole celebration within a 'homey' atmosphere; oftentimes deep, personal sharing; good camaraderie. Faith on these occasions is almost palpable.

A scripture group meets weekly to come to an understanding of the Sunday readings. There is some introduction to the scripture background, then time given to apply its message to people's own lives. The richness of faith expressed, the perceptiveness of what its application implies, the attitudes, decisions, activities arising from the reading can be startling in their sincerity. In the group, age is no barrier at either end.

An expression of the real faith of the people is their genuine compassion and sharing with each other. Somehow there always is enough to share some, however little materially. Again it may be a listening ear (and heart), a supportive word, an understanding smile. Or the occasion may be the illness of a child, the hospitalisation of a family member, an accident, death, birth, wedding. First reception of the sacraments is still an event of great importance in the family and preparation of parents to participate more fully in these big days has everything to recommend it. Their involvement in the lead-up to children's reception of baptism, first communion, penance and confirmation offers invaluable occasions for re-evangelisation and we are not fully exploiting them.

The eucharistic celebration is still the central religious celebration in the lives of our people, and for them, in a sense, everything flows out or leads up to it. So the Sunday congregation commemorates the opening of a centre and/or prays for its annual general meeting. The Community Festival Week commences after Mass at 12.00 noon. The concluding of a workshop may best be highlighted by an intimate celebration for the group, when the insights and enrichment gained are expressed in liturgy. The Celtic aspect of our spirituality is still with us, where every feature of daily life was linked with prayer, and worship could include the whole of living. As one committed member of the community aptly (and sincerely) worded it, 'my work is my religion'.

Our locality has a high proportion of young families and, quite naturally, a big percentage of our population is under 18 years of age. This presents its own difficulties and its own challenges. Generous community members interested in youth and in sport have given considerable time over the years in training teams, preparing for competitions etc. Only within these last months, with the provision of indoor and outdoor facilities, has it been possible to organise clubs and other additional forms of leisure activities. In this respect, the number of adults (parents and others) who have come forward to act as adult leaders and take training sessions themselves has been very re-assuring. The overall organisation in the hands of a youth worker, youth chaplain and community garda eases considerably the sense of limitation, deprivation and boredom on the part of youth, and concern in the community generally in their regard.

What keeps the voluntary workers working? A sense of self-satisfaction in achieving results, although these may be little and spaced. But to have helped a person one step forward in human life gives a good feeling. With companions there is the sharing of experiences, of humour in times of difficulty, of get-togethers and social outings which renew the spirit. There is also the consciousness of helping to bring about a better world, a more equitable society, where people can live with dignity, honesty and pride – a world where the vision of Jesus may be brought nearer to fulfilment: 'I have come that they may have life, life in its fulness' (Jn 10:10).

EMPOWERMENT
Contributed by Irene Bailey, LSA. on behalf of
The Community-Family Training Agency, Ballymun

The Community Family Training Agency was founded by the Little Sisters of the Assumption in 1987 – to provide a training service to organisations, groups and individuals. The need for a specific group to provide this specialised service became clear as a result of active involvement, over the years, in community development by a member of the Little Sisters of the Assumption, local people, and others committed to the Ballymun community.

Different programmes were designed around the felt needs of people – groups in Ballymun. In 1993 the following training courses are being run by the agency:

1. Basic home management courses for women

The participants in this course are by and large in touch with local health workers – nurses, social workers, community welfare officers. The objective of the programme is to provide training that will build participants' confidence and enable them to learn new skills and provide group support. The hope is that, through this experience, people will have more control over their lives and be less dependent on others. This transformation we have witnessed with our own eyes.

2. Courses for the unemployed

As the percentage of people unemployed in Ballymun is three times the national average, the needs of this grouping are a priority for our agency.

For a number of years we have been involved in a FÁS sponsored scheme for unemployed men and women. To date over 70 people have participated in our scheme. The objective of this programme is to build confidence and motivation to re-enter the workforce. Each participant is supervised in a work project – e.g. secretarial duties, book-keeping, computers, creche work, home decorating. As the projects are locally based, a useful service is rendered to the community. An integral and important aspect of the programme is the additional training provided by the agency for the participants – input on personal development, job seeking skills and starting your own business, social analysis, continue for the duration of the course, further enhancing the prospects of securing employment.

The outcome for the participants has not always been the securing of employment – (some participants are now in employment) – due to the existing labour market. However, all have found it a very positive experience in building confidence and self-worth. Many have become involved in voluntary work in the local community and so feel they have a contribution to make to society.

3. Community development – leadership training

Ballymun has a long history of community development. Local people, together with professional people working in the area, have for many years acted on the social issues that were manifesting themselves in the community. This has resulted in the formation of our 100 community groups/projects. There was therefore a need for ongoing training of local community leaders. The programme we provide – sponsored by FÁS – is a 6 month fulltime course in leadership training, based on the philosophy of Paolo Friere – developing critical awareness and skills for participative education. This course covers confidence building, communications skills, assertiveness, project initiation, organisational development, development of resourses, networking with other communities, administrative skills, social analysis etc.. Participants are drawn from existing projects. However, many new projects have been initiated by participants as new community needs were identified. A number of people who have completed this course are now committed community activists.

4. Back to work course for women

Due to the large number of redundancies for men, women are now becoming the breadwinners as their skills are often more marketable in the existing labour market. We therefore have become involved in a part-time FÁS sponsored course, which aims at assisting those women, who wish to move from work in the home back into a paid labour force. This course covers confidence building, classification of one's own skills, new career options, job seeking skills, practical training on word processors and computers and work placement. Many of the participants of this programme are now in paid employment.

5. Course for men

Over the years, it has been relatively easy to initiate/sustain women's groups – numerous women's groups exist in Ballymun and are sharing resources through an establishment network. Initiating men's groups has been more difficult – our programme is aimed at men who are not in any other grouping. The course is of eight weeks' duration, covering topics like pressures on men in today's world, coping with stress, financial management, dealing with anger/conflict, communications, listening and assertiveness skills, day-to-day living in relationships or alone, practical skills.

6. Married couples course

Knowing the needs of young married couples, we have been involved in a programme designed to meet the needs of couples who attend this course – offering ways of nourishing relationships, mutual decision-making, and growth building experiences. This course is run by members of our staff, who are marriage counsellors.

In all these programmes we aim at enriching peoples lives, by building self-worth/confidence, helping people to become aware of their potential, passing on skills, forming community, and helping people to see the contribution they can make to the wider Ballymun community.

The agency staff structure is designed to blend professional expertise and local talent in training, administration, and management. This blend of professional and part-professional skills has proved both efficient and effective in providing a training service, a person centered atmosphere for the trainees and a consultant management style – sensitive to the needs of individuals/groups.

The faith dimension

Believing in the words of Jesus: 'I have come so that they may have life and have it to the full' (Jn 10:10), we see our attempts to create a climate where people can grow and experience community, as participating in the ministry of Jesus. As a group of committed Christians, aware of the mission of Jesus, we feel this awareness permeates who we are, and what we do. Like Jesus, we strive to have a preferential option for those most on the fringes of society and to take action where possible, in the area of structural injustice. This has changed our spirituality over the years. We now feel more at home with the Basic Christian Community model of church and with the concept of God as liberator – being with us in the struggle for liberation.

As many of the people we encounter, at times, are apathetic, alienated, angry with the church, it is difficult to proclaim the word of God explicitly. However, we are convinced that, if we ourselves are trying to live and work out of gospel values, this in itself is the proclamation of the good news. At times we have been able to run short workshops for those who desired them, on the life of Jesus, within his own historical context and his orientations.

While we do not work from the official church structures, we have many positive links with church leaders, especially when working on local community issues. We have participated in formation programmes organised at parish/diocesan levels which have been life-giving. Some members of our staff are members of their local parish councils.

At times we become downhearted – because of the slowness of this type of work, through lack of resources or because of interpersonal conflicts and power struggles which are all part of the human condition. However, belief in our project and past experience of life that has been created and knowing we are not alone – 'He walks with us' – spurs us to continue our journey toward life and wholeness. Like Martin Luther King, each of us can say:

'I have the audacity to believe that peoples everywhere can have three meals a day for their bodies, education and culture for their minds and dignity, equality and freedom for their spirits. I believe that what self-centered people have torn down other centered people can build up. I still believe that one day humanity will bow before the altar of God and be crowned triumphant over war and bloodshed and non-violent redemptive goodwill will proclaim the rule of the land and the lion and the lamb shall lie down together and every man shall sit under his own vine and fig tree and none shall be afraid. I still believe that we shall overcome.'

ADULT FAITH DEVELOPMENT
Contributed by Ciarán Earley for
Partners in Faith, *c/o DIAE, Mountjoy Square, Dublin 1*

'Partners in Faith' is a twenty-eight session process of adult faith development which is run with six groups from six parishes over a year. It is led by a team of four from the Pastoral Department of the Dublin Institute of Adult Education.

For the present course, in the late summer we entered into contact with pastoral agents from adjacent parishes in the Tallaght area. It was decided to run the course in the community hall in Jobstown. In each parish, someone took on the task of inviting people to take part in the project. A group is made up usually of four parishioners and a pastoral agent, sometimes more, sometimes less. On a week night in September the groups assembled in a room in the parish centre and the journey began.

The idea for the course emerged six years ago. Our institute has a mandate to develop pastoral projects which are evaluated and communicated to others. We are searching for a way of giving people an opportunity for faith education in the context of community with an action dimension. Faith, community, action, all the elements of basic ecclesial community. We had in our minds the sowing of seeds for the development of small faith communities.

Five of us, three adult religious educators and two theologians set about devising the project. As we struggled to create Partners in Faith, the elements of our vision emerged, embodied in the activities which can take place each night:

a) Experience of Christian community

We firmly believe that God intends us to live in solidarity with one another. The church, as the sacrament of God's dream for people, must embody this vision in structures of communion and participation. This is why people do not come to Partners in Faith as individuals but as members of groups who grow in unity and love over the year. Every night each group has a task to do at the service of the wider gathering – reporting, commenting, leading prayer, linking the course with current events, serving tea, tidying up and, by the time the last sessions arrive, the groups themselves are running them and we, the leading learners, become participants.

b) Essential Judaeo-Christian message

Each night, focussing on a certain theme, the participants reflect on their experience, converse about it, test it against an input and then decide is there need for change. The first themes explored are their own experiences of mystery and their image of God. In the next sessions they compare their image of God with the God of Moses and they compare their dreams for the world with God's dream for people as revealed in the bible. They then look at how in the bible, as in life, the dream is only partially fulfilled and there is call for prophetic action to begin to bridge the gap between reality and vision.

In the second third of the course they compare their image of God with that of Jesus who revealed God as Abba. They also compare their values, life projects and actions with the stance of Jesus who made the kingdom transparent among us. What happens next is described under the heading:

c) Action for the kingdom

In the last third of the course, each group identifies a concern of the larger group. After dialogue about that concern they research and plan action to help the whole group deal more creatively with that concern. The intention here is to enable the groups as communities to embody their faith in God through action for God's dream in the context of service of the wider community. The method for action is based on the philosophy of Freire. Through all this they engage in activities which allow them to reflect, celebrate, pray, deepen and reinforce their humanity and their faith. Gradually they blossom in confidence even in such a short while.

The people on the present course are ordinary working people from Tallaght and Clondalkin who participate with the leading learners on the basis of equality and dialogue and who shape the sessions, through the tasks they engage in, their comments, their criticisms and their eventual co-ordination of the sessions. They are usually excited at the whole idea of God's dream for people which translates into an egalitarian society of which the ten commandments are the constitution. They are amazed at their own creativity in terms of the bible. They are refreshed by the concrete manner in which we explore the vision and action of Jesus in his own country and time. Finally, they are surprised by their own ability to plan and lead sessions and respond to people's concerns.

Spirituality

In Partners in Faith we define spirituality as the art of listening to God revealing Godself and of responding to God's call according to our gifts. What shapes and moves my own living of this is the kind of God revealed in my experience illuminated by the Bible. This compassionate, liberating God, present in life and history, who has dreams for an egalitarian society, shapes and moves my own poor struggles. In a way, my work and my life are not too far apart. I couldn't really be doing faith education on the basis of any other theology than the one that influences my personal choices. On the one hand, Yahweh/Abba nurtures my being and, on the other hand, the dream/kingdom challenges my action. This influences how I vote, how I spend, how I work, whom I work with, how I organise church, how I repent.

Effects

I think the people, the priests and sisters and religious who take part in Partners in Faith are all inspired and encouraged by their participation, even though it's only 70 hours spread over a year. They are active on behalf of the kingdom and many are involved locally in church life. The bonds, dreams and actions of Partners in Faith continue to echo in their consciousness and affect their choices. The problem to be faced concerns the ongoing nurturing of this faith and love.

The church in Dublin is struggling to retrieve its fundamental inspiration and to find new ways of embodying itself in the lives of people, in new language and new structures. It is taking a long time. There are problems of faith vision, theology, structures and authority, but everywhere there are new dreams and new grass-roots gatherings struggling to grow and blossom. I think Partners in Faith is an experience which contributes to the emergence of ecclesial communities which are more nearly salt, leaven and light for the kingdom.

TOWARDS BASE ECCLESIAL COMMUNITY
Written by Gemma McKenna in dialogue with the
Fig Tree Prayer Group, Fatima Mansions, Dublin 8

The Fig Tree group has it roots in the efforts in the 1980s to build up the Fatima Development Group here in Fatima Mansions. During ten years of struggle, the Development Group prevailed on Dublin Corporation and other statutory bodies to work with them to change things for the better in the flats. Several major problem areas were named and tackled: improving the sewerage system, improving lighting, providing creche and play facilities, initiating a women's education project, residents having a say in the allocation of flats, the refurbishment and landscaping of the flats, employment schemes, co-operatives. As these external changes happened, people began to have a better image of them-selves and to experience power through effectively influencing bodies like the corporation, funding agencies and the media. It was a movement for dignity and justice: a struggle to reduce the effects of poverty, unemployment and internalised oppression.

Faith connections

In 1987 some people tried to make explicit the link between trans-

formation and the kingdom of God: a week of 'directed' prayer
was organised in the local school. Everyone from the flats who attended got a short gospel passage each day to pray and talk about
with a director. On the final evening, at the eucharist, a few said
they would like to keep meeting and so the Monday night prayer
group was formed. A small group has continued to meet each
Monday for six years. The format is simple: we meet in one of the
flats; after quiet music and a bit of relaxation led by one of the
women, we read a short gospel passage (usually from Luke). People single out words or phrases that strike them and repeat them.
The passage is read again and each one says why a particular
word or phrase struck him/her and what the passage in general
seems to be saying to us. We end with prayers for different needs
and for situations around us that have been mentioned in relation
to the gospel text. We round off the sharing with a cup of tea.

When President Robinson came to visit Fatima, the prayer group
was asked to meet her and explain what we are about. We formed
our reflections into a prayer-poem and found our symbol: the fig
tree:

> We cannot speak of who we are
> Unless we speak of one who gathered us
> and another who shares her home
> and here we are at ease, sit in candlelight
> and safety.
>
> Among us is Jesus and in and through our lives,
> ancient words breathe hope.
>
> He tells us we are precious; he
> embraces us, raises our heads and
> we struggle to keep them high however
> weak we feel, in spite of officials
> who refuse our people work, refuse
> to acknowledge our needs and talents,
> in spite of government's broken promises.
>
> He reveals to us a dream that can
> unite our people, move us to act for change.
>
> And the times we see this dream being lived,
> we give thanks to God. We bring into prayer
> our people's hurt and we know that we have
> been wronged.

It is our belief in the dignity of each and
every one and our right to challenge
those who trample on us
that will sustain us as we work to let go of
past injustice
and build a community based on equality and freedom!

'I am there whether you rise or sit; whether you go out; or come in' (2 Kings 19:27).

Small Christian Community

The elements of small Christian community can be traced in our meetings:

1. A coming-together: trust growing deep among us, enabling each person to be free to speak her mind, knowing she will be respected;
- freedom to comment on the gospel text without fear, in our own words, as it strikes us tonight: as need be, getting light about the text from a commentary;
- expressing in our own words how we experience God.

2. Knowing ourselves; through the trust and the sharing of stories we learn mutual support and self-esteem.

3. Knowing God; moving gradually away from the false image of a God who is super-critical and condemning, to a more liberating image, as we become free to accept and trust the glimpses we have had of a God who is loving, struggling with us and delighting in us.

4. Knowing the gospel; losing the fear that kept us from it;
- interpreting it in terms of our own struggle;
- challenging the gospel to speak more meaningfully to our lives;
- noting the passages that are key to our struggles;
- beginning to find 'words never heard before' to express the meaning of the gospel in terms of the reality of Fatima.

5. Celebrating. Each meeting is a celebration of ourselves as valuable people; at times like birthdays, etc. the 'ordinary' communion among us takes on eucharistic aspects; actual eucharistic celebrations in the small group are appreciated deeply and strengthen us as Body of Christ and Christian community.

6. Outreach. In a small vital way, what has been happening on a

larger scale in the flats is beginning to happen micro-style in and through the prayer group but with an *explicit* link made by the members between the kingdom of God and working to make things better. The experience of God's love and respect for us, tangible through the prayer group, has moved us to want to get involved beyond the Monday night meetings.

This impetus is coming while the problems of unemployment and lack of significant involvement for young adults are still with us in the flats, when there is an increase in drug-trafficking and drug addiction and when the energy of the organisers is running low in face of apathy and reduced funding.

Activities springing from our vision

Since last June, on two evenings a week, children from the nearby Blocks come to learn how to make something they like and so build up their self-esteem. This has become the 'Sunflower Club'. A plot of waste ground has been dug with help from a farmer and gardener and vegetables have been successfully planted. The children have been involved in minding it. We have joined the Fatima Development group in their efforts to deal with the drug problem by demonstrating against pushers, joining the addiction support group and joining meetings to plan the resurrection of adult education activities. Each Monday the 'fall-out' from these involvements gives a new dimension to our gospel sharing, sometimes putting on the brakes – as when we asked ourselves whether we could achieve much by an aggressive stance– and mostly giving us a reason to go on acting despite setbacks.

What keeps us going, despite the smallness and fragility of our efforts, is the support we get from each other, the co-operation stemming from mutual trust and the encouragement from the way Jesus acted. Faith helps us hang in there together.

Our Strategies

1. Trying to build up each other as persons and taking time to do this.
2. Becoming more free to act positively in our own favour (greatly enhanced by trips to *An Tobar*).
3. Claiming the gospel as our own and God as on our side.
4. Beginning in small ways to make a difference in the community and not dismissing what we do because it is small.

Our spirituality

The core of it is the realisation that each person is loved and cherished by God. Five points expressed during our review in August 1992 contain the seeds of our spirituality:
- In all the changes God is there, all the time faithful to us.
- God is binding us together in love and trust.
- God is healing the past hurts and turning those bad experiences into a powerful gift.
- God is taking delight in each one of us.
- God is calling us to move out to do something for others.

Links with the wider church

The faithful presence of the local curate, searching with us, learning from us, enlightening us and sharing our struggles, goes a long way in countering the slowness of most professional Christians to understand and value what we are about 'at the edges'. The Fatima experience invades the marrow of my bones and vitally influences what I do and say in other pastoral contexts.

Major difficulties

1. Apathy and hopelessness that so easily rear their heads, even when projects are under way.
2. When to assess the movement to push and challenge ourselves beyond where we are at.
3. How to make the link between kingdom and community development when people are 'shy' of the bible connection and the 'prayer bit'.
4. For ourselves, how to remain content with the pace and the fragility of it all.

A personal reflection on what the journey has done for me

- I have met a new face of God: passionate, vulnerable, struggling.
- I have discovered God in and through my own vulnerability as a stranger in my own country, needing to build up a sense of who I am as a Christian woman in a conservative church.
- the comments made in the group about God and the meaning of the gospel have challenged my more controlled, rigid, 'heady' ideas.
- the gap between faith and life, prayer and action has narrowed.
- I have been taught how to celebrate.
- I have seen the power of gesture: as when the people of Fatima

marched to the *Sunday World* offices to show the 'good side of Fatima on Good Friday.'

- I have seen how people blossom when they are granted space and respect to be themselves.

- I have learned to be contemplative: to let God reveal Godself through the people and events that surround me and not precipitate into action.

- I have experienced the value of solitude balanced by weekly group meetings;

- I have come to see the fragility of any kingdom effort: God alone gives the increase.

> The Jagged Edge
> The jagged edge is uncomfortable, unsafe,
>   unclear, liminal
> a no-person's land;
> But from and around the broken shards
> seeps the glue of blunt, awkward companionship,
> a steadying force to hold you
> clear
>   comfortable
>   safe
> in periphery land.

EXODUS
Contributed by Susan Gannon and the
Exodus Group, Basin Street, Dublin 8

After the death from AIDS of a young man in our area, I noticed a deep sense of powerlessness and despair. His death seemed to have raised many questions one of which was: 'If even with all our efforts nothing changes, what is the point?' So with community leaders and organisations in mind, I wrote a framework of reflection on the book of Exodus, believing that the story of the Hebrew people was a rich starting point to begin the process of answering this question in our own lives and the life of the community. I took ideas from a section of a book called *Partners in Faith*, which enables people to explore their image of God. With this, I then invited several people to come together, including members of our parish team. One member turned up but could not continue to be part of the group. Within a few weeks, what emerged was that although we drew meaning from community activities and projects, something bigger and more constant is needed to sustain us.

Here we are, a year and a half on, four women and one man who meet in each other's homes to reflect on our lives in the light of our faith and scripture. This is how we do it;
- relaxation, becoming aware of 'God with us'
- select a passage, use part of the 'Seven Step Method' to get familiar with the text.
- A closer look at characters and events in the text, imagining the feelings, reactions and thoughts involved.
- Some background information using *Partners in Faith* and a theological commentary on the text.
- Questions about how the text speaks to our lives. How it affirms, nourishes, challenges. How it can shape our personal lives, our community and its organisations.

These steps sometimes followed in one night or over a period of weeks. I have planned and led the greater part of our meetings, mainly due to the fact that other people in the group had little or no experience in reading and praying with scripture. This set up was accepted and welcomed by the group. Gradually this has changed and people have more confidence, more belief in their own experience, faith and their right to make their own of the bible. Therefore, they are willing to plan and lead our meetings. These gatherings have, on a personal level, helped to heal some very deep wounds. We have developed strong, supportive relationships which never cease to bring life and hope to our daily experiences. This then spilled over into our extensive involvement in organisations such as community response to AIDS, enterprise development and youth projects. Not only were we concerned about the community, involved in the community, but we were continuing to do so because we are Christian. We were being inspired, challenged and nourished through our faith, becoming much more aware and critical of our situation, as well as the use of power; all through reading scripture.

However, except for one person in the group, our involvement in community organisations has come to a standstill. This is firstly due to growing belief that our attentions must be more focussed on people within our community who are usually overlooked: whose lives remain untouched by the policies of our organisations. Secondly and sadly, it is linked to a painful and destructive interaction with a member of the parish team within a project.

This almost crushed my own and another member's confidence and sense of worth. It is impossible to be involved in community organisations in our area without being limited to, dependent on, influenced by the parish team and their resources. This can be a wonderful vibrant sign of community and church partnership and, to some extent, it is just that in our area. But it has become an obstacle for members of our group who are really struggling to translate into action what we believe in and are commited to. At first, we dealt with this obstacle by public evaluation of the project and then we resigned from the umbrella group. Then we simply stayed out. We are not in the process of developing and gathering resources, skills and confidence to address and respond to issues in our community that continue to be overlooked. So rather than being separate from other organisations we see ourselves, at this stage, as being underneath or on the edge of the ways of development and of being church that are in place.

What sustains us in our commitment to each other? A spirituality that has been forged out of the meeting point of living struggle, scripture and faith. Also our desire to be a source of hope, solidarity and change. A sign of 'God with us' in our community. The verses from Is 61:1-4 best expresses what we struggle to live in our daily lives. What we dream can be the essential ingredient in the formation of an organisation that seeks to create a space with those people who have been ostracised by our community. A space that accepts, supports and enters into a dialogue to begin responding to our many needs. Our contact and periodic meetings with the Fig Tree Group in another parish also sustains us, as we know we are not isolated. In fact, it is my own membership in the Fig Tree Group that made the formation of the Exodus Group possible. Another source of support and way of stretching us further is a priest who is open to doing a study programme with us, to help deepen our knowledge of the bible. Our celebration through being creative with drawing, clay and writing, eucharist and the occasional good night out are a great source of joy and keeps us going!

So all this together enables us to survive difficult situations, to have a sense of our own worth and, therefore, raises expectations for our lives and relationships. It also calls us to live to the full, to be part of the process that makes this possible for ourselves and for our neighbours.

DRINKING AT OUR OWN WELLS
Written by Patrick Galvin CSSp.,
An Tobar, Ardbraccan, Co Meath

I am here at *An Tobar* having chosen to live with a group of Spirit-
ans and to work on a team composed of Seán Ryan and myself.
The purpose of our centre is to provide for the more deprived
people of our society. Our main aim is to provide a facility and be
available to meet the needs of groups who chose to use it. The emphasis is on the groups' own agenda and what they want to do
during their time here.

My first concern when groups are coming is to see that basics like
heating, kitchen facilities and bedrooms are in order. I also check
to see that garbage bags are in place, tea towels are available as
well as a sufficient gas supply. It also maybe necessary to provide
videos, markers or a chart for paper. There is also work when the
groups leave like clearing garbage and laundry. Most groups
when leaving take a lot of care to see that the place is clean and in
order for the next groups. I spend time too with maintenance; like
finding a way to mend a leaking pipe, providing fuel for the fire
or finding the culprit for the mouse droppings. These are some of
the basic physical things I am doing.

Groups booking our centre usually do so months in advance and
normally by phone. I get information on the number in the group
and the purpose for which they are coming. I also enquire 'what
do you want from us while you are here'. The answer to this var-
ies considerably from group to group and also depends on how
well they know Seán and myself. Groups come with varying
agenda. Some come in order to get away from family pressures or
surroundings to find space for themselves. Some come to reflect
on their surroundings and environment while others come for
human development, while still others come for a retreat. Often
groups bring their own facilitator which then leaves us free to
meet people at a more casual, though no less important level.

My approach to working with groups, whether it be in the area of
social analysis, human development or retreats would be present-
ing some input and then processing with the group. This means
preparation and finding suitable material and techniques. I invite
them to process what's going on for them through sharing their
experiences or through drawing and the use of symbols. A simple
exercise like putting all sorts and varieties of pictures on the floor

and then have them choose a particular one could be the beginning of a whole session for reflection and sharing. These sessions also give me the opportunity to share my own story, be it the struggle and pain or the joys and hopes.

One of the most important qualities I find in my work is to be a good listener. I find I do a lot of this from small chat right up to group processing. I hear mothers share a lot about their children, their pride and their disappointments. I hear a lot about prices and where to get the best bargains and the whole struggle of making ends meet. I hear people's pain of a drunk spouse or of broken relationships. I hear people share about their own inner struggles their desire to be free and at peace and yet finding themselves anxious or depressed. I hear people looking for a peace within or for a deeper relationship with God. I offer people an opportunity to reflect on what's going on for them as they take a walk through nature or as they meditate on a passage from scripture. If they so wish, time is given for them to share what is going on for them. A useful exercise I find with groups who relate to God is by asking them to share when they felt closest to God. I find this can bring home to people that God can be found in all sorts of situations and in the bits and pieces of daily life.

A high point for many groups is the eucharist. It can become a gathering point for a group over a weekend. Time is given to preparation of readings and inviting as much participation as possible. People, so they tell me, find such celebrations alive, personal and with a sense of belonging.

WE ARE THE CHURCH
Contributed by Tom Carlin (its first full-time lay co-ordinator) for WATCH (We are the church) c/o, Presbytery, Wexford Town. One of the main architects of the process was Teresa McCormack IBVM, who became its full-time co-ordinator from 1986 until September 1988. At that time Fr Jack McCabe, Administrator during these developments, was appointed PP in another parish and Fr Hugh O'Byrne was appointed Administrator.

In the early eighties the two parishes of Wexford Town began to initiate a joint process of radical re-structuring triggered by a number of elements:
– Bishop Herlihy, at a meeting of priests and religious of the town, encouraged them to explore ways to work together as a local church.

– among people, a growing sense of dissatisfaction with society and a desire to do something about community issues was articulated.

– within the Church, the impact of ·Vatican II was having some effect and there was an increasing number looking to the Church for change and an up-dating of policy and practice.

The result was an assembly of the priests who minister in the town's two parishes and almost one hundred religious. This assembly took a decision to conduct a survey of the town looking at its economic, political, social and cultural situation. The group (priests and religious), rather than bring in professional bodies to carry out the survey, decided to do it themselves.

The structures shaping Wexford town: (i) history; (ii) economic; (iii) political; (iv) cultural; (v) social.

(i) Wexford has two natural resources – land and water. These created its economic growth in the nineteenth century. From 1850 to 1885 it was the port of Wexford that brought many benefits to the town and made it prosperous. The wealthy ship owners were willing to spend their profits on improving local amenities and services. This led to an infra-structure and standard of living that was unique for a medium-sized Irish town of that time. The sea trade, however, had declined by the end of the century.

This decline was off-set by an increase in agriculture-based industries. Foundries, Iron Works, Engineering Works were all established to manufacture farm implements, not just for the local and national levels but also for export.

By the 1970s, the harbour was closed and the majority of the agricultural industries had gone. These were initially replaced by new factories and new types of industries which catered for foreign markets. Most of these have moved to other countries.

For tourist reasons, the focus has now been placed on the importance of the Viking era as a significant contributor to the development and shaping of Wexford Town. Other significant contributions have not been over-looked. For example, some of those are the skilled workforce who lived in the community and contributed significantly to the development of a small/medium-sized rural town.

(ii) The industries, business and services that existed at the time of the survey were examined from the perspectives of:

- who owns them?
- who controls them?
- how many people work in them?

In 1983/1984 there were seven international companies employing just over half the people at work in major industries. Since then there has been a steady decline in the major industries operating in the town. Note also that at this time there were only two major industries controlled by Wexford families. The survey helped us discover that the major businesses in the town are dominated by family concerns and that they, together with the service industries, provided for 36% of the total number employed.

(iii) In doing a social analysis of Wexford, we looked at the political structures affecting the town. Who have power, what are their aims, what do they do, what influence have they got, what concerns have they? The study was limited to two groups – politicians and trade unions. The politicians listed among their most important concerns the following social problems:
- unemployment
- housing
- growing marriage breakdown
- alcoholism

Trade Union officials and Shop Stewards listed them as:
- a decent work atmosphere
- a wage structure in line with the national average
- to make jobs more attractive in status and pay
- to keep as many jobs as possible
- to look after the unemployed

(iv) So what gives meaning to Wexford society? We decided to look at religion, education, media and community organisations. In 1983 we concluded that most people felt part of the parish but were not happy with communications between priest and people. 87% felt that lay people should take more active part in the parish. Of the people who go out for leisure activities, 87% go to the pubs. The number of young people who drink is higher than those who smoke and marital breakdown is on the increase.

(v) We discovered that, because of increasing population, there will be an equivalent pressure for more jobs, houses and shop facilities. There exists a great sense of community in Wexford town and among residents there is a high sense of social awareness and

concern. There is also a large number of voluntary groups working to improve the quality of life in the town. The following are the major social problems mentioned by most groups questioned:
- unemployment
- poor housing
- marital breakdown
- alcoholism
- drug taking

This process took two years. Not only were the participants helped in carrying out the survey, but groups also met to develop a common vision of church for the town. The next stage was the decision to present these discoveries to the people and, at the same time, to invite them to discuss their hopes about the sort of Wexford they wanted and what kind of church would help them bring this about. At these meetings, which took place in ten pastoral areas, the people were invited to actively join the process by establishing a leadership team in each of the 10 pastoral areas. By 1985, teams were established and operating in each of the ten areas, organising gatherings every month to which all residents of that area were invited. At these assemblies, plans were laid to tackle issues according to the needs expressed by the people. A Steering Committee of the whole town was also established with final responsibility for the whole process and for community development in the town.

The survey process led to a clear conviction that the traditional church structures were also in need of transformation towards a model which would take on board the theology and direction of Vatican II and, in particular, the full implications of the statements:

'all baptised belong to the people of God'
'the real context of the people of God is the parish'

Consequently, the parish also re-organised itself and developed a structure that was community orientated. This was captured in the name WATCH (We are the church). It was the title assumed by the parish and signalled to the community that together we are in the process of building community – we are in the process of developing a church which is relevant and effective – one which responds to the prophets call: 'Act justly, love tenderly, walk humbly with your God'.

A significant number of initiatives, both community and church based, developed as responses to the indications of the survey. Actions were taken at the levels of community development, work initiatives, setting up a community response to security problems, establishing an open learning centre geared to respond to the needs of a specific community, the involvement of people in liturgical developments, parish preparation programmes for the sacraments of initiation with a community dimension, special care projects.

At this time, Wexford parish was unique in Irish church life because it looked in an analytical way at its own situation; not because it articulated a dream/vision for the parish; not because it devoted time and energy to the development of a structure that was respectful of the right of each person to participate, but because as a parish it has combined all of these elements and interwoven them into an alternative way of being church. This uniqueness was further enriched when, in September 1988, the parish appointed a member of the laity to the position of full-time coordinator.

A beacon had been lit in contemporary Irish society. On the one side, it signalled that the human construction of society is not secular in the sense of being outside of God's plan, but intimately connected with it and, on the other side, it signalled that the mission of the church is with people in society in an intimate, real and on-going way. For Wexford, our new thinking leads us to explore key concepts, such as empowerment, participation, discernment, collaboration, reflection, action, celebration.

In 1993, we are beginning to engage ourselves in the process of renewal, taking a serious in-depth look at our development. We are discovering:
- that, despite the provision of resources and support, many continue to feel less than comfortable with the truth that ministry is a communal (team) calling to all baptised. This includes priests and laity of all ages.
- that attempts to enliven this sense of community are most successful when the need being responded to is one experienced and identified by the respondents.
- that people, on the one hand, long to belong and play a part, yet on the other hand are driven by individualism.
- that team ministry is more difficult than we imagined, especially when the starting point is listening to people as they find the cou-

rage to intimately describe their experience of living.

- that for most people 'church' life seems to be one more thing to be squeezed into a busy schedule.

- that we cannot go back to the way things 'used to be'. We are on a journey of discovery regarding Christian discipleship in the modern world.

- that the way things are is not the only way things can be.

- that we need to keep struggling, telling our stories and finding ways to support and challenge one another.

- that by working/collaborating together we can achieve more than by each person doing his/her own thing.

But where is the church at national and diocesan level? Where are the pastoral plans that clearly identify goals and targets for authentic partnership so that as church in Ireland we can act justly, love tenderly and walk humbly with God into the twenty-first century? The church needs to be the countersign to individualism, not the supporter of a corner stone of the western model of development. The church must promote, encourage and resource community development.

BUILDING A PARISH COMMUNITY
Written by Fionnuala O'Sullivan OP, with the collaboration of the parish team in Firhouse, Dublin 16

As a parish team, we believe that we have a role in developing a concept of leadership as service. We do this by:

- Meeting regularly as a team (at least weekly).

- By sharing on what is going on for us and with the people.

- By sharing scripture together weekly and by trying to see what we do of maintenance and formation in the context of the real needs of people and in the light of kingdom values.

- By a monthly planning meeting followed by a celebratory lunch.

- By keeping each other reminded that the future of the parish is in the hands of lay people.

- By constantly encouraging people to become involved and to use their gifts in service of others, in a spirit of mutuality.

- By setting up courses in personal development, adult religious education, scriptures, parenting, etc., or by recommending others available in the area.

- By regular, systematic visiting of homes.

- By formation of small groups: two small Christian communities;

separated support group; twinning group; parish office service team; C.R.A.M. (for cleaning, repair, adornment and maintenance of Church building); baptism team; bereavement team; plus several connected with liturgy.

- By regular contact with the schools (two primary), pupils, 34 teachers and by small group meetings of parents (in homes) before confirmation and communion.

- By outreach to others and by raising awareness of justice issues in small Christian communities and by twinning with a parish in Molo, Kenya. And by reference to justice issues in preaching and in the parish newsletter.

- By a full day annually for the team, to evaluate the year past and to sketch a plan for the coming year.

- By a monthly parish newsletter prepared by one of the team and a lay woman.

- By regular meetings with the Pastoral Council, its Executive Council and by in-service days for the members.

- By celebration of the liturgy, sacramental occasions, street Masses, special events in Lent and Advent.

- By ordering from England and having available for sale a very attractive, inspirational booklet, *Advent Extra* and *Lenten Extra*.

What are we trying to achieve?

Under the guidance and inspiration of God's spirit, we wish to play a part in the formation of a vibrant local Christian community, where people will be involved in taking decisions and in seeing them through.

To move from a version of church that is mainly motivated by law, fear and/or formalism to one which frees people to be fully alive in Christ and where a commitment to social justice and community will be stronger than personal piety, individualism and conformity, with educated lay people taking responsibility for their own decisions if they are informed and trusted.

To set up a supportive infra-structure that will be flexible yet appropriate to enable people to continue to respond and to grow as Christians in spite of society's values (or lack of them), changes of personnel on parish team or the attitudes of official church leaders outside the parish structure.

To be aware of and together to find ways of responding to new needs – impermanence of relationships, unemployment, secularism, violence, the growing chasm between rich and poor etc., and to network with other parishes and interest groups in trying to respond in a courageous way to these needs.

The decision-making process

At parish level the decision-making group is the Pastoral Council. Our council is in existence since August 1987. The members hold office for three years. Our second council is coming to the end of its term. The council meets five times a year. The executive meets every other month and prepares the agenda for council meeting. The council is chaired by a lay person. It is made up of the parish team, a representative from every 100 houses and a representative from a few other organisations. Over the years there has been a noticeable improvement in participation at council discussions but there is still a reluctance among the lay members to initiate new ideas or projects. Issues are mainly raised by the team, discussed by all members and ratified or not by the council. To date, not all members give their views or seem to be aware of the overall needs of the community but, through experience and in-service days, there has been development in this area.

Development of spirituality

- For one not raised on scriptures, a growing towards reading it personally and in pastoral situations.
- A sharper awareness of the need to include the people of the parish in my prayer.
- A growing desire to reach out to and include in some way those who are not church-goers.
- Awareness that if our preaching is to be relevant, we must relate it to life today, and have input from our lay people.
- A conviction of the need to take a stand for justice in our local church community, inclusion (young, old, male, female, pious, impious, etc.) just salaries, attitude of partnership, power 'with' not power 'over' etc.
- The need to make a conscious, creative effort to include the people from new areas (where houses are still being built) in the life of the parish community.

Our greatest obstacle to date has been an attitude of fear of change from good practising Catholics who have no scriptural or theological foundation for the faith that is in them.
- A fear of leaving the old tried ways, practices and devotions.
- A fear of not really being wanted in the new ministries, (the

priest is saying it because he has to, but he doesn't really mean it).

- A fear (or hope!) that the next Parish Priest will go back to the old ways of the priest deciding everything, holding all the power and getting (or allowing!) lay people to 'help father'! A lack of realisation and/or conviction that God's people share Christ's mission by right of baptism.

-A lack of vision of a new way of being church among good people taught for years in a rigid authoritarian system.

Our experience has confirmed us in our belief that to be effective we must work as a team, build community between team members and between team and people. Our experience gives us the hope that, where people have the will to work together, new initiatives can be taken in spite of lack of leadership at wider church levels.

What sustains us in difficult times?

- Being part of a team in a relationship that allows for constant informal contact and exchange of information and views .

- Feeling encouragement and affirmation from each other.

- Humour – the ability to laugh together.

- To see lay people grow, take initiatives and be free gives us heart.

- The knowledge that, no matter how gloomy the scene may seem at times, God in Christ is faithful to the promise to be with his people until the end of time.

WOMEN OF VISION
Contributed by Claire Murphy on behalf of the
Christian Feminist Movement – Ireland

The third 'International Interdisciplinary Congress for women' was held in Dublin in July 1987. On the last day a session conducted in the Mansion House was entitled 'Religious Women, Women of Vision'. Four Religious Sisters told of their work among the marginalised in New York. Margaret McCurtain OP in responding, expressed appreciation of what she called the 'domestic work' of the church and then focused on the title *Women of Vision* and suggested that there was a need for further exploration of the role of women in the church. Those interested gave in their names.

Two months later, Maura Dillon, Columban, and Eleanor Dargan, Sacred Heart, arranged a follow-up meeting. Eleven women attended, of whom ten were religious, the eleventh being Mary

Doyle of Carrigaline, Cork. At the end of the discussions that evening, it was felt that Ireland needed a feminist voice. To find out for whom this voice would speak, it was decided to hold a Christian Feminist Conference the following May. Through the pages of *Womanspirit*, a new Irish feminist magazine, the idea of a Christian Feminist Movement in Ireland was floated. Seven women's groups around the country responded, offering suggestions for a Conference topic and workshops.

Two hundred women attended that first conference held in Milltown Park, in May 1988. It proved an opportunity for feminist women to meet, to share and to discover how much they had, and had not, in common. More study support groups were set up but it was decided to take no further organising steps for a year. That October the Cork Feminist Spirituality Group hosted a weekend at which travelling women and women theologians spoke. The aim of the weekend was to inspire and inform.

In October 1989, the organising conference was held. Opinions were divided as to whether it should be a more inclusive Feminist Spirituality Movement or a Christian Feminist Movement rooted within the churches. This distinction caused great heartache and soul-searching till finally a name was agreed, 'The Christian Feminist Movement – Ireland'. Several names had been submitted including *Aisling Íosa*, (The Vision of Jesus), but it was decided to keep to the term used in church documents. Some women unhappy with the Christian emphasis left the C.F.M.I. and continued in spirituality groups. Contacts are kept open and mutual support given for specific objectives.

The 1990 conference advertised itself as an opportunity: 'to enable feminist women within the Christian Churches in Ireland to come together and organise and, in the light of the gospel, to discern and to respond to areas that call for renewed effort in realising the vision of Jesus in the life of the Church.' At this conference, old disagreements were aired again but, finally, during the year the following Statement of Identity was agreed:

'We, members of the Christian Feminist Movement, are women of Ireland working together to become a voice for our Christian Vision and Values. The aims of the movement are:
- to raise consciousness among women and men
- to open channels for dialogue
- to support affiliated members and groups
- to help bring about changes in the churches

- to explore new prayer rituals and liturgical forms
- to work toward changing structures which cause poverty and powerlessness, especially in the lives of women
- to network with other feminist groups

The northern groups took responsibility for organising the 1991 conference in Belfast. Bridge building was the theme chosen. Again differences arose. Some groups objected to men attending the conference, believing women still needed a 'safe place' until they found their voice. However, the Northern women felt there were enough religious and political divisions in their area without adding another, so Saturday was declared an Open Day, three men attended, and Sunday was reserved for members only. As a result of a proposal made at the Sunday session, the National Committee sent an explanatory letter to all the bishops in Ireland and to the Congregation for Divine Worship in Rome making the following request:

'The Christian Feminist Movement in Ireland considers that biblical texts about the subjection of wives to husbands should be avoided in the liturgy and should be omitted from the next edition of the Lectionary.'

A few supportive letters were received from the bishops but no word as yet from Rome. By Holy Family Sunday, 27 December 1992, the phrase 'Wives be subject to your husbands as is fitting in the Lord' was either omitted from the Reading of Colossians 3, or Pope John Paul's explanation on mutuality in marriage read, (*Dignity of Women* n. 24) in some of the dioceses of Ireland.

1992 saw the women gather in Knock, Co Mayo. The number of proposals presented showed that the movement was finding its voice. Concern ranged from the amount of violence committed against women in Ireland, especially within Christian marriage, to the patriarchal distortions printed in children's bibles. An extra day was needed in Dublin to deal with all the proposals. The central committee undertook to become more media conscious and it was decided to hold a separate business meeting annually some weeks after the conference.

After five years, the movement now has a logo, an information leaflet is in process of being designed, and a sub-committee is planning a book of prayers and rituals expressing women's experience of the divine at work in them.

THE FEMALE IMAGE OF GOD
Written by Maureen Brazil on behalf of Sophia

In the mid-1980s more and more women in Ireland began to realise that there was something wrong with the way the church treated women. It was difficult to pin-point what exactly was wrong and different aspects caused problems for different women. But the unifying aspect was a growing consciousness that the church was anti-women. Clear language is not readily available to express a new consciousness and the 7 or 8 women who came together at the beginning of 1986 were aware that the very fact of meeting together was itself a statement expressing their new consciousness, that Christian church authorities were on the wrong track as far as women were concerned. The group was ecumenical and open to all Christian denominations but it was women from the Roman Catholic Church who took the initiative in setting it up.

After six months we had given ourselves the name *Sophia* and defined ourselves as a study and support group, with group action focussed on educational and communication areas. We saw our long term aim as working towards enabling women to participate in leadership and decision-making roles in the church. One or two women, who were more interested in the wider feminist movement than in the church, left the group and new members joined. It is sometimes said that all women who are critical of the church should leave. We believe in staying in the church and working for change from within.

We wished to be a group of well-informed people educating ourselves and others about the fact that Christian women were rejecting the false idea that they were created inferior to men, and replacing it with the truth that humanity, male or female, was created in the image of God. The Irish Bishops' Pastoral of 1985 said that Christian feminism should reject what is contrary to the gospel. That is acceptable. But the reverse side is that the official church should reject what is contrary to the gospel in its own attitudes to women. There is a great reluctance on the part of the official church to admit that there is anything in its attitudes to women which is contrary to the gospel. That is the core of the problem and there is no mechanism for dialogue or communication between women and the official church.

Sexism and patriarchy

Women brought up to believe that churchmen are holy, honourable and honest, suffer a multi-dimensional shock on learning about the kind of things such men have been saying about women for many centuries. Some fairly typical contemporary churchmen take it all in their stride and laughingly blame 'society' for the whole phenomenon. 'Awful things about women were said by society long ago and churchmen picked up the bad habit.' Women soon discovered that, far from picking up a bad habit from a God-less society, churchmen were telling that society that God created woman inferior to man, and that all women (with one exception) are thoroughly bad.

In the third century, Clement of Alexandria: said 'The female sex is death's deaconess and is especially dishonoured of God.' Thirt-een centuries later, Ignatius Loyola said much the same thing: 'The devil conducts himself as a woman.'

The fairly typical modern churchman will comment 'So what? Eve was created after Adam and Eve sinned first.' The shocked woman will say that Christ redeemed Eve's sin. But the church-man will tell her to remember that woman was created inferior to man and will always remain so. Sexism is the belief that one sex was created inferior to the other. Patriarchy is the belief that the female sex was created inferior. As the above quotations show, patriarchy has been embedded in Christian thinking for a very long time. Christian feminism aims to rescue Christianity from patriarchy and sexism. Both sexes were created equally in God's image.

The creation stories

The belief that woman was created inferior to man blocks the gos-pel message that Christ freed women from subjection to men. This is why that fruit of Christ's redemption has remained hidden until now. Women's subjection to man was a consequence of sin (Gen 3:10) and was not part of God's created order. Christ's re-demption restored the relationship between men and women to one of equality, unity and harmony. When that restored relation-ship is claimed and lived, the old relationship of male dominance and female subjection will wither and die.

Unfortunately, distortions of this are still with us as evidenced by Eucharistic Prayer IV which contains these words: 'You formed man in your likeness and set him over the whole world to serve you his creator and to rule over all creatures'. In 1988 the Sophia

Group expressed its concern about these words to the Irish Institute of Pastoral Liturgy and received a reply saying that the International Commission on English in the Liturgy had prepared an inclusive language version of the prayer in 1981 which referred, not to 'setting him' over the whole world, but to creating humankind, male and female and setting 'them' over the whole world, but this was not approved by the Congregation for Worship on the grounds that inclusive language is a very delicate issue and that they were studying it in depth. The real difficulty with the above prayer is that it changes the Genesis story of creation. The corrections do not require study and should be made without delay. Failure to do so demonstrates the blindness of decision-makers to their own mistakes concerning women.

The following resolution was proposed by the Sophia Group to the annual conference of the Christian Feminist Movement in Ireland in 1992 in relation to the distortion of the text of Gen 2 by the addition of the words 'the woman is dependent upon the man', as well as other additions and omissions.

'The Christian Feminist Movement in Ireland wishes to draw attention to the distortions of the creation stories which appear in some children's bibles and requests Christian church authorities to take action in the matter'.

The resolution was passed unanimously and is being followed up at present.

What we are seeing in various instances of tailoring the text of Genesis to fit male supremacy is the destructive effect which patriarchy has upon men. It saps their integrity as human beings by making them succumb to the illusion that they are a higher form of humanity than women. The next step is the illusion that male supremecy is God's plan for the human race.

Men's conferences

In this generation, more and more men are rejecting the illusions of patriarchy and are giving support to Christian feminism. The Sophia Group organised a 'Men's Conference on Christian Feminism' in 1988 which was well attended and led to another one being held in 1989. After that conference, several men decided to meet together on a regular basis to think things through and discuss the ways in which their own lives had been affectd by patriarchy. One of the points concerning the church which had been brought up at the conference was the false edifice which had been erected on the Scriptural passage which says that man is the head of woman (1 Cor 11:3-16). It is interesting to note that in the Papal document *Mulieris Dignitatem* of 1988 this passage is included in a footnote to paragraph 24 with the other six negative passages about women which appear in the New Testament.

The Lectionary

One of the subjects brought up at Sophia meetings at the very beginning was the upset caused to women by readings at Mass saying that wives should be subject to husbands. It was incomprehensible to women why the church should choose these readings and at the same time claim that it supported equal partnership in marriage. Furthermore, women knew that these readings are misused by men to justify aggression.

In 1987, the Sophia Group wrote to the Secretary of the Irish Episcopal Conference making the case for omitting these texts from the readings at Mass and including the point about aggression. The reply received expressed disbelief about aggression and said that no generation has a right to rewrite scripture. We, of course, had no wish to rewrite scripture but simply to see some texts omitted from the readings in the same way that the text about slavery had been omitted. So we pursued the matter by looking up research done in other countries on the link between the misuse of biblical texts and wife abuse in the Christian home. In 1991 we prepared an information leaflet containing that research and sent it to every parish in the Dublin diocese with the request that the text of Eph 5:22-24, listed for 25 August, be omitted. The response was minimal.

Yet the U.S. bishops (1988) do accept that there are husbands who use the bible to justify wife abuse. 'Traditionally the abuse of a wife by her husband has been considered not only a family matter, but virtually a husband's prerogative. Many abusive men hold a view of women as inferior and believe that men are meant to dominate and control women.' The part played by the Christian church in forming such attitudes has to be acknowledged before it can be reformed.

Christian marriage

Generation after generation of men absorbed the message that they had divine authority over their wives. It was the 'created order' that was being maintained when the church supported the

State in sanctioning wife-beating. But what if the created order did not confer authority on the male sex? Then, of course, the whole concept of divine male authority collapses. That happened in this generation. What was the key factor in bringing about this development? As far as the church is concerned, the key factor was the refusal of women to tolerate being treated as goods and chattels. In 1963 Pope John XXIII said: 'Becoming ever more conscious of their dignity as human beings, women will not tolerate being treated as goods and chattels. Instead they demand to exercise the rights and duties belonging to a human being, both in the home and in civic life' (*Pacem in Terris*, 41).

In recent years the U.S. bishops have publicly acknowledged that 'over the centuries even leading theologians and influential pastors have interpreted the Scriptures as teaching that in some respects women are naturally inferior to men, weaker in the face of temptation and as such rightly subject to male domination.' They named sexism as a sin and called for personal and corporate contrition for the sins of sexism (*Draft Pastoral* 1988). There were objections to this from churchmen in Rome and, following lengthy consultations and revised drafts, the U.S. bishops decided in 1992, not to issue a pastoral at all.

In Ireland there has been no dialogue between women and the bishops and the Sophia Group would like to see some communication developing particularly in the area of marriage. In May 1992 *Sophia* organised a Seminar on the subject 'What is Christian Marriage?' Recommendations were made at the end of the Seminar and copies were circulated to all the bishops. Some encouraging feedback was received.

Ordination of women

The Sophia Group hasn't devoted time to the question of the ordination of women, not because it is against the idea, but because it believes that the first priority is to help to get the church off the wrong track regarding women. It has, however, become clear to us over the years that the church's opposition to women priests is holding it back from reform in other areas. This is particularly so in regard to marriage. There is a strong view among some churchmen that what they call the 'proper' subordination of women to men precludes women not only from ordination but also from equal partnership with men in marriage. They are of the opinion that to concede equal partnership with men in marriage is to leave the church without any defence against ordination. The point is made bluntly in the book *Women in the Priesthood?* by Manfred Hauke, which is highly thought of by some senior churchmen in Europe, including Ireland: 'If the subordination of women were to have disappeared just as the subordination of slaves has done, despite having also been defended by appeals to the New Testament household lists, then might not the prohibition of female priests, which was already linked in the New Testament itself to the notion of subordination, collapse in a similar way?'

This sort of thinking is obviously one of the reasons behind the paralysis of the church regarding the new teaching on marriage by Vatican II. They are afraid to talk about equal partnership in marriage for fear that this would open up the debate on women priests. But that debate is now going to open up in any case following the Church of England's decision to ordain women.

Reconciliation between male and female

Christians of all denominations need to repent of attributing to God the distorted relationship of male domination and female subjection which has endured for so long. Having now found the truth, the present generation has a special responsibility to promote reconciliation between male and female in a relationship of equality and harmony which is the fruit of Christ's redemption.

MNÁ LE CHÉILE
Written by Ben Kimmerling in collaboration with Mná le Chéile, Foxford, Co. Mayo

In Autumn 1990 a group of approximately 30 women met in my house. We were a random group – the kind of middle of the road rural women on whom the present and future church depends. Our objective was to initiate dialogue with the bishop and priests of the Killala diocese about the needs of women in the local church. Having ascertained that a public meeting with the clergy of the diocese would be possible, our group spent its first year working together in preparation for this.

This account will focus on that first year. It will describe the raising of our awareness, our empowerment through storytelling, the surfacing of questions, the re-thinking and broadening of our objectives and our eventual arrival at consensus on the vision, values, activities, strategies and future direction of our group.

At our first few meetings, we identified issues which concerned us. These were collected in a document which we planned to use as a basis for discussion with the clergy at a later date.

However we soon realised that change would not be brought about through purely intellectual debate. The energy to work for change is released when people get in touch with burning personal issues – issues which Paulo Freire calls generative themes. So, in order to get in touch with our own burning issues and to tap into this energy, we decided to engage in storytelling.

Some of the group volunteered to share their stories with us. We agreed to listen silently – without judgement or comment – while each woman spoke. For the first time ever, some of the women spoke the truth in public about the circumstances of their lives. We were deeply moved and at times deeply shocked by what we heard.

The issues which surfaced were without doubt burning issues – not just for the storytellers but for the entire group. Indeed we soon realised that these most deeply personal stories – stories of birth and death, of marriage and separation, of violence and tenderness, of abortion and sexual abuse – were also universal stories. They were the stories of women everywhere.

And even more startling for some of us was the realisation that these were the untold stories of many women right here in our local church.

We decided that we would like to explore the pastoral implications of these stories with the clergy at our joint meeting. So we selected four which could be told. The four stories were (a) the story or a birth (b) the story of the death of a child, (c) the story of a violent marriage and (d) the story of an abortion and marital breakdown which were the direct result of childhood sexual abuse.

There is not room here to retell those stories. But, in order to illustrate how the sharing of stories can raise awareness and evoke questions about existing structures, I will comment briefly on two.

On one occasion, we shared our stories of birth. We discovered that the moment of birth is a moment of breakthrough into a new world for the mother as well as for the child. Here physical experience is religious experience. Our sharing convinced us that birth is a sacramental moment – a moment when God breaks through into our lives. We asked why our church never officially marked that event by a sacramental celebration of some kind? We asked if children were delivered of fathers would the church have a sacrament to mark the event?

As we explored our lives further, we found there were other moments which call for recognition. We asked how could we mark these events? So we began to devise our own prayerful rituals to celebrate significant life events. These celebrations are very meaningful for us. They have given us new insight into the significance of liturgical events. However, they have also made us acutely conscious of the contrast between our creative and active participation in our own celebrations and our passivity and virtual exclusion from the official rituals of the church.

So gradually, through reflecting on our small pool of stories, we were raising our awareness and discovering that women's experience is a rich though largely untapped theological source. We decided that, in our dialogue with the clergy, we would draw attention to and state our dissatisfaction with this.

However, what disturbed and energised us most was the experience of being personally exposed to women's pain. This raised big questions for us. And, although our focus was on women, our exploration opened up issues which are of concern to other marginalised groups.

As we listened to some of the stories, we were confronted in the starkest and most personal manner by the depth of the victimisation of women – a victimisation which if started early in life (as it usually is) is then compounded a hundredfold as a woman's life unfolds. For example we learned that women who are sexually abused as children may have been conditioned to see sexual availability as a prerequisite for acceptance and love. When this pattern is established in childhood, it's not surprising if it continues into adult life. Symptoms of abuse – surfacing perhaps as depression and withdrawal or alternatively in teenage promiscuity or pregnancy, in ruptured relationships or abortion, in marital breakdown or physical abuse – are likely to appear.

As we listened to these stumbling stories, we could see clearly that the pain of remembering – and therefore re-living – the experience inhibits or even prevents speech. We became aware too that most sexually abused women can't stand up alone to name this evil because the threat of violence makes it too dangerous for many victims to speak.

But there is more than the pain and threat of violence keeping abused women silent. There is the fear of disbelief. Disbelief is the ultimate violence. Disbelief is the last straw which breaks minds and spirits and pushes desperate women over the edge. Yet how often has a disbelieving world (or the institutional church) labelled an articulate woman crazy (or a sinner) rather than face up to the horrifying reality that thousands of silent women live in hells like this? How often does society (or the institutional church) administer pity or medicine (or forgiveness and compassion) to such women, rather than stand alongside women in their fight against the sexism which is the root cause of sexual abuse?

For the first time, we became acutely aware of the deep silence which, in our church, surrounds certain aspects of women's lives. Where women's sexuality is concerned, communication in our church has been all one way.

We wondered if those who are in authority in the church realise that many women, if invited to do so by an open and listening hierarchy/clergy, might be glad to tell and might experience more healing in telling their full history in public without shame, rather than privately whispering an isolated incident in that history with guilt, in the confessional? Do clergy/hierarchy realise that if they listened publicly, collectively and with respect to the stories of such women, they would be collaborating with women in the public uncovering of the root causes of what is now so often deemed to be solely women's sin?

The storytelling was a turning point in the life of the group. We discovered that the act of standing up and publicly speaking the as yet unspoken truth liberates and empowers a person or a group. We discovered that the act of listening with openness is a truly Christian act – because it offers the belief and respect which enables that unspoken truth to emerge. We discovered too that when a person, a group or an institution agrees to listen deeply to the reality of others, they open themselves to change and to growth. Conclusions, positions and ideas which have been firmly held up to that point, have to be re-examined and reformulated in the light of the new reality which has been disclosed.

We asked if women and other marginalised groups find this kind of redemptive listening and the openness to change which goes with it, within the institutional church? And we had to admit that it did not always appear to be so.

And so we committed ourselves to fostering a spirit of openness within the church. We decided that, from this point onwards, we would speak our own truth openly as women, without fear, within the local church. We also decided that, where possible, we would create listening spaces within the Christian community where other peoples' truth – especially, but not exclusively, women's truth – could emerge.

We took a first step in that direction when, one year after we first came together, sixty women – our group plus friends and supporters – met with the bishop and priests. What happened there is I'm afraid, another story! All I can say here is that, whatever about the effect of our presentation on the clergy, the experience of speaking our truth as women in public to the clergy was a freeing and empowering one for us.

Now, two and a half years later, dialogue with the clergy has become a less immediate, though still desired objective of our group. While we have been heartened by the response of individual priests, we now realise that the pace of the public dialogue is outside our control. It's dictated (according to the priests themselves) by an enthusiasm for meetings – and we suspect for women's issues – which is, to say the least, some degrees less passionate than our own! We have learned that – in spite of the openness of individual priests – we must not depend on the clergy as a body to promote justice for women. It's we ourselves and other groups like us who will be the agents of change in the church.

Consequently, at the end of our first year, we started to re-think and eventually broaden the focus of our group. We began to take initiatives ourselves. In our second year we decided to network with other grassroots people on issues of justice. And we organised a Partners In Mission course (based on Paulo Freire's psycho social method) for forty people in the local church. So now, two and a half years after our initial meeting, while the clerical dialogue slowly simmers, the grassroot pot is on the boil!

YOUNG ADULTS ARE ALSO THE CHURCH
Contributed by the team of
Teach Bríde, Tullow, Co. Carlow

'When the church is truly present to young adults, it is able to listen compassionately and lovingly to them.' This type of listening is one that leads to understanding and mutual growth. It is a stance leading to three important outcomes. First, listening carefully to the faith questions and spiritual journeys of young adults enables us to proclaim the gospel in such a way that it will bring healing and strength to the life situation of these people. Secondly, we need to be aware of the growth that takes place within us if we truly open ourselves to the stories we hear from young adults. Finally, having accurately heard the voices of young adults, we can then become advocates for their needs to the larger community.

Goals of Youth Ministry
Youth Ministry is a multi-dimensional reality, but all of its varied facets are brought into focus by a common dedication to the following goals:
1. Youth Ministry works to foster the total personal and spiritual growth of each young person.
2. Youth Ministry seeks to draw young people to responsible participation in the life, mission and work of the faith community.

Vision
To promote Christian ministry to young people.
To promote Christian community's care of its youth in Kildare and Leighlin.

Why?
a) To discover the potentialities of young people and to seek to liberate them from what oppresses them and to empower them to build up communities that can support and transform themselves, their community and the world in order that all may have life and have it to the full.
b) In order that young people may become part of communities which work for the liberation and transformation of the world in the light of God's dream for people.

Who?
1. Adult Christian communities that have concern for Youth Ministry including young adults themselves.
2. Young adults with leadership potential.
3. A special ministry for young adults themselves.

Teach Bríde, in Tullow, Co Carlow was founded in 1981 as a
Christian House of Welcome for Young Adults. In its initial years
it developed its attitudes and strategies in relation to giving
young adults (18-25) a place where they can (re)discover their personal 'faith' story and share this with their peers in an environment which places value on the diverse and unique views of
young adults. Today, eleven years on, Teach Bríde, has evolved,
in response to needs of young adults, society at large and the community of church, into a resource centre for youth ministry. The
focus has moved from the building to the community; from the
'experienced' to the 'possibility'. Co-ordinated by a team of youth
ministers, the aim for our ministry is to reach out to communities
and encourage and empower them to embody the concern and
care which their young adults deserve and long for. Our main
focus is on young adults themselves. By means of leadership, reflection and action programmes, we seek to discover (with the
young adults themselves) the potential for change which they
possess:
- to liberate them from that which oppresses them.
- to empower them to build up communities which can support
and transform themselves, their community and the world.

We do this 'in order that all may have life and have it to the full'
(Jn 10:10).

We have a special ministry to young adults themselves, while
working primarily with young adults with leadership potential.
The larger circle is that of adult Christian communities which
have concern for youth ministry, including young adults themselves.

Our main strategies are embodied in the type of programmes
which we run:
- At parish level we involve adults, including clergy, in leading
programmes such as *Faith Friends* or the Y.C.W. movement and
encouraging them to reach out to young adults and involve them
in such programmes.
- We also work within the school forum, especially at Senior cycle
level. This puts us into contact with leaders who have already begun work with young adults in a Christian framework, namely
R.E. teachers, chaplains and others with responsibility for the integral development of young people. This also gives us a contact
with parents from time to time which is very crucial in our larger
plan.

The main structures by which we achieve our aims are:
- *Faith Friends* which is a Christian leadership programme for young people and has two focal points, i.e. confirmation and first communion. We train parish teams to run these two programmes in their parishes for young adults and in the first communion programme, specifically for 16 year olds.
- The *Meitheal* programme is a co-operative leadership training programme for senior cycle students who are commissioned by the bishop to build up a more caring community in their schools.
- We are also responsible for resourcing and developing the Young Christian Workers (Y.C.W.) movement in the diocese. This international movement brings together groups of young adults at local community level where they reflect on the reality of their life and plan actions to improve it.
We also resource the development of new and established folk groups in the diocese of Kildare and Leighlin.
- In all of this, we continually create an awareness of the need for communities to take up responsibility for the concern and care of all its members, and especially, in this generation, of young adults.

The spirituality which we encourage is that of the early Christian communities and of the modern thinking in the church, reflected in books such as *Partnership in Parish* by Fr Enda Lyons (Columba Press 1986). It is that of encouraging one another to see our Christian lives as relevant and intrinsic to our faith once we work for the liberation of the oppressed, the bringing of good news to the poor, the release of those held captive by society or structure, and to proclaim the Lord's favour to one another in our actions, our care, our respect, our responsibility, our community.

At present *Faith Friends* is actively working in almost all of the 55 parishes in Kildare and Leighlin. *Meitheal* is now an integrated part of 14 secondary schools in the diocese, the Y.C.W. is developing in leaps and bounds in Carlow, Laois and Kildare and folk groups have adopted structures to provide for the ongoing care and training for their members and have networked with other groups through the diocese.

The team
The team is composed of 5 adults who work together while having singular responsibility for different areas. We also live in an apostolic community (separate from formal work) and support one another in our celebrations, concerns, experiments, successes and failures.

As a team, we meet once a week to share our experiences and receive suggestions and critique of our work, individually and collectively. The director has an individual 1:1 forum with each team member and is himself responsible to the bishop for the overall running of Teach Bríde. This support structure, along with the community living, is what helps sustain our commitment along with the inspiring responses which we continually encounter in our work and in the diocese.

Celebration is a natural and vital part of our work and this happens formally at the end of a phase in specific programmes, and seasonally, e.g. Christmas, Summer recess, Easter and also informally in our prayer, our team-work and our community activity.

Youth ministry is still a developing young adult itself and, as we continue to care for its growth and share concern for its difficulties, we are confident that it is already making a difference to the lives of communities and individuals and that it will do so in the foreseeable future.

A PILGRIM PEOPLE
Contributed by Michael Murray CSSp.,
24G Fatima Mansions, Dublin 8

The history of my own involvement in Pilgrimage Walks goes back five years. It began because of a desire to have closer contact between Irish and English vocation teams. An initial meeting between the two vocation teams took place in London in 1989 and as a result we decided to co-operate with one another in so far as we could. Our English colleagues had long been involved in Pilgrimage Walks because their vocation apostolate was not based on a schools' visitation programme as operates here in this country.

They were certain that direct vocation promotion in schools was a waste of time because it was based on a number of false assumptions. The primary assumption which underlies vocation promotion in the strict sense is that the youth to whom you speak have the faith. Our English confreres knew that this was not the case in their own milieu. So they began to look around for ways and means of fostering and nurturing faith in young people. One of the avenues which they explored was the Pilgrimage Walk. These Walks were set up in Scotland and England and I decided to take part in these Walks to experience what went on during the week's walking.

On the basis of what I had experienced in Scotland and England, I decided to set up a similar Walk in Ireland. There were many reasons for taking on such a venture and I will try to share them as best I can. There is much talk about youth and young adults in Ireland. My own experience in travelling around the country left me with the conviction that there were serious questions to be faced in the whole area of youth ministry. Many young people see the church as out-dated and irrelevant to their needs. Consequently, they feel reluctant to become involved at a serious level in their own parish. To the eyes of young men and women, it appears that the facilities and resources of the church are at the service of an older generation whose faith needs are satisfied by the more traditional worship forms. Their overall experience of church, God, Jesus, etc, is very negative.

With the above in mind, I decided to set up a Pilgrimage Walk in Ireland. The purpose of the walk was to give young people a lived experience of faith in a way which affirmed them in their own search for God. Ireland is full of Christian symbols and the route was chosen in order to take full advantage of our Celtic heritage. The Hill of Slane evokes ancient memories of St Patrick's confrontation with the druids and the lighting of the fire on the Hill is part of our opening liturgy. The celebration of the eucharist in such a setting begins bonding the group as each walker is invited to take a log and throw it on the fire. The spirit of St Brigid is still alive and well in Kildare and those of us who are from Ireland know well the connection between St Kevin and Glendalough. Every step of the journey reminds the participants of the rich Christian tradition which is part and parcel of our country.

There is a challenge in walking 100 miles and there is pain and suffering involved along the way. Sixty young people set out every August to walk the roads from Slane to Glendalough via Kildare. Those who can are invited to carry their rucksacks. There are 'water-stops' every hour or so and each day is lived out as a repeated 'journey to Emmaus'. It is important to provide water to the walkers on a regular basis from a medical point of view, but the 'water-stops' have a further purpose. After each stop the walkers are invited to walk the road with someone they have not yet met. The result of this request is generally apparent after two or three days on the road because by then those on the Walk know one another and the challenge of walking long distances bonds the group closer together.

The participants are always divided into smaller groups at the end of the first day's walking. The leaders of these groups are always young and there is an even ratio between male and female. If there are older participants in the group they must defer to their group leader because the Walk is primarily for the youth. Responsibilities for liturgies, the route, preparation for breakfast each morning, etc., are shared out on a rota basis to each group. Voluntary groups provide the food in some of the towns through which we pass and the overseas participants get a glimpse of the wonderful hospitality which is synonymous with our people. Hotels and pubs provide the nourishment when local groups are unable to look after our needs. There are two swims and two ballad/singing sessions during the course of the week which enhance the overall sense of vitality experienced in the Walk.

A theme is chosen for the Walk each year. The focus of the group work and liturgies centres on the theme. The experience of walking the roads gives the groups much insight into the chosen theme. It is wonderful also to see how young people minister to one another. At the beginning of the Walk there are many participants who have little understanding of how to prepare a liturgy of the Word or eucharist. However, by the end of the week, they have become proficient in drawing up a programme for any liturgy. Drama, liturgical dance, nature, the experience of the Walk, etc., become part of the daily routine. Peer ministry is used in a positive way. In an average group of young people, those who are trying to live out their faith tend to keep their thoughts and reflections to themselves for fear of being ridiculed by others. However, the opposite happens during the course of the Walk in that those who would often be in a minority in ordinary society find themselves affirmed in their own search for the Lord.

The walkers are often asked what they are doing by those who meet the group on the road. People are amazed to learn that the young people are actually on a Pilgrimage Walk. The participants come mainly from Ireland, Scotland, England and Germany. Other nationalities have been represented on the Walk and the experience of sharing the joys and pains while on the road breaks down many prejudices. At the end of the day's walking, the group sleeps in school halls and community centres and this is another factor in bringing the group together. There is no preferential treatment for anybody on the Walk. However, if a participant for one reason or another cannot walk, he/she will be given a lift in the vans or cars which accompany the walkers. It must be pointed out that the Pilgrimage Walk is not an endurance test and those who cannot walk are always part of the group. There are many opportunities to live out one's faith during the course of the week and it is wonderful to behold the transformation which takes place in such a short time to the group. The 'flesh-pots' of television/radio and other creature comforts are forgotten as the Pilgrimage takes people out of their normal daily routine and there are generally many tears when the time for departure arrives.

There is much preparation needed well in advance of the Walk. Accommodation much be arranged as well as the meals. Participants are invited to contribute £35.00 for the Pilgrimage Walk. This covers all the meals and other activities over the course of the week. However, many of the participants take extra pocket-money with them but whatever they spend is their responsibility. The walk is patrolled by a medical van, a 'water' van/car and a luggage van. This year I hope to introduce 'walkie-talkies' so that there is instant communication between the back-up team and the walkers on the road.

It is important to have insurance for the Walk and, where necessary, to inform the Gárdaí about the route. Publicity for the Walk has not been a strong point but this year a committee will look after this side of the Pilgrimage Walk. There must be a strong road discipline when the walkers are on the roads. Two-abreast is the desired number but when walkers get tired they can forget about their own personal safety. It is the responsibility of the back-up team to remind people of the dangers if they are straying into the middle of the road.

During the course of the week, the participants become part of one another's lives and this is something which invites reflection on organising some follow-up to the event. In many ways people are on a 'high' at the end of the week and we are still trying to evolve a fully satisfactory way of helping the participants in the processing of their experience. Many return to parishes where their faith experiences on the Walk cannot be incorporated into their own parish life and liturgies. The resulting alienation can upset the young people more than if they had never been on the Pilgrimage Walk.

RECONCILIATION WITH THE OTHER
*Contributed by Rev Samuel Birch in collaboration with
Cornerstone Community, Springfield Road, Belfast*

The Cornerstone Community is a small inter-church group working for peace and reconciliation in the Shankill–Falls areas of West Belfast.

The Community was formed in 1982 in response to the growing alienation of the Protestants and Roman Catholics in the area and the rising level of violence between them. Christians from different churches were grieved by this polarisation and wanted to express and demonstrate their unity in Christ, having experienced this in a very deep way in a joint prayer group over the previous 7 years.

Five members came together in a pair of semi-detached houses on the Springfield Rd., on what had become known as the 'Peace Line'; a physical barrier which separates the two communities. The other 12 members pledged themselves to meet with these five once a week and, by sharing each others lives and faith and prayer, to do whatever God opened up to them as a means of healing the rift between the two communities.

Over the years we have been led to take a number of small initiatives, but we believe that our being together, Catholic and Protestant, sharing the joys and sorrows of West Belfast and living out our common life of prayer and service, is in itself, our most important work, a sign of what the Lord desires of his people. Sometimes we feel like an icon shining as a beacon; at other times, we are more like a voice crying in the wilderness, as the hatred and fear give rise to murder after murder.

When a person of whatever background, is killed in our area, we try to visit the home; a Catholic and Protestant together. In trying to convey our personal sorrow to the family we are also expressing a collective pain that the groups from which we come are doing this to each other and we believe that we can say that this is not the wish of the majority in our community. This seems to be of some small comfort to those who pass through these harrowing experiences. They often express the comfort that expressions of sorrow from 'the other side' bring to them. We believe that we are all God's children and a hurt to one is a hurt to us all.

The apartheid in which most people in N. Ireland grow up leads to great fears and misapprehensions of one side of the other. We

have tried to draw people from each community together to listen
to each other's hurts and views. We have had a number of conferences for clergy at which we have tried to look at divisive issues in
a calm and friendly and open way. Many who have attended
these have discovered how great have been our misunderstandings and prejudices and have been led to re-think their attitudes
and relationships. Similar experiences have occurred in our weekends for lay people, especially when people who have passed
through experiences with para-militaries have shared their story.

Believing that bridge-building needs to happen at all levels, we
have developed a children's work in two small after school clubs
and share in a senior citizens' lunch club where people from each
side can meet and share. These are by far the easiet groups to mix.
We have had much less success in trying to bring young people
and young adults together, though we have visited a number of
schools and urged them to be more open to each other and we
have mounted a number of courses for youth leaders with some
success.

In the face of the terrifying gulf of fear and hatred of the divided
communities, these small initiatives seem utterly futile, but we
believe that such small steps can be very significant in changing
people's perspectives and enabling a slow change of attitude and
action to take place. One example of this was when a small group
of Protestant ministers went to the funeral of a young Roman
Catholic man who had been shot by a loyalist group. Their presence was noted and much appreciated by the local clergy and congregation and enabled us all to affirm the sacredness of every life.
Our working together has also encouraged others to do the same.

As well as trying to bring people together, we have found it helpful at times to move into the 'other camp'. A Catholic woman became a member of a mothers and toddlers group in a Presbyterian
church on the Shankill and a Methodist minister worshipped in a
Catholic church for a period. Such little steps indicate that the
walls of separation do not reach to heaven. There is a way
through if we have the courage to take it. These small breaches in
the apartheid life of the communities can make it easier for others
to move out of their camp.

One of our members is very interested in spiritual healing and has
been able to draw together an inter-church team to develop two
healing services at which both Catholics and Protestants share.

This kind of common service to suffering and needy people is a helpful means of breaking down barriers both in the recipients and in those ministering. It would point to the value of inter-church co-operation in tackling some of the social problems of society.

Three or four times each year we try to challenge the local community in a more public way, by inviting them to share in an ecumenical service or act of witness. We believe that the churches especially have an opportunity and duty to lead in the healing of the divisions in our society and these events enable the local churches to give this lead. Unfortunately, they are not widely supported and do not have the impact they might.

In these and many other ways, we seek to live and work out our calling to be peace-makers in our community. We cannot claim much success in bringing about reconciliation in the Falls-Shankill area though we have challenged some and strengthened others. One of our members continually reminds us that we are not called to succeed but to be faithful to our calling.

In this mission we are supported, encouraged and comforted by the other members of the community. Meeting regularly, we reflect on the life and happenings around us, praying for God's wisdom and grace to respond in ways that will be helpful and healing. We are glad to know that there are many other groups working for the same goal in many different ways and, where we can be supportive and encouraging of their efforts, we are happy to lend our aid.

Over the years we have been able to attract volunteers from many different countries to help, especially in our children's and youth work. These young adults have made a particular and very valuable contribution to our life and witness. They bring an international dimension and a different cultural outlook to the community and almost always say how very much they have grown in the process.

The Cornerstone Community is a totally independent group but we seek to have good relations with the churches. Each member of the Community is encouraged to play as full a part as possible in their local church and many do. At the higher level of the churches we are known and encouraged, but there are many Christians, especially on the Protestant side, who disapprove of us and our efforts, believing them to be destructive of true Christian faith and dangerous to the future well-being of the church and country. On the Catholic side, we are generally regarded as well intentioned but some would see us as largely ineffective in making any significant difference in the situation. They would accuse us of wanting people to be reconciled without addressing the real political, economic and justice issues which lie at the heart of our problem. Our reply is to say that no one group can deal with all the ills of our society and each group has to tackle the part that God calls them to confront while acknowledging that the other areas must be addressed.

We in Cornerstone all believe that sharing as we do has immensely enriched our own spiritual lives, widening our vision of the church and enabling us to appreciate and appropriate to some degree, the particular gifts of each tradition. We have also been enabled to see some of the weaknesses of our traditions in comparison to others. Most members feel that they have gained a new appreciation of their own church and have begun to understand better its history and contribution. Some, however, have felt a frustration with rules and traditions which seem more suited to another age and are grieved that the churches are taking so long to fully recognise each other's validity.

In the practical running of the community, we try to keep things as simple as possible. All major decisions are taken by the whole group talking through until there is a consensus. A small executive looks after the rest. Because the government is keen to promote good community relations, we have been able to secure major funding from it for our work, raising some 25% ourselves.

Many visitors come to us from all over the world and we are constantly surprised that they find us worth a call. Perhaps they recognise in us something that we ourselves cannot see, as one French nun said, 'You are like a little seed, the promise of something good to come, God's people as one family sharing their lives and witness and service together for the sake of the reconciliation of the whole world.'

RECONCILIATION WITH ONESELF
Contributed by Miceal O'Regan O.P. and the staff of
Eckhart House, Institute of Psychosynthesis
and Transpersonal Theory, Clyde Road, Dublin 4

The ethos and structures of our society tend to fragment the human

person. The effects of this inner and outer fragmentation are seen in the rise in unemployment, increase in substance abuse, dissatisfaction with available education and indifference to spiritual and religious values. Many people and groups experience confusion and inadequacy in their daily lives. Today a different context or different structures are needed by many in which to speak and work through their dilemmas. The vision of Eckhart House is to create a context for:
– reflecting on the mystery of the human person and on the meaning and purpose of life.
– exploring the theory and practice of psychosynthesis, transpersonal theory and faith.
– guiding personal change through reflection and practice as a basis for change in society.

1. Reflection on the mystery of the human person

In the Judaeo-Christian tradition one speaks of the self in terms of body, feelings, mind, soul, spirit, will, development, conscious, unconscious etc. How one tells and shapes the story of the self within a tradition gives rise to different accounts. Therefore within the Western tradition there are stories of the self different from that told by psychosynthesis. In Eckhart House, using the insights of psychosynthesis, we tell the story of the self as a network of relationships, inner and outer. The inner relationships are those that exist between body, feelings, mind, soul and spirit. Each of these words is filled with meaning within the tradition. When the energy between them is flowing and appropriate, a sense of inner justice or wellbeing is experienced. When there is inner injustice or oppression of one by the other, suffering, pain and disease are experienced.

To say the self is relational is to say it is in constant process of give and take with its environment, within, between and around. To say that relationship between people is essential is to say it is more than useful or a good thing. It is more than a social contract. It implies that a self or person is not a monad or self-contained system, but rather, in its very essential structures, calls out for and to the other.

The self, complex and relational, is also dynamic and embodied. To construe the self as dynamic is to point to the fact that a person develops through phases and stages. Within each stage different structures of relating to life emerge. Later structures transcend but include earlier ones. Transcendence in development is by way of inclusion rather than exclusion.

To construe the self as embodied is to give an account of a person as essentially in the body. It is to suggest that every human action, whether inner or outer, is embodied. Self-realisation and God-realisation do not occur within a person but rather are embodied between persons.

II. Reflection on psychosynthesis, transpersonal theory and faith

1. Psychosynthesis and transpersonal theory:
Although the story is never fully told, nevertheless there are greater approximations and more satisfying tellings. Psychosynthesis is one way of telling the story of the mystery of the self. It is a map to guide us in giving an account that includes the complexity and singularity of a person. Synthesis as an explicit thrust of the psyche is not an idea exclusive to Roberto Assagioli, the founder of Psychosynthesis. In fact the word itself, in relation to the work of therapy, may have been used first by Buber, as a way of seeing the parts in terms of the whole, as contrasted with building up the whole from isolated parts. In so far as Assagioli included in his account of the person, experiences beyond ordinary human well-being or self-actualisation, he is part of the fourth school of psychotherapy that included Jung, Maslow, Frankl and Grof.

The fourth school of psychotherapy is sometimes referred to as the Transpersonal. Transpersonal theory points to a deeper unifying dynamic within the person, to what Assagioli calls spiritual synthesis. It views the spiritual as the highest possibility of human fulfilment and explores the relationship between spiritual and psychological perspectives.

2. Faith
An account of the whole person needs to include the reality of faith. Faith, as it is understood in the context of Eckhart House, is more than correct doctrine properly formulated, more than correct moral behaviour. It is the capacity of the human spirit to recognise and respond positively to the graciousness of the Divine within ourselves, in the people we meet and through our environment. This activity of faith has its roots in the human spirit, beyond thought and image. Nevertheless, the human person can facilitate, nurture and experience its effectiveness in daily life through practice.

III. Personal change through reflection and practice as a basis for change in society

1. Personal change and change in society

The focus of work in Eckhart House is on personal change as a basis for change in society. It is a kind of personal asceticism. The dichotomy between initiating change at personal or at group level is an unnecessary one. Each level with its own laws and procedures is part of the one system. While psychotherapy and other forms of inner work will not resolve political, social, economic injustices in society, neither will political, social or economic analyses and interventions bring about deep change and transformation without the insights of psychotherapy.

Change at a personal level does not seem to come about through analytical knowing but from a knowing that is close to Yeats' understanding of knowledge:

> God guard me from thoughts men think
> In the mind alone;
> He that sings a lasting song
> Thinks in a marrow bone.

One could have much training skills and conceptual clarity and yet lack the art of 'thinking in a marrow bone'. It comes only through reflection and practice, a practice of attention to what is happening within and between, a practice of mindfulness that is from the heart rather than an abstract staring from the mind alone or the feelings alone.

2. Meditative practice and reflection

Deep change and transformation are facilitated by meditative practice which has two elements, awareness and action. Awareness without action is disembodied, while action without awareness is mindless. The two together reveal the whole person, body, feelings, mind, soul and spirit. Hence we promote a meditative attitude to life rather than merely teaching meditation techniques.

We foster personal somatic knowledge rather than disembodied or impersonal knowledge. This mode of knowing, knowing how I embody who I am, involves nurturing the symbol-making faculty or creative imagination. For this reason, meditative practices such as guided imagery, body work, symbolic art work, journal keeping and especially skills of concentration, relaxation and reflection are used in our courses. These help us to experience how we see ourselves and our world.

IV. Practice of presence to self by community of workers, in courses offered and in psychotherapy

Some courses focus on psychosynthesis and transpersonal theory and practice while others emphasise the religious – faith dimension. There are morning courses, evening courses, week-long and year-long courses. Eckhart House also offers a four year training in psychosynthesis and transpersonal theory for those who wish to use this perspective in their work or as therapists. As suggested, psychosynthesis is essentially a perspective, a way of construing a person. Assagioli writes: 'If we now consider psychosynthesis as a whole with all its implications and developments, we see that it should not be looked upon as a particular psychological doctrine, nor a single technical procedure. It is first and foremost a dynamic, even a dramatic conception of our psychological life.'

Practice of presence in psychotherapy

The story of the self as desire, (complex, dynamic, embodied and relational) proceeding, stretching, and evolving is not necessarily a smooth one. It has its own knots and ramblings. Any strand whether of the body, feelings, mind, soul or spirit, might be knotted and in need of untying at any of its different stages of development. Likewise, the absence or diminishment of any thread affects the overall weave of the story. Therefore it is important to place the human problem or disorder in its proper place; to decide where in the story the knot occurs. To misplace a human problem is to create category error. Some experiences and suffering that properly belong to an earlier phase in life might be construed as belonging to a later phase. For example, the desire for an experience of love, peace and security might be nothing more than a regression to an earlier phase of non-separation. On the other hand, it might indeed be a response to the call and promise of a greater and fuller life. It is the art of the clinician in dialogue with the person to decide which. All healing and transformation occurs in meeting. In this sense, pathology might be construed as the absence of relationship, and healing as a turning to the other, a metanoia. There is nothing more frightening than the vacant staring of despair of a person locked up within himself or herself. It is a looking without seeing. Dante's description of hell is of a place full of noise and effort but without relationship.

Healing is the opening up to the grace or presence of the other. It is to feel oneself spoken to and addressed as subject. It is to know there is a hand outstretched to help and hold on to. A healing dialogue or presence is more than the mere use of technical, skilful or abstract knowledge. It is a guiding from the manic pursuit of certainty – whether of being loved, understood, healthy or holy – to a more compassionate understanding of ambivalence. The pursuit of certainty leads to tension, intolerance, addiction, violence and finally breakdown. A compassionate acceptance of ambivalence leads to relaxation, humility, tolerance and a joy of living. It is the experience of living from a position of plenitude and fullness rather than from a position of scarcity and emptiness. It is a focus on the mystery of the one who suffers and is wounded without denying either the suffering or the wound.

Within the temenos or sanctuary of the healing dialogue, a greater life appears and manifests itself to both client and therapist. A transparency occurs within and between so that the deep inner life reveals itself even in the apparent ruins of a shattered life. The process continues outside the therapeutic session as the client learns to live daily life by witnessing to this deeper life, i.e. by remembering, through attending to and expressing, the greater life that enfolds each individual life as the ocean enfolds the wave and the tree the leaf. Such a transparency for and surrender to a deeper life may not get rid of the painful symptom or erase memories, but it does allow for the possibility of an experience of oneself as greater, deeper, beyond, unfathomable and mysterious. The client comes to live daily life in gracious co-operation with the inevitable.

For this to happen, the story may need to be told many times over until it sounds and reads right to the storyteller; until it reaches some gestalt or closure that makes sense. The safety of the therapeutic sanctuary allows the telling of the story to echo and re-echo in the many chambers of the storyteller. The events of the story may remain the same, the words and images used may sound the same as in the beginning, but eventually it echoes and resonates and sounds complete. There are no new pieces of information but the voice of the one telling the story has changed. Perhaps only the tone is different or the hues of description different, but nevertheless the one who tells the story hears it differently and begins to tell and write the story forward. In this process, the therapist is no passive or silent element but becomes another character in the story. He or she may embody not only roles from the past but also something of an icon that embodies, opens up and points forward to a deeper life beyond and between. This iconic quality is not primarily encapsulated within the therapist but rather in the dialogue and commitment between the client and therapist. The therapeutic situation itself is the icon of the larger and deeper life.

V. Conclusion

Psychosynthesis as a theory and practice often has a different configuration or style in different institutes. As with the project of any synthesis, this too has its limitations and strengths. Without a strong psychoanalytic base, psychosynthesis may be presented as too speculative and disembodied, while without the insights of the traditions and perennial philosophy it tends to trivialise the spiritual dimension. For this reason, it is a safeguard for the community of Eckhart House to be in dialogue with, and accountable to, the living tradition of the wider community.

The house is called after Meister Eckhart, a fourteenth century Dominican whose seminal idea of 'letting be', 'releasement', 'doing by not doing', influenced such diverse figures as Heidegger, Jung, Suzuki, Fromm and Merton. This perspective or idea of learning 'to care and not to care' (Eliot), permeates all the work done in Eckhart House.

THE COMMUNITY OF LABOUR
Contributed by Gill McCarthy, Paulbeg, Shillelagh, Co. Wicklow

Sitting here on the side of this lovely hill, looking out on to this early Spring day, and with all the hustle and bustle of the Nursery going on around me, it is hard to know where this story begins. All of life is a continuous rhythm of interweaving threads, and ultimately a mystery. Sometimes I see our lives as a wonderful tapestry made up of the most myriad of colours and textures, all interwoven in a most complex way. We can never see the entire picture, for God is the Artist, we are his design. When we come together in work, play, love and family, so often in our attempts to organise ourselves pragmatically we fail to hold that fundamental awareness of our own unique individuality, our specialness, and how we all have gifts and graces to share for the common good and for our own enrichment. That is the spirit and basic ethic we try to apply here in our working environment, and which we try to share with others whilst still addressing all the practicalities of working and business life. Perhaps if we have any basic premise it is this: 'Caring values come first.' That provides us with our touchstone and our inspiration.

This approach to life and work began for us long before we arrived in this beautiful place, and found ourselves living amongst these fine people; before also I experienced that 'resurrection' of the spirit which led me to baptism as a Christian in 1989. I realise clearly now that its roots are, however, drawn from 'kingdom' values which suggests that Christ was present in my heart and life long before I was ready to recognise and articulate his presence. However, an event took place in Summer 1991 which enabled us to put shape and form to our fundamental beliefs, so that we could translate them into working practices that had a viable working future. By a series of events, that I now consider providential, I was invited by Donal Dorr to participate in a workshop which proved to be a water-shed experience.

Our belief is that every day is valuable and can never be recovered; it is gift and should be treated as such. This stems from a desire to enjoy and celebrate each day and to share that enjoyment; plus the more mundane practicality of having to earn a living and finding a great deal of challenge and fulfilment in working with and amongst others. Our experience had shown us that the combined talents and commitment of an entire team have to be a stronger unit than that of a hierarchical 'pyramid'. Fundamental to this however, is a belief that each person has a voice that has a right to be heard. Each time we gather together for a working day we are moving through time that we can never recapture; the contribution of each and every one of us must be respected, valued and rewarded, both in terms of personal satisfaction and in fair and equable remuneration.

We came to live here in May 1985 and, things being what they are, we had to earn a living. We had bought a domestic shrub nursery impulsively (we had no background in this work), having decided to leave city life after twenty years in the business world of London. However, we soon realised that the future for our enterprise lay in forestry, which was a relatively new industry in Ireland at that time. We began to build a team of experienced foresters and set out to develop the business. We now have a basic team of thirteen, which rises to twenty-eight between November and April; from June through August to approximately fifty. Our hope and aim is to be able to increase the full-time staff to at least twenty and to be able to offer security of employment and a positive and viable future to us all.

We consider the principal resource and strength of this group are the combined energies and talents of all who gather here. We believe in a working structure that allows for flexibility and enables each member of staff to have a voice which can be and is heard. The disciplines of this business are formidable. We all need to have a high level of commitment and dedication. We have to be conscientious and skilled, and to work together harmoniously with mutual trust and confidence, both within ourselves, with each other and within the structure of the business. We consider our special responsibility is to provide an environment where these prerequisites can flourish. All staff receive training and an opportunity to take part in planning strategy and work practice. We try to encourage everyone to work at all times as a team, where each link is valued for the strength it brings to the whole. The saying goes that 'a chain is only as strong as its weakest link'. By encouraging an atmosphere of mutual trust and confidence, we try to ensure that the burdens are equably shared, so that all links are as strong as their ability permits. Each section of the nursery is encouraged to build its own team, to employ staff members at its own discretion as and when required. The weekly core group meetings provide a place where worries, problems and dilemmas can be aired and shared. We try to encourage people to help and support each other and to ensure that all points of view are aired and considered. Our experience suggests that most people are eminently fair and just – they don't wish to be 'right' for the sake of it; more important is to feel they have been heard respectfully. The atmosphere we try to promote is one of mutual support and respect, rather than that of competition.

We do not have a 'middle management' as such. We try to promote a climate where special aptitudes and talents have an opportunity to be expressed, developed and acknowledged, and people who are willing are able to take up the responsibilities they are most suited for. The reality shows that, as confidence develops, people are more than willing to take up responsibility, both for themselves and for the good of the enterprise, and will tend to identify and articulate for themselves what needs to be done and what are the appropriate boundaries and parameters.

We have the business structured in a 'total participation' way. The nursery is loosely divided into four main activities. They are (a) nursery (b) brokerage (c) drivers and delivery (d) grading, with the staff from each section interchanging if and when necessary. We have a 'key' facilitator responsible for the liaising and smooth running of each section. Once a week, these 'core' people meet for a maintenance and planning meeting which is conducted according to a planned agenda. At each meeting two additional members of staff join in on a rota system.

The weekly meeting assesses the previous week's work, plans ahead for the next week and deals with any issues arising. Decisions and plans made at the previous meeting are reviewed. We also have a 'problem-solving' section to each meeting, where any member of staff is entitled and encouraged to put on the agenda any specific problem or difficulty. Administrative problems and/ or misunderstandings are also addressed under this heading. Every person present is encouraged to contribute ideas, comments and suggestions and to feel open to express 'gut-level' responses. The atmosphere is specifically enquiring, experiential and informative, not accusatory and 'blame-seeking'.

The principal aim of these meetings is to build *esprit* and trust between all members of the company, as well as to ensure the smooth running of the business. It also affords an opportunity for people to reveal talents and initiatives that all can benefit from; feelings and opinions can be noted and addressed. The aim and result is that hopefully every person on the team can know and believe that they have a real and valuable contribution to make to their working day.

A key aspect of this working model is that staff are encouraged to understand and appreciate all aspects of the business and how each person's contribution is considered vital, important and worthy of consideration. It is to show that each and everyone of us here has a part to play which is crucial to the strength of the whole. It also enables those willing and able to take responsibility to contribute significantly and dynamically, whilst those less able are still recognised and valued for the contribution they make in the overall scheme of things.

Where does this life we live here on the side of this lovely hill fit in with the Christian concept of transformation? For me it started in the welcome and acceptance I found in the small village of Shillelagh when I arrived so tired and 'burnt-out' from my frenetic city life. There is a pulse and rhythm to the life and community here that wrought a miracle deep within me – I feel I have learned what it is to be truly alive for the first time.

In his book, *The Truth In Love*, Vincent MacNamara says: 'To accept the otherness of the other – that each other exists for himself/ herself with similar desires and hopes and a similar destiny to our own – is a shift in consciousness. And yet it is interrelatedness that is the key issue for us. It is a piece of Eastern wisdom that where there are others there is dread; we see them as a threat rather than a gift. It is in the resolution of this that the fundamental drama of our lives is lived out and that in the end our response to God is given or refused – 'as you did it not to one of the least of these you did it not to me'. It is only when we accept the community of others and recognise our responsibility that our own humanness becomes possible.'

Perhaps in the work-place we have an unique and special chance to live out this truth. Teilhard de Chardin wrote in *The Divine Milieu* that: 'The knitting together of God and the world has just taken place under our eyes in the domain of action. No, God does not deflect our gaze prematurely from the work he himself has given us, since he presents himself to us as attainable through that very work. Nor does he blot out, in his intense light, the detail of our earthly aims, since the closeness of our union with him is in fact determined by the exact fulfilment of the least of our tasks.'

In the way we gather here together in our working lives, perhaps we have been granted a God-given opportunity to reconcile and harmonise all these truths; the irresistible call to 'Live the Kingdom now'.

CONCRETISING THE GOSPEL
Written by Patrick Cogan OFM., on behalf of
Respond, Luke Street, Waterford

Respond began in 1980-81 when, in my role as Spiritual Assistant to the Secular Order of St Francis (the Third Order), I was concerned that the members of that Order may have been seeing themselves as types of mini-religious; religious to the extent that they sought a spirituality which was in the main internalised in prayer and communal devotions and cut off from the 'world', and mini- in that they thought that their secular status was less than perfect and would not enable them to be as holy as 'real (or 'first order') religious'.

So we set about looking at practical ways in which the Secular Franciscan Order (SFO) might have a greater impact on the real world. Eventually we opted for a proposal to set up a Housing Association. We made this choice because of the long housing lists of elderly persons and young families in Waterford at that time, as well as the fact that I had had some exposure to how effective such housing associations could be in preventing the exploitation of young families.

However, the Housing Association notion was flatly rejected by the SFO governing body because it was deemed to be too financially risky. I suggested to the other sub-committee members that, if they were willing, we could set up an association on our own. They were and we did; and it was formally incorporated as a company, limited by guarantee, with charitable status, and approved by the Department of the Environment as a Housing Association in 1982.

The main objective of *Respond* is to provide low-cost, good quality housing for low-income households and persons, young or old. We set out to build not only houses but communities: sheltered, for those who needed a safer environment (elderly and homeless persons) and community interactive, to enable families determine their own environment.

When we began, there were no government sponsored voluntary housing schemes to assist us. So, we put together two packages: one, in partnership with Waterford Corporation, is a cost-sharing scheme for 15 dwellings for elderly persons, completed in 1983; the other, an agency scheme of our own making, whereby we worked with low-income young families and prospective families, as their agents, to handle all their dealings with builders, local authorities, consultants etc.

Respond has operated since 1984 under the Capital Assistance Scheme, building some 143 dwellings for elderly, homeless and disadvantaged persons. The former scheme we still operate for young families and have provided 50 homes. However, the agency type package was not allowing *Respond* to really meet its objective of providing housing for the lowest income earners. Indeed, this scheme was being perceived by some families, who may well have been able to afford their own home on the open market, as simply a good bargain.

We had presented several proposals to the Department of the Environment and to the Construction Industry in 1987. One of these proposals was a 'Shared Equity' deal which was unanimously accepted by the latter Board and adopted by it as one of its recommendations to the Minister. The latter's new 'Shared Ownership' scheme unfortunately presents too many unkown and financially dangerous possibilities to low-income people, and we have indicated that we cannot support it.

However, we have given full support to the other schemes announced in February 1991, under 'The Plan for Social Housing', particularly that known as 'The Rental Subsidy Scheme'. This scheme allows *Respond* to work with the very lowest income earners and the most socialy vulnerable households. *Respond* has a major programme in hand under this scheme over the next few years.

Respond has been disappointed that, in spite of offering our services to local authorities, we have been unable to provide purpose-built and community-integrated housing schemes for the travelling community. We still live in hope!

The inspiration

A concern for social justice is the pivotal value for *Respond* in all its work. This is coupled with the realisation that Irish housing provision over the last 50 years, while providing – except in recent years – good quality housing for virtually all citizens, has also created and reinforced class distinction and segregation. This has contributed to the exclusion of the lowest socio-economic families from equal opportunities to education, work, dignity and power.

So, *Respond*'s concern for social justice must not be channelled along the old paternalistic (and 'Catholic Action') pathways of simply pulling people out of unsheltered holes. Rather, we seek to find ways to integrate low-income people into a programme of housing provision, whereby they can fill in some of those holes with the concrete foundations for new estates in which they play a vital and active management and maintenance role.

This is why *Respond* has been so energetic in supporting the Plan for Social Housing over the last year. Our fear is that if the housing lists became too long too quickly due to the cutting of the public housing programe and the ineffectiveness of the non-profit sector to meet the housing needs, we might well return to a form of doctrinaire and paternalistic socialism which, while certainly providing more houses in the short-term, would simply perpetuate the dependency of low-income households upon the state and continue their exclusion from the exercise of local democratic power.

The programme

Respond has offered its services to over 20 local authorities to provide housing under the Plan for households on their waiting lists. Our programme includes the following elements;
- the provision of good accomodation, at the lowest possible cost, for low income families;
- a finished house, carpetted to the wishes of the family, which will allow each family to enjoy a standard akin to any other on the estate;
- an estate design which will allow the tenants to 'own' it;
- a design which will seek to integrate the residents with the residents of other estates, be they private or public;
- the provision of a creche/pre-school play-group on almost every estate available to the children of the estates and the neighbouring estates as well;
- the provision of a 10-session pre-tenancy management course for the prospective tenants which includes such topics as, budgetting, rent control, community responsibility, integration with the local community, resolution of community conflict, vandalism, training for child-care, running of meetings etc.
- the course is set to enable the tenants to form an Estate Management Board with *Respond*, controlled by themselves for their own benefit. In some developments, *Respond* also provides a day-centre, run by the residents or the local committee for the needs of elderly and other residents, and users, of the estate.
- *Respond* has offered its services to local authorities, under possibilities opened up by the 1992 Housing Act, to put in place tenant management training programmes among local authority tenants. There has been some positive response – not a lot;
- we are also looking at possibilities of integrating some job-creation initiatives with our building and management programmes.

Respond's Team

There are four volunteer directors who oversee the work of *Respond* at monthly meetings. One of the directors is also the full-time volunteer manager of the association. (He values his involvement as priestly ministry and not only as social work). We consider that the 'voluntary' input into an organisation such as *Respond* is vital, and allows freedom to the directors and manager to decide a programme of action on the principal basis of what is most in keeping with the objects of *Respond*, rather than any other motivations – and there are many motivations available in the building trade!

The 'voluntary' (or charitable) nature of *Respond* should not be confused with a non-professional or an 'optional extra' approach to our work. As a charity we do the work, not of 'charity' but of justice (we are a 'justity'), and we seek to set and maintain high standards. For schemes reliant on voluntary income, *Respond* has been more than generously helped, even in the worst of times, by the general public.

Church influence

As a limited company, *Respond* does not avow any denominational or 'religious' values. Indeed, religious categorisation is an element we exclude from our assessment of housing need. We are 'Christian' to the extent that the justice we seek is very much an integral part of the 'justification' won by Jesus and we seek to build a human city that is truly human, and consequently, by Christian definition, Christlike.

This wide definition of our 'Christianity' is often not appreciated by church authorities. The more traditional 'Catholic action' organisations act overtly and specifically from a Catholic perspective and usually from within a Catholic locality, the parish. Accordingly, *Respond*'s resistance to being confined to parish boundaries or parish-based institutions is not always readily acceptable to the official church, clerical or lay (more by the former than the latter).

In the truest sense of the word, *Respond* seeks to build 'Christian' communities: communities of poorer people, integrated among themselves and with the people around them, in estates where 'God does not have favourites', and where there are agreed programmes and forums for interaction and the exercise of mutual concern. Though most members of these communities would probably be 'practising' Catholics, *Respond* does not presume this, nor do we presume that the relationships in which they are involved are 'regular'. These communities in time, may well become 'ecclesial communities' inspired by gospel values and prayerful reflection: this will not happen from any overt action of *Respond*, but from the desire of the people themselves, provided the larger 'church' in which they are set, allows them such an expression. For *Respond*'s part, we seek to provide them with the natural ground-work upon which their own 'grace' may build. It is to our frustration that the generous spirit of creativity and mutual concern which we are witnessing among the residents of these new estates is not being harvested by the official and local church. Unfortunately, the official church is still very much concerned with numbers, practices and ecclesiastical boundaries.

Sustaining the effort

All of *Respond*'s personnel are concerned to build more than houses: we look to the wider creation of community, and in particular to the needs of the poorer sections of our society. This is what has sustained our efforts in difficult times. Some of the difficulties we have encountered since our inception are:
- the perception among the politically involved that the provision of housing is part and parcel of their constituency work and their consequent reluctance to cede this power to any other bodies; since housing is a statutory right, so the argument goes, this right can only adequately be met directly by the state;
- the parallel belief that the state's only function is to provide houses and that it has little role in the creation of communities;
- the widespread perception, even among volunteers, that 'voluntary' means non-professional, unreliable and optional;
- the perception, among our client-group, that all they want from *Respond* is a house and their reluctance, at times, to be open to *Respond*'s community-creating agenda;
- all the difficulties created for one-cell housing associations by the departmentalised and multi-cell structures of local authorities:
- the reluctance felt in government departments to pay seeding monies for the emergence and training of a professional non-profit housing sector: the attitude obtains that 'if one is there, then support it', but only with mortgages and after most of the preparatory work and worry has been undertaken free of charge to the exchequer.

Celebration

Our celebrations, as an office team, are confined to Christmas celebrations and the office party. As a project team, we celebrate at the launching and opening of every estate and when we see a new community-based Board of Management begin its functions.

We are conscious of the need to constantly renew our spirits, but particularly in recent years, under pressure to take advantage of 'the signs (benefits) of the times', we have not been able to put aside requisite times for this.

TOWARDS AN ALTERNATIVE SOCIETY
Contributed by Dara Molloy SM., in collaboration with the community of An Charraig, Inis Mór, Oileáin Árainn, Co. na Gaillimhe

I am one of a group of 12 people who have come to live on Inis Mór, the largest of the Aran Islands. We can be identified not so much through what we do as how we try to live. The kernel of our identity is in our way of being in the world.

We live in households scattered across the island. Being scattered helps us to integrate with the island. People themselves choose where they want to live and with whom they want to live. A number live alone. We avoid all tendencies to institutionalise people's personal lives. We do have committees for various purposes and these often bring us together as a large group for such things as: worship, celebratory meals, parties and musical evenings, outdoor rituals, discussion forums, workshops, guest conversations, etc.

I live in the household called An Charraig. This was the original household, when there was only one, and it still plays a key role in the wider network. It is a small, rented, traditional, thatched cottage. At present, five of us live in this household and we practically always have guests staying. Other households are quieter, even contemplative.

Our way of being in the world could be roughly summed up as:
- to be rooted in the Celtic;
- to live in right relationship;
- to work for transformation.

To be rooted in the Celtic

Like a tree, we want to sink our roots deep into the soil – not just the soil of place, but also of culture and of vernacular and indigenous spirituality. Our activities, in order to do this, include:
a) becoming practised in the Gaelic language:
b) learning to celebrate with traditional music, singing and set-dancing.

c) practice of traditional arts and crafts. At present among us these include: Aran knitting, spinning, dyeing, weaving, candlemaking, button-making with Celtic designs, greeting cards using the Gaelic language and Celtic designs, cheese-making, wine-making, jam-making, bread-making, stonewall building, thatching, etc.

d) celebration of Celtic feasts and holy places. The Celtic feasts include the older feasts associated with solstices, equinoxes and seasons and also the feasts of the Celtic Church – mainly the feast-days of Irish saints. We give special attention to St Enda, St Ciaran and St Colmcille – all of whom lived on the island.

To live in right relationship

This is the visible, tangible, day-to-day part of our lives – relating to each other, relating to the divine, relating to nature, to food, to animals, to money, etc. We are searching for the right way to live with a clear perception that relationships in the western world are out of harmony and that this disharmony is producing very bad fruits.

Our relationship to the divine
We give expression to our relationship to the divine in an explicit way through prayer. Various forms of prayer used include meditation, shared prayer, the eucharist and rituals that we create for special occasions. Input into these forms often include music, dancing, readings, poetry, spontaneous sharing, spontaneous worshipful singing (praise), silence, symbolic objects, symbolic actions, dramatisation, etc. Some of us in An Charraig also join with local people in the daily Mass and rosary.

Fasting also plays a part in our lives and on Wednesdays and Fridays we do a traditional Irish fast. This is to delay the breaking of the fast – in other words, to delay breakfast. On Wednesdays we fast until 2 pm, and on Fridays until 6 or 7 pm. We promote a consciousness of the divine element in everything that we do.

Our relationship to nature, food, animals
We have worked hard on our relationship to nature, food and animals as we see just how far modern life has become dysfunctional in this area. On Aran, the beauty and power and mystery of nature is all around us. We are careful in how we live, not to damage it or treat it with disrespect. This has meant for example that we use energy and other materials from the earth sparingly. We try to avoid pollution of the air and of the water and of the land. We pre-

fer smokeless fuel. We compost whatever we can and recycle whatever we can and we use natural fertilisers on the land (mostly seaweed).

In An Charraig we grow our own food and buy very little from the shop. This gives us independence but also means that we are not giving tacit support to many foodproducing practices that are damaging to our health, damaging to the environment, or possibly oppressive and unjust to poor people. Where we do choose to buy, we are careful from whom we buy and what we buy. Our preferences are for purchases produced ethically and fairly, produced locally and produced with a minimum of processing and packaging. Home production of food includes: potatoes and a wide variety of vegetables all the year round, eggs, milk, honey, tomatoes, cheese, wine, chutney, jam.

We keep animals – household cats and a dog, fowl (chickens, ducks, geese), goats and sheep. Other animals will come with time. Our primary purpose in having these animals is to be in relationship with them, to give them a fair life suited to their nature, and to learn from them about ourselves and about God.

Our relationship with each other
Where difficulties in relationships arise, within our own household or with others, we try to deal with them in a healthy way. This may involve gathering for a meeting, asking a mutually acceptable person to facilitate or when speaking of emotionally charged issues, applying the rule of thumb, 'I felt A when you did B because of C'. We find that this allows people to own their feelings while at the same time linking those feelings to the behaviour of someone else, though not in an accusatory way.

Hospitality
In the An Charraig household, hospitality is a major part of our work. We practice it as a traditional Irish virtue, for which the country is famous. I have come to see it as even more than a virtue. It is the gospel command 'Love your neighbour' in an inculturated Irish expression. Its essence is an openness to and recognition of the divine in the other. Our guests are invited to become full participants in the household and way of life for however short a period. They usually contribute roughly the cost of their keep.

While households each welcome their own guests, together as a wider group we own a house of welcome called Killeany Lodge or Brú na mBuncloch. This house can welcome guests in larger numbers as well as being a facility for us as a group. In order to buy this house we formed a company called Aisling Árann Teoranta. Membership of this company is open to those of us on the island and others among a wide network who share our vision. We have used the company to run a number of Social Employment Schemes, to fund-raise, and to help establish a printing and publishing works that includes *The Aisling* magazine.

Our relationship with the island
With the people of the island, our neighbours, we work to become totally integrated. Through a commitment to the island that for many of us will be lifelong, and through our commitment to the spirituality, language and culture of the island, many of us hope to end up more Árannach than the Árannaigh themselves. We fully participate in the social events of the island and many of us are members of various island committees and volunteer teams.

Our relationship to money
We try to avoid the use of money as much as possible through living simply and producing as much as we can ourselves without having to buy it. In this way, our money needs are slight. Each of us earns money in different ways. Some of us are ex-professionals and offer services on a part-time or contract basis (on and off the island). Others of us are skilled craft-workers and sell our produce to tourists or by mail-order. There are part-time and casual jobs available on the island, especially in the summer. Work in our house of welcome and on the magazine produces a basic income for some others.

To work for transformation

Transformation begins with ourselves. In coming to live on this island we have removed ourselves from lifestyles, value-systems and institutions that were not life-giving to us. In giving ourselves the space to choose differently, we have opened ourselves to various other influences both within ourselves and around us, choosing them carefully and allowing a creative process of transformation to take place. Nonetheless, difficult situations have arisen from time to time for each of us. By attempting to respond positively to these, with the help and support of others, many of us have had to deal with major turmoil within ourselves. These have often led to big changes taking place. In the course of these experiences and through subsequent study, a number of our group have become skilled in spiritual discernment, understanding the psyche, and counselling.

Our mission

Our missionary spirituality, if we have one, is that of the Celtic monks rather than the standard European model. The Celtic monks chose to be missionary by being 'the light on the hilltop' and 'the salt of the earth'. By concentrating on the quality of our own lives, and allowing that be visible to others in a non-egoistic way, we believe that we can perform a transformative role in society around us. Actions speak louder than words.

In line with the Celtic monks, who copied and illustrated texts in their *scriptoria*, we in An Charraig have established a publishing and printing business called *Scriptorium Press*. We publish and print on the island both a newsletter and a quarterly magazine as well as doing other printing work. The newsletter, 'An Charraig,' is a 52 page booklet that comes out 2-3 times a year. 700 copies are printed and it is sent to a wide network of friends in Ireland and throughout the world. Our magazine, *The Aisling*, is an 80 page quarterly publication that sells by postal subscription and through shops. To us, these publications link us to a long tradition and are also an expression of hospitality, creating links of friendship and allowing ourselves to be seen, known and understood.

Our 'Aisling'

The word *aisling* means 'vision'. The vision that we share is of a transformed church and a transformed society based on community. Here on Aran we do not call ourselves a community. Rather we say that we are working towards community. Community in this sense is the kingdom of God – with us already and yet still to come. This transformation that we work for begins with ourselves, personally and communally. Much of what we try to do is done in the consciousness that it might inspire, encourage or simply inform others. In this way a light might be taken from our light and carried somewhere else, where it itself becomes a light for others.

Ultimately, the precedent for what we are doing is in the monastic model of society and church proposed by the Celtic monks exactly 1500 years ago. The patriarch of this movement was St Enda or Éanna who came to Aran around 485 AD. Aran quickly became a monastic island with over ten monasteries situated on its small and barren landscape. Many people came and stayed. Others came to learn and to be inspired and then moved on to found their own monasteries. St Ciaran, St Colmcille, St Brendan, St Sourney and St Jarlath all spent time on Aran and then took the fire elsewhere.

The monastic movement in Ireland was a community movement that was not just for monks, celibate or otherwise, but for everybody who wanted to participate. It was a movement that not only transformed church and society in Ireland, but had a major influence for good throughout the known world. This is the tradition in which we want to continue.

PART THREE

Reading the Signs

CHAPTER ONE

Towards an ecclesiology

'Hear, you who have ears to hear, what the Spirit says to the churches'(Rev 3:22). If we were to listen closely to the Spirit today, the very first thing we might hear would be her plea to be included. The overriding concern of the church universal at the moment seems to be a pre-occupation with Catholic identity – ever more narrowly defined, clarity to the point of unwavering uniformity in moral and doctrinal teaching, unquestioned obedience to norms and canons and an increase in traditional vocations. These pre-occupations are closely mirrored in the priorities here at home. The code word for this, first enunciated by Cardinal Ratzinger, and the real agenda, is 'the restoration of pre-Vatican II values'.

The institutional face of the church is relentlessly organising itself in pursuit of these goals and its system of recruitment, appointments, expenditure and communication is ample evidence of this. Leaving aside the possible betrayal of the spirit and even the letter of Vatican ll implicit in this process, there is an even greater danger in all of it. It is the danger of being so well organised that there is no longer any felt need or indeed any room, for the Holy Spirit. If everything is judged in terms of a Canon Law enacted, promulgated and interpreted by the same elite; if the agenda for all synods and gatherings is determined by a select few; if discussion and contestation are dismissed as disloyalty; we may succeed in simply stifling the Spirit. The ecclesiastical edifice is strengthened but the body of Christ is weakened.

Church in the power of the Spirit

What follows is based on the assumption that the initiatives presented in the Part Two are, broadly speaking at least, the fruits of the Holy Spirit and through them and the currents of creativity and commitment they represent, God is speaking to the church. Theologically, these commitments represent the 'reception of Vatican II'. It is in the lives and action of such groups that the motor and dynamism for the renewal and reformation of the church is to be found. Given the sense of depression that pervades Ireland at the moment, the fact that they can emerge and continue at all is itself a triumph of grace, as well as an invitation to hope, and even to conversion, for the church as a whole.

Is it possible to discern what the Spirit is saying to the church? Perhaps we can only begin to do so in the conviction that others are listening too and that it is only in the to-and-fro of a shared dialogue that the whole truth can begin to emerge. In essence, I believe that the Spirit is calling the church into a deeper Christian identity so as to incarnate itself as a community of hope and of authentic human values in the secularised society that Ireland has become. The importance of the initiatives presented in the previous section is that they embody this hope. Its further realisation will allow the church to become a counter-cultural movement for personal and social transformation, imaging in itself the structures of participation and community to which it wishes to invite all people of goodwill – and not least those who in practical terms, can no longer see in it a sign of their liberation and salvation. This will entail reforming its priorities, structures and ministries.

The basic shift is the one we are discussing here. It will be a church in the power of the Holy Spirit – who blows where she wills – rather than a church so tightly organised around a formalistic doctrine of sacraments and an over-exalted code of Canon Law that there seems to be no need for anything innovative.

This church in the power of the Holy Spirit, feels itself constantly called forward to a deeper depth of human authenticity and a fullness of life. Only in this way can the church reappropriate the theological virtue of hope whereby the discovery of the presence of God is inseparable from the longing for a new kind of sociopolitical order, developed by and for people who are experiencing the call to personal conversion and transformation.

Hope is the church's forgotten virtue because when faith is cut off from its roots in transforming love and reduced to adherence to doctrines, there is no longer any place for hope. Hope means creating the future out of the promise and the contradictions of the present – in social structures, in relationships and in our own hearts – through seeing differences and potentialities for change, as opportunities to respond to grace. Theologically this seems obvious, yet it requires a leap of imagination for so many in the church. Unconsciously at least, the church looks backwards, not exactly to Jesus, but to an idealisation of the High Middle Ages, as a result of which it tends more towards the reconstitution of the past rather than the creation of the future. A rediscovery of what it is to hope allows the church to root itself in the present and that means analysing the social structures and ideologies which consolidate that present reality in order to know how to contribute towards transforming them in the light of the gospel.

A church of hope seeking to co-create the future is one which is in the service of God's kingdom rather than in the service of itself. It never fails to realise that it is the servant of something beyond itself. In terms of universal history or even the state of the world today, the church is the extraordinary and not the ordinary means of human salvation. But although it exists to be a sign and a servant for others, it seems excessively preoccupied with itself. The enormous energy – and finance – expended on issues which do not impinge on the essence of the church itself, never mind the salvation of the world, and allow it to distract itself from its Christ-given mission, is a scandal. In existing for others, it is not neutral and has a clear priority: the poor. The church is certainly for all people but not all in the same way: the true Church always speaks from the perspective of the poor.

This paradigm shift – from organisational rigidity to community of hope – which is already taking place in the church, as illustrated in the experiences presented – includes a turn from an institution which is heavily masculine-patriarchal towards a movement which is markedly feminine-inclusive. As soon as we accept the practical consequences of the realisation that grace works only in and through freedom and co-responsibility and the openness to community, then believing that both male and female are created in the image of God, while still upholding the subordination of women to men in the church, becomes a contradiction. More than this, it becomes a theological and sacramental impoverishment because the action of the Holy Spirit in over half of the church's committed membership is, for the most part, not allowed to address and therefore empower the people of God.

With this shift to the feminine and to the poor will come an even more profound movement: from a strongly empirical or materialistic view of church life to a more mystical one. Rooting itself more adequately in a wider and profounder experience and notion of God, the church will begin to see its vocation more clearly in terms of a quality of loving service to the world expressed in witness, prophetic action and the ministry of reconciliation. This will allow it to free itself from the heresy of numbers and the illusion of computing its salvific significance in primarily statistical terms and institutional solidity. In this regard, the importance of initiatives such as *An Tobar* which facilitate a genuine and reflected spirituality of the people cannot be overstated.

The consequent detachment from socio-political status and numerical strength will allow the church to relocate itself at the heart of the common human search for meaning, authenticity, justice and reconciliation. This church will no longer need to be a bastion of conservatism or indeed a bastion of anything at all. This will be a grace; freeing it from the supposed task of being the guardian of the world's morals and free in turn to live out its own truth. For the Christian faith is not primarily a morality but a mysticism empowering a morality and the heart of that mysticism is the experience of love as forgiveness. Rooted in this experience, the church can carry out its ministry of reconciliation, not out of its own supposed moral self-sufficiency, which can so easily give the impression of self-righteously judging the world, but by speaking to the world of its need for reconciliation, with a sensitivity born of its own lived dependence on forgiveness.

The context of this conversion is a world controlled by the transnationalisation of capital and the dehumanisation of culture which follows in the wake of the resulting consumerism. In this context, the church is called to be avowedly counter-cultural. When consumerism becomes the international ideology, then the human person is no longer a subject. Jobs, houses, rights and even life itself at all stages, are all expendable. The unnegotiable is production and consumption: 'I consume, therefore I am'. This form of advanced capitalism is destroying the eco-system, marginalising the Third World in a cruel poverty that only increases as the West consumes more. Even in the so-called developed world, the greed for profit renders an increasing number of people unemployed and therefore marginalised. Welfare, far from being empowerment and inclusion, becomes a way of life sinking its recipients further into dependency, exclusion and despair.

The church can no longer challenge this world out of its own institutional aspirations. Where it still seeks to do so, it is immediately swept up into a power game which demands that its prophecy be balanced and measured; then it must be prudent and inoffensive and finally, for the sake of institutional interests, it must be silenced. The institution survives but the gospel is not proclaimed. Not long ago, a prominent businessman in this country, was quoted as saying that he saw the role of the church as providing order in society. It was a moment of illumination for many. For what does 'providing order' mean in a world of institutionalised oppression and inequality? The church's challenge to this system will come not from institutional self-interest but from the simplicity of its own life and its unambiguous links with the victims of this system.

This means a listening church rather than a promulgating church. For how can the church speak for and with the oppressed unless it first listens to them? Surely, one of the gifts the Spirit wishes to give to the church at this present juncture is 'a disciple's ear'. God's view is the view from below. That is the meaning of the cross. Only a church that can listen to the victims can listen to God. Only a church that can critique the system in the name of the excluded, can address it in the name of God.

A counter-cultural church in the power of the Holy Spirit will be a community of communities rather than primarily a hierarchy. Obviously, there will be a ministry of leadership in this church and that ministry will be episcopal and in communion with Peter. But on what basis should bishops be chosen and ordained? In a church genuinely desiring to minister in the power of the Spirit, the single most important gift in a would-be bishop might be the gift of discerning and developing the gifts of the Holy Spirit in others. The bishop's role would not so much be to consolidate the institution and administer its patrimony as to animate the emergence and life of communities. Needless to say, we are not speaking here of institutionalised forms of community such as those in which many religious have been obliged to live, but rather of a sharing of vision and purpose, leading to a sharing of time and goods and then the deeper sharing of the journey of life. This is not simply an optional adornment to Christian life, but is actually essential to it. There is no church life and no Christian life that is not community life. We are not saved as believers nor do we grow as human beings, merely as individuals, but within the relationships that form community. Even union with God is always mediated through relationality – and, as the Eckhart House experience emphasises, is embodied in it. There is a strict and inseparable unity between our love for each other and our love of God.

For this renewed church, life itself in all its complexities and ambiguities is a primordial locus of the sacred. Purposeful action in the secular world then is the primary means of knowing and loving God. The contemplative life is the call to love this world more deeply. The church's liturgy proposes, focuses and celebrates this and calls people to a life of prayer and worship in order to deepen and sustain it. The sacraments become privileged moments of internalising and celebrating this essentially contemplative involvement in secular reality, as distinct from some supposedly 'supra-natural' sacred space outside of which God is not accessible. This is the Copernican revolution in the church's understanding of sacrament of which Rahner wrote years ago. Now, for the first time almost, we in this country are forced to consider it. Life itself with its struggles, ambiguities, joys and failures, and not the sacraments of the church, is the primary locus of the sacred and it is there that the common human vocation to holiness is lived out. The sacraments are those privileged moments when we confess, deepen, personalise and celebrate what is everywhere true but seldom recognised.

Rooted in reality

The actions of Jesus, the options of the New Testament communities and all genuine reform movements in the church flow from a love for God but are always rooted in the reality of the moment. The gospel is not a religious ideology but the news that the justice and compassion of God are unconditionally offered to all in the here and now. Without reading the signs of the times, we cannot perceive how grace is being offered to humankind. Not to analyse is not to evangelise.

As in all periods of history, so today, grace and 'dis-grace' are locked in apocalyptic struggle. There is a New World Order yet unprecedented violence and militarisation. It is a time of record production and consumption yet coupled with massive and increasing poverty, as well as the accelerated destruction of the environment. In Europe, we have achieved the Single Market and, together with it, catastrophic unemployment, not to mention the further impoverishment of the South. It is a time of alleged consensus yet brokenness, division and the collapse of a moral basis to society is everywhere evident. It is a culture where freedom is trumpeted but the abuse of women and the manipulation of youth as paying consumers for the false message of their freedom, are its hallmarks. We in Ireland have bought into this – perhaps irrevocably. We did so because of greed; convinced we would gain. A few have and will continue to do so; many more will join the list of its victims; some of us must urgently make the decision as to whether we wish to contribute to legitimating or challenging it.

The work of the Justice Commission of the CROI and the current of thought and action it represents in the church, must not be seen solely as an optional involvement of church personnel. This kind of action is constitutive of evangelisation. A church that would not so act would be merely a religious sect. Political options and the financial budgets and social policies which implement them are also places where grace and sin abide. There would be something pathetic about a church that would have something to say about where contraceptives may or may not be sold but would not consider the assumptions and decisions of the budget fit material for examination in the light of the gospel. There are difficulties here certainly. There is the distinction of competencies: economic strategies must be critiqued in economic terms, but the human and moral assumptions that lie behind them must be unmasked in ethical terms, for what they are. There is the unfamiliar vulnerability of consciously taking sides. Concepts can remain general and inclusive but not so practical decisions; so whose side are we on? There is the reticence to offend the Government. But is that not to render to Caesar something more than his due?

To make recommendations, to surpass generalities, to take sides, to leave behind a facile neutrality: there is no other way to proclaim the gospel in a situation of division. Indeed, there is no other way to trust in the power of the gospel. One of the most courageous and encouraging aspects of the bishops' pastoral, *Work is the Key*, even though it still needs to carried through in practice, was its willingness to name what it considered to be the cardinal issue: namely, the divisions in our society between the haves and the have-nots and then to allow this to be an interpretative key for analysing our socio-economic reality.

Reading social-reality from the underside is not surrendering the gospel to a secular ideology. If aspects of ideologies can help us to do so more scientifically, all the better. But the option itself is profoundly and unmistakeably Christian. It is the option of God in the Exodus experience to which the Prophets constantly recall us, the option of Jesus throughout his ministry and is a fundamental aspect of Catholic social teaching. The gospel is not an aid to the order sought by the powerful. Neither is it a legitimation of the management strategies of the public services. Rather, it is the spiritual basis of action for transformation in favour of a new and inclusive quality of human solidarity.

But this analysis takes place at local as well as at national level. We must 'think globally but act locally'. The Moyross, Ballymun and Wexford initiatives are examples of first seeking to know in a structured way what are the forces and influences shaping life and attitudes in an area, before seeking the gospel response to these situations. But this analysis that precedes gospel-based action has to be equal to the complexities of contemporary life. The distinction between the personal, communitarian, and societal, adopted by the *Partners in Mission* movement, is instructive here, though it probably needs to be amplified into a four-level distinction to include the institutional. Our lives are shaped by many institutions which are neither small groups nor structures of wider society.

Many strategies are shortsighted and unproductive because they focus exclusively on, or ignore, one or other of these levels. The church, for example, has generally stressed only the individual in its moral teaching, and the institutional in its message of religious faith. It has generally overlooked the structures of the wider society and the forms of community and communication to which they give rise. Equally, it can sometimes fail to grasp the moral and social significance of the manner in which certain institutions operate in its name. Many political movements leave out the personal and interpersonal aspects of the human person's being-acting in the world. The present political agenda in Ireland is depersonalising people by reducing all relationships to commerce. In contrast, different kinds of renewal movement in the church seem to emphasise solely the personal experiential aspect of transformation. Diocesan and parish attempts at renewal have much to learn from a vision and strategy based on the interdependence of these four levels.

Church doesn't exist for itself

Like the human person and the Sabbath, the gospel does not exist for the church but the church exists for the gospel; and the kingdom of justice and compassion which God wishes to inaugurate. As soon as the church can accept – in its allocation of resources and not just in its lecture halls – that it is not the quasi-exclusive means of otherworldly salvation for a select number, but the sign of salvation for all, then its priorities and organisation will change. At the moment, it would not be difficult to demonstrate that these resources go more into consolidating its own structures than into its mission. That the church is not an end in itself is part of its own teaching. Yet, in this area of Christian doctrine, we have the same phenomenon that occurs in relation to key aspects of the church's social teaching. An established and dogmatically certain aspect of its doctrine is not allowed to penetrate its imagination and policy-making, just as its social teaching is rarely applied to its own structures.

The sentient base of the church's decisions in relation to allocation of resources, training of ministers, matters demanding public commitment and the expenditure of time and money operates in terms of a view of salvation which is no longer the official doctrinal position of the church itself. For the church believes and teaches that all people share in the Paschal mystery and in the grace of Christ. The mission of the church is not therefore to ensure the salvation of the few or the many who belong to it but to live a life of witness to that salvation permanently offered to all which is mediated through the struggle for integral liberation.

Centuries of over-spiritualisation and domestication lie buried in our whole manner of thinking and speaking in religious terms. What the *Partners in Faith* experience reports is easily verifiable: it comes as a source of amazement to people that God in Moses and in Jesus was concerned with real live issues and structures and offered salvation mediated by human liberation and transformation to be concretised in an egalitarian society. Whe,n in the light of this realisation, they can, in the words of the *Fig Tree* base community, claim the gospel as their own, religion becomes a dynamic, exciting and empowering experience which is actually Good News.

What Scripture reveals to people such as the *Fig Tree* and *Exodus* groups and those who take time out in places like *An Tobar*, people who pray with the text in view of the real issues of oppression and hope that exist in their communities, is that (i) God calls us into a movement of emancipation and solidarity, (ii) fidelity to this call and to the action and community it entails, is always the heart and soul of our covenant with God and (iii) fidelity to this covenant and the commitment it entails evokes in us the need for and the call to a life of faith, prayer and liturgy. History has bequeathed to us the bones of the third, only formally connected to the second and dislocated from the first. We almost need an experience of defamiliarisation with the symbols of religion so that we can discover God in Christ anew and know God, as it were, for the first time. In meeting God anew, we need to pay special attention to the way she/he is perceived by women, by the poor and by people of deep spiritual experience of whatever tradition.

The whole concept of catechesis needs to be rethought in the light of this. It can never be reduced simply to a matter of establishing the credibility of Christ or the church in theoretical terms or of demonstrating the suitability of the church's sacramental life. It has a more basic context from which it can never be cut off, and that is learning – especially as adults – to act purposefully for the reign of God in the world. Christian doctrine cut off from this does not possess any content of its own. 'You cannot even say "Jesus is Lord" except by the Holy Spirit.' But the Spirit is not present in some static Euclidian point in our souls, but only in ourselves as acting persons, in our praxis and in the fruits of that praxis. We may never allow ourselves to think about Christ and the church in a manner that permits us just to think about them.

Yet it is the opposite that is often the case. *Respond* reports that work for housing which is about building communities and not just physical plants and which seeks social integration rather than the consolidation of class distinction is not seen as church work. Yet it is a form of praxis more likely to generate a Christian spirit of creative concern and community not always apparent in more recognisably church structures.

What we are seeing is a call from the Spirit to avoid becoming closed in upon ourselves. A church existing for itself easily degenerates into clericalism. This not only distorts the church but impoverishes it by denying it its most valuable resources. It also results in a massification of the people of God, who are no longer allowed to be subjects in the church but instead are consigned to passivity. Today, people would rightly reject the institutional form of a movement that would offer them only this.

The most the church could ever aspire to in this model is paternalism. It can never be community and never be prophetic: hence it can never be the church. Under the onslaught of the market forces at work in present-day Ireland, which cannot be controlled from within the country and owe no loyalty to the historical or social goals of the Irish people, the institutions of the State will need less and less legitimation from the church. Up to now, there has been a sort of tacit concordat between church and State in both parts of this country, whereby the church stayed out of politics and the State allowed the church certain privileges in education. But the church's role in education is rapidly declining and education itself is being rethought in terms of the technological requirements of an advanced capitalist economy. Ethics are being replaced by technocracy.

From now on, if the church wants a traditional role of sharing influence with the State, it will have to do so increasingly on the State's terms. But what kind of State is it that leaves children homeless and, in practical terms, remains indifferent to so much inequality and the degradation to which it gives rise, as Fr McVerry asks, and does the church really want to share influence and power – and thereby legitimate – such a State? How, in fact, can the church be a sign of the kingdom of God in a situation where the vast majority of the people practice their religion and yet vote for and support a political system which is increasingly materialistic, less caring and more oppressive?

Somehow religion and 'real life' are still being kept separate and always will be as long as the church thinks of itself solely or even firstly in merely 'spiritual-religious' terms. A community shy of face-to-face involvement with the homeless and the one-quarter of our society they symbolise; a community that, unlike *Cornerstone*, will stay clear of the uncontrollable interface and retreat to the familiar; a community that will not allow itself to be reconstructed by integrating the stories of women believers: such a community, however large, is a religious sect and not the church.

This partly explains the very ambivalent experience that many innovative groups have of the involvement of priests. They appreciate support but fear control. Many share the experience of the Killala group: there is often a marked difference between the openness of individual priests and the body of the clergy as a whole. The problem on the priests' side is, often though not always, a question of power or security. Frequently, it is a matter of a deeply internalised sense of loyalty that does not distinguish sufficiently clearly between the mission of the people of God and the institutional form of the church.

By contrast, this goes some way to explain the very real difficulties that some progressive groups have in identifying themselves as church. For surely one of the great scandals of Irish church life and a constant source of amazement to visiting Third-world theologians, is that the very people who take the stance that Jesus took in his society, have often the greatest difficulty in identifying themselves with the church or even as church. And it must be said that the major difficulty lies not in some incomplete degree of reflection on their part but in the perception, too general to be without foundation, that 'the church', unconsciously at least, has different priorities.

There is much food for reflection in the choice of target groups implicit in many of the initiatives presented and explicit in some. Energy and communication are first directed to those who are visibly poor and disadvantaged; secondly, to those who live and work in some kind of solidarity with them, and thirdly, to those who are broadly sympathetic to their struggles. This vision and strategy has much to say to the quite different attitudes to the poor and oppressed found within the church.

Firstly, there is the attitude of helping 'them'; the dynamic is donor and recipient; the church is not poor and the poor are not the church. Secondly, there is the attitude of including 'them'. Dependency is being surpassed, but not paternalism. 'They' are being allowed into 'our church'. Thirdly, there is the more theologically coherent vision of actually constructing the church out of the struggles and yearning of the poor for a transformed world and out of the poverty of spirit of those who sustain an option to share in that struggle. For there is such a fundamental reciprocal relationship between the liberation of the poor and the Good News of Jesus, that they cannot be conceived except in terms of each other.

Women: the silenced majority

As in life in general, so also in the church, women do more than half of the work and get less than half of the recognition. Yet even in the very way this short observation is couched there is a sort of residual paternalism; as if the most the committed female Christian could hope for is adequate recognition from the male hierarchy. Still, it must be clearly stated that both in traditional church life and in most of the initiatives for renewal, including the ones discussed in Part Two, it is women who participate most frequently and most faithfully.

There is a quality of participation vital to the survival and sustenance of innovative groups which can be summed up in a comment of the *Cornerstone* community that we are called to fidelity rather than to success. For a variety of reasons, women seem to grasp this more readily than men. The Firhouse group observed that, apart from scouts and sports, in all other initiatives, most of the participants were women. One place where men were the majority was in the clientele of *CentreCare*. While mobility may have something to do with this, it also points to the terrible brokenness in men who cannot live up to the norm of masculinity and success demanded by our society. For a society which oppresses women also oppresses men.

Patriarchalism in the church represents an objective injustice and in the light of the findings of the human sciences in relation to the historical subjection of women, it can no longer be condoned. What was once largely unconscious has become conscious and to persist in it now would be to persist in sin. The experience of the Sophia group amply illustrates how women repeatedly experience themselves allowed to participate in church life only if they implicitly accept a subservient role. Undeniably, many would wish to keep things so. When one reads neo-conservative theologians today it is difficult not to conclude that a literalist interpretation of the Pauline and Pastoral Epistles – not to mention a distortion of the text of Genesis – has contributed considerably to endorsing this.

If one wants to know Paul's real attitude to women in the church, then just consider his relationships with Phoebe, Priscilla, Chloe, Eunice, Lois and Lydia and the manner in which he valued them personally, theologically and ministerially. Paul's perspective was always one in which 'the fashion of this world is passing away'. To use his words to attempt to give the status of revelation to historically-conditioned cultural assumptions is a serious misrepresentation. There is indeed – relative to the feminism of Jesus and Paul – a process of repatriarchalisation in the churches of the pastoral epistles. But this simply represents a process of inculturation such as we will later see in relation to imperialism, feudalism and liberal democracy.

Theologically, it is an attempt at a culturally intelligible catechesis within the worldview of that epoch. Paul would never have seen such a worldview as either binding or adequate for those who 'live in Christ'. Ironically, the very same reasons that made it legitimate in those circumstances, demand that it be superseded in the circumstances of today. Just as the New Testament does not simply repeat the words and actions of the historical Jesus, but in order to proclaim their significance in a new situation, expresses them in a new way, so the church at the end of the twentieth-century cannot merely quote the pastoral epistles – either in relation to women or to slavery – as if the context of that catechesis had remained unchanged.

The great danger for the church today is that it will lose reflective women who are socially and religiously sensitive, just as it once lost the politically aware element of the workers' movement. The process of distanciation from the church is in fact, well underway among feminists and the experience of the *Christian Feminist Movement* reflects just what a heartache it is to try to hold commitment to women and to the church together. It would be altogether too superficial, and perhaps even self-serving, to be content to dismiss, in a solely theoretical way, the premises of the various currents of post-Christian feminist religious thought. The writer shares many misgivings about religious movements cut off from the memory of Jesus and the tradition of the church, but that, for the moment at least, is not the central point. The real issue is the manner in which the stubbornness and sense of threat of the church leadership has made women despair of ever having their voice heard. It should not come as a surprise that many women feel the need to form their own groups. The experience of women seems to be that, whether inside or outside the church, they first of all need to find their own voice.

If the rest of the church can learn to listen to that voice and, having really heard what it has to say, only then attempt to dialogue with it, the whole church may be blessed. Since women, no less than men, are created in the image and likeness of God, then women's stories, as the Killala group insists, are stories of God. Women need to tell and hear these stories to vindicate their own womanhood as a locus of God's revelation. But so too does the rest of the church. The one-way communication that is an effective denial of the mutuality of the sexes, both in ordinary life and in the plan of salvation, is also an impoverishment of the church as a whole. Since both male and female are together in the image of God, a church that would not express this mutuality in the communion between its members and in its structures of ministry and decision-making, would not image God.

One danger in couching the debate on women in the church in terms of common versus distinct humanity of males and females, is to lose sight of the mutuality and interdependence of the masculine and the feminine, in community and in each human person. It is constitutively, in the search for this mutuality and coresponsibility for the church that we can create 'the communion in the Holy Spirit': neither domination nor separation. In a postfeminist world, a church that persists in systematic patriarchalism, is cutting itself off from half of its own spiritual and theological resources and by elevating the other half to the status of a quasicomplete version of revelation, may well be running the risk of simply creating a god in its own image and likeness.

Certainly, the implications of properly integrating a feminist reconstruction of theology may be awesome and one cannot help suspecting that a fear of this lies buried in the moves to block it. The fact is that it is not possible to predict the results of such a process but, in all probability, it might result in a sea-change in the consciousness of the church. But only the truth in love will make us free. Who can now doubt that the voice of women needs to be heard more clearly in the elaboration of sexual ethics? And if as seems likely, the stilling of that voice in the sexual area amounts to silencing the victim, then what, in fact, would be constructed without that input?

Alternatively, a feminine input into theology and decision-making in the church may create not so much a new doctrinal system as a new style of being church; less legal, clerical, formal, fixed; more open, inclusive, practical, flexible – and dare one say it? – more honest. A new emphasis on communication and mutual comprehension might well pave the way for a post-authoritarian exercise of authority. This, in turn, may make it possible for the core Christian values in the area of sexuality to be once again taken seriously in the wider debate.

Crucial as the issue of women's ordination may be, many Christian women do well to recognise that it is not necessarily the most fundamental issue in the feminist debate in the church, even though it may well be one of the ways of addressing it. The more basic and ultimately far-reaching issue is the recognition of the female and the feminine as equally revelatory of the divine as the male and the masculine and then allowing this its proper input into reshaping the consciousness, priorities and structures of the church.

Women whose real agenda was, consciously or unconsciously, a share in the power of the institution as it now operates and who had not critiqued and surpassed the manner in which power is understood and exercised in society and in the church as it stands, would be just as unlikely as many of their male counterparts to effect renewal. Yet until public ministry is also exercised in the church by both men and women who have integrated the masculine and the feminine both within and between themselves, and in so doing, have surpassed an authoritarian exercise of authority, the church cannot express the communion towards which it seeks to call the world. For this reason, the issue of women's ordination is crucial and must be faced. [2]

From the materialist to the mystical

On two occasions in its history, but in completely different ways, has Catholicism become a World Religion. One was after the Constantinian peace and the other was at Vatican II, especially in the decrees on non-Christian religions and on the church in the world of today. By means of the first it sought the world's salvation by seeking a share in ruling the world in the name of God. By means of the second, it seeks the world's salvation by identifying itself unreservedly with the joys and struggles of the whole human family. Behind the first lies the assumption that God's grace is given only to certain people under certain circumstances. Behind the second is the conviction that 'grace is everywhere' and that God's kingdom comes by means of all forms of human authenticity.

The first gives rise to a materialist phase of church history with the emphasis on numbers, uniformity in organisation, sacramental theory and law, all in the service of an expansionist understanding of mission. The second gives rise to a mystical phase in the church's presence in the world, with the emphasis on imaging and witnessing God's unshakeable fidelity to God's creation and to all creatures. In the first, the secular is disparaged for the sake of the sacred, but under this sacral veneer, the church may have many worldly goals. In the second, we come to see with Bonhoeffer that it is not the 'religious' act which makes the Christian but the participation in God's suffering love in the secular world.

This represents a difficult shift for the church and it should not surprise us that it is resisted. What we are witnessing in the present restorationist tendencies within the church is the reaction born of fear, that unless we hold fast to a certain way of organising the church, it will lose its identity and have nothing to offer the world. Apart from the mistake of identifying the church with a particular historically-conditioned institutional form of ecclesial organisation, there is a deeper theological issue at stake here. God needs the church as a faithful sign and life-giving embodiment of what has been offered to all people in the life, death and resurrection of Jesus. But God does not need the church as if only – or even especially, in some quantitative sense – in it, is the grace of salvation offered. The church must not do with baptism what the Judaisers sought to do with circumcision.

Like a person in the middle of life's journey who having developed and expressed her/his personality as the emerging ego seemed to indicate, can move no further in a particular direction but must pause to integrate all s/he previously felt obliged to overlook, in the new project of becoming one's true self, so too the church. An inestimable amount has been contributed to the world by the church, but in the process certain aspects of its true self have been overlooked, if not to say repressed. In the task of picking up on these, there may well be a period of disorientation and unfamiliarity. But that will surely be the opportunity for that deeper journey into the mystery of God in Christ, where alone the church can find its true identity. Indeed, the very darkness and uncontrollability of that journey may be its moment of grace and creativity. St John of the Cross reminds us that to go to a place where we have never been we must go by a route we do not know.

This may well take the form of an on-going conversion to the 'other' – the repressed antithesis of what was assumed, without regard to its limitations, to be 'the thesis'. It will be first a journey from the limited to the whole. It will be a journey to the sacredness of all of creation where matter itself is being divinised by the cosmic Christ. Part of the reason why the sacramental life of the church appears so vacuous is that bread and wine, the pouring of water or oil and the uttering of words cannot mediate the sacred unless that sacredness is venerated in the heart of all materiality. Can we pour oil in an act of healing if our spirituality is suspicious of the body? How can we communicate the sacramentality of infant baptism if we cannot adore the glory of God in every human birth? How seriously do we believe in the sacredness of life and motherhood, if mothers may not preside at the celebration of the Christian mysteries and if one third of all mothers and children are systematically denied the right to participate in the normal structures of society? How can the breaking of the bread be visibly – and sacraments are *visible* signs – the creation of communion when the socio-political structures of our society, supported by churchgoing people, systematically deny communion to a quarter of the population?

The conversion to the other means seeing the 'poor person' (*Centre-Care*), the 'employee' (*Shillelagh*), the 'enemy' (*Cornerstone*) as a 'person'. This is an experience of great theological depth, for that person's 'otherness' mediates the 'otherness' of God. The act of listening with genuine openness is a redemptive act, a serious indication of the desire to be evangelised. Correspondingly, speaking one's own truth openly is a form of prophecy. A church in the power of the Holy Spirit wishes to mediate these forms of empowerment and rejoices that people can – as in many of the groups encountered in Part Two – claim the gospel as their own, convinced that the greater truth to which it will be thereby summoned will bring it closer to God. In this way, we can hope for a genuine lay spirituality which will not be just a watered-down version of religious life but the articulation of an experience of God rooted in a purposeful attempt to address the real world.

This move will also be characterised by a greater appreciation of what is small and authentic coupled with a resistance to the desire to be powerful in a physical and visible sense, at the cost of attention to a deeper authenticity. It will not be an abdication from the vocation to be relevant and effective – and, if necessary, confrontational – but a conviction that this is achieved more by the networking of communities which are focused and faithful rather than by expanding institutional dominance. For the priority for powerful institutions quickly becomes the protection of their own interests. This option for authenticity brings with it and is nourished by a spirituality of God's faithfulness, God's abiding, nurturing, empowering and sending – all born of lived experience and not just handed down by an external authority. The willingness to be small and tentative, if that is what authenticity demands, and to prize fidelity over success, is a crucial part of the spirituality of a local church seeking to relocate itself in dependence upon the Holy Spirit.

The move to the mystical will also be a reappropriation of many aspects of our forgotten ecclesial past in the Celtic church. After two decades of revisionist history, explicable in part as a reaction

to the manner in which the myth of the 'Island of Saints and Schol-
ars' was manipulated in a previous generation, it has now become
possible again to explore and rejoice in what we once were. There
is no call to idealise the Celtic church. It too had its decadence as
well as its glories; but when one visits the ancient monastic sites,
especially those in remoter areas, one is always struck by the
profound spirit of contemplation that still lingers on. There is a
palpable thirst for God, yet set in a harmonious connectedness
with nature and the environment: a rejection of the selfishness
and violence of the world, yet a capacity to see even these distortions of God's will in the context of God's compassion. Anyone
who has sat silently alone in a *clochán* and thought about what it
was that drove people to seek this kind of solitude and rootedness
in the divine, will know what I mean.

For at the heart of all of this flowering of the gospel in the Celtic
church was a unshakeable desire to possess and be possessed by
God. Centuries before Teilhard, the Celtic monk knew that the
cosmic Christ was the vision he contemplated in all things and, at
the same time, was the High-king of his heart. Reconnecting with
this is to reconnect with ourselves.

A counter-cultural church

One of the important issues the experience in Inismor asks us to
consider is how the monastic spirit of the Celtic Church may be
lived out by a post-clericalist Church in a post-Christian secularised Ireland. The *fuga mundi* of the early monks was geographical.
Ours may well be counter-cultural. Knowing what people really
value is the key to understanding their culture and what the people of this country seem to value above all else right now is consumerism. The core myth that gives shape to the emerging culture is
that of human happiness achievable by increased income, consumption and leisure in an ever-expanding economy that is part
of a world trade-bloc with unlimited resources. The fact that the
expectations to which this rather crude materialism gives rise remain pathetically unfulfilled for many people does not seem to
have substantially reduced the blind faith the people and their political representatives have in this myth of progress. For a myth,
and an unrealisable one at that, is what it certainly is.

The relationship between Christianity and culture is not a simple
one. In different circumstances, the Christ of the church seems to
point us towards, above, against, in dialogue with or in opposi-

tion to culture. Catholicism in general, because of the medieval experience, has a bias towards the concept of a Christian culture and because of the early history of the state, this is also the case in this country. When John Paul II speaks of Christianity as the heart of the cultural values of the new Europe from the Atlantic to the Urals, he is speaking out of the same model. But this whole way of thinking may well be a carry-over from the now defunct Christendom model of church. Does the church really want or need the protection of the new Roman Empire? In fact, organised Christianity is increasingly irrelevant in continental Europe and in a post-religious world, the new Empire will not need the legitimation of religion. A church seeking an harmonious relationship with the New World order will do so in the hope of re-shaping that order's value system from within. But it may well be that the increasingly naked worship of Mammon will make it virtually impossible for the church to do so without risking a fundamental compromise of essential elements of the gospel.

A survey of the values contained in the initiatives presented in Part Two points in the direction of a counter-cultural church. The transformation for which these groups are working, involves changing the socio-economic structures of society. This is seen as an explicitly religious task in the light of the realisation that God's dream for humanity includes an egalitarian society. Throughout is a philosophy of empowerment and the attempt to construct alternatives to the endemic dependency and destructive consumerism of the emerging culture. There is an explicit shift from a church of paternalism to one with a denunciative prophetic role in relation to injustice. This prophecy goes beyond denunciation in attempting to articulate and construct alternative practicable models of work, communication and organisation. It is a search for the integration of the feminine in all aspects of life rather than merely the inclusion of females in the existing power structures. It seeks to be the voice of the voiceless and to channel rather than still that voice.

All of this does not have to remain at a theoretical spiritual level but can and does have serious economic implications. The economy is more than money; it is above all, human labour. The gospel and Catholic social teaching, in particular, both assign a clear priority to labour over capital. In analysing an economic situation, Christians abandon the gospel if they allow the myth of the market to be the sole or principal criterion of economic truth.

The *Shillelagh* experience illustrates this. Caring values come first because work and economy are human, ethical, purposeful endeavours. People do not cease to be human persons when they work because the employee is not simply someone who sells his or her labour and whose value may then be computed in solely financial terms. When the work-place is conceived of as a human community, one of the first discoveries is that the principal source even of organisational and productive strength is the combined energies and talents of all. Allowing talent and aptitude to be expressed and developing a community of participation and shared responsibility increases purposefulness and productivity. Conceiving of work and entrepreneurship as a participation in community-building and the common good is the one and only way to tackle unemployment. Self-reliance points towards valuing the common good over individualism. Dependency, by contrast, always produces fragmentation and division. As long as we go along with the fallacy that the right to increase profit margins supersedes the right of others to work, and build our future accordingly, we condemn our people to disaster.

Contrast the thinking here to the endemic dependency on transnational corporations and our apparent willingness to hand over our collective future to them more or less on their terms. In early 1993, the Galway subsidiary of the TNC Digital announced a 'restructuring' plan which involved the loss of 780 jobs. As Digital was the largest employer in the city and its hinterland, the announcement was devastating. At the same time it emerged that a similar factory at Ayr in Scotland was to keep its job quota, not least, it was alleged, because of behind-the-scenes manoeuverings by the British government. The whole event was undoubtedly a real tragedy for the people involved and, in all likelihood, for many more as well. Would it have been less a tragedy, even if less immediately so, if the job losses had occurred in Ayr? The whole scenario of dependency was played out in the attitudes and actions that followed. A Minister of State from the Labour Party flew overseas to beg from a multi-national; the then bishop-elect stated that everything possible was done; an opposition politician blamed the government for not acting as their counterparts in London were alleged to have acted and, most indicative of where power really lies, the Taoiseach went to pains to let the nation know that he personally telephoned a businessman to look for his intercession with the TNC.

All of the thinking remains within the parameters of assuming that this kind of dependency is a human and fruitful way to build the future. The bottom line seemed to be that if the jobs had been lost in Ayr then all would have been well. Hardly anybody seems to see that we are going deeper and deeper into the process of simply surrendering power over ourselves to institutions which will never feel any loyalty either to the Irish people or to working people anywhere in the world.

It is time for the church to rediscover that part of its mission is to contribute towards defining the moral basis of the political order as a whole. The church shouldn't be involved in politics in the sense of seeking to become itself a political power or seeking political power for its own institutions. But it most certainly should be involved in politics in the sense of helping to clarify the human and ethical options implicit in different political choices. This has already been stated in all the social encyclicals, as have the criteria according to which it may be attempted: justice, equality of opportunity, respect for life and human rights, the priority of labour, the common good, reconciliation, the wider solidarity of the human family, the integrity of creation and the preferential option for the poor. It is difficult to see how even one of these ethical values is in any way a significant element in the political order and the culture of the 'fast track' towards which our economic and political leaders long to lead us and towards which we appear to want to be led: to stand with our begging-bowls, dependent and demeaned.

Community of communities

In a depersonalised and alienating culture, the creation of community becomes an act of evangelisation. Because of the nature of Irish society, up until recently it was not possible to adequately communicate the idea of the Christian vocation as a vocation to create community. People already lived in a form of *societas* which passed for community; the difference being that it was a communal adherence and internalisation of an external norm rather than something freely created through dialogue, participation and co-responsibility. In the secularised society that Ireland has become, Christian community can no longer be simply equated with the local unit of population but must be chosen, co-created and sustained in the light of a Christ-centred vision of transformation.

The communion in the Holy Spirit (*koinonia*) which is the soul of community, is at once the communion within God, between Christ and his community and between ourselves in the process of becoming community. Only if the church is a networking of communities does it exist in the image of God, for God is community: that is part of what the doctrine of the Trinity means. Theologically speaking, this is the reason why the practice of the bishop or priest living in effect alone and not organically part of a real community of life, and presiding over a church where real community between its members is not considered essential to their church life, is a very suspect one, apart altogether from being humanly unsustainable. There is something theologically sound about the central team of *Teach Bríde* choosing to live together as an apostolic community. One wonders indeed if there can ever be a theologically sustainable model of pastoral leadership that does not contain a real community of life as a constitutive element. We might do well to re-read the New Testament texts on leadership in the light of these reflections.

Renewal and reformation in the church will always be a rediscovery of community and this is something strongly present in all the initiatives presented in Part Two of this book. Creating community in society; integrating the abandoned into community; reconciled communities as servants of reconciliation; training people in teams, to be community builders; proposing the creation of caring community in the school or club here and now; building local community in the service of transformation; emphasising the building of trust in communities as a prerequisite for sustained action. What this points to is a renewed church which, instead of just pronouncing on community, will image it in its own structures.

In shared Christian praxis at the most foundational level, we are all both donors and recipients; all participants and therefore all fundamentally equal. This involves for all of us a conversion from a monological to a dialogical way of relating. It involves new forms of decision-making and a new openness to being inclusive, representative and valuing consensus. Although it is true that the church is more fundamentally as well as more ultimately a mystical reality (*mysterium*) rather than a socio-political one, endlessly repeating this assertion can easily mask an ideological attempt to block renewal. For it all too conveniently leaves out how this mystical reality shall incarnate itself in a given historical epoch. It is contradictory as well as ridiculous to debar democratisation as an expression of communion (*koinonia*) because democracy is a political rather than a mystical concept and then persist with a monar-chical structure which is not only political, but outmoded and anti-participative. The people of God includes a hierarchy but it is not a hierocracy.

It is interesting though not surprising, that alongside excitement and appreciation, innovative pastors – as the Firhouse experience notes – also experience strong resistance to attempts to carry these values into reforming their parishes. Generations of internalised authoritarianism do not fade away easily. This is especially so in a situation where people interested in a participative style of church and of life in general, are more likely to be distanced from the existing model of church than those who value order and con-tinuity. There is a temptation for leaders to allow themselves to believe that order and authority are what 'the people' want. To go down that road would be a great mistake. It will produce civil religion rather than the church of Jesus Christ. It will plunge the church so deeply into conservatism that it may permanently alienate the very people it most needs.

One of the groups of people it needs most is creative, reflective young people. Just as the church needs to be converted to the poor and to the feminine, it equally needs to be converted to the young. It really is time to consider whether, if we really want young peo-ple to participate in the church, it has to be entirely on 'our' terms. The first step is to realise that the real concerns of young people are the only religious concerns they can have. Their concerns may sometimes include the concerns of 'the church' but just as often may not. It is only in their attempts to be authentic in relation to the decisions facing them that they can find God. Just because 'their' questions may be different from 'ours' does not make them any less real nor any less a potential disclosure of God. How can they encounter God except in terms of that which is real for them? Or must they be always obliged, no less than the poor and the women in the church, to meet God only in dealing with issues pre-determined by people with different questions?

What both the *Teach Bríde* experience and the Pilgrimage Walk ini-tiative illustrate is the crucial importance of peer group ministry, especially among the young, as well as their remarkable capacity to appropriate the faith and celebrate it creatively. All classical theologies were once local theologies and all liturgical rubrics were once creative local initiatives for worship. What a tragedy that so much of the church leadership still views as fringe and sus-pect what is the very lifeblood of renewal!

All of this points to a model of church as a wider community of Base Ecclesial Communities, or as they are sometimes called, Basic Christian Communities. Essentially, these are groups of Christians attempting to work for the transformation of society at local level in the light of the gospel. To this end the members sustain some form of sharing of life between themselves fed by scripture, prayer and eucharist. The *Partners in Faith* experience is invaluable because it points to the fact that the only way the church can build up such communities is by a pedagogical process which itself includes the values and form of Basic Ecclesial Community: trust, sharing, self-worth, analysis of the social reality, reading scripture in the light of this analysis, reading action for transformation in the light of scripture. Then, in continuity with this project, searching for a sharing of life which is inclusive, respectful, dialogical and mutually empowering as well as prayerful, eucharistic and in communion with the wider church.

Community of reconciliation

'For when I am weak then am I strong', was one of St Paul's core insights into his own human and spiritual journey. Could the converse also be true; 'when we are strong then we are weak'? When we reach the top of the mountain, we have to come down the other side. The church has climbed the mountain of organisation, spirituality, theology, law, clarity, ritual and mission. In each historical choice and reorientation something is lost for something else to be gained. With each dogma, each development, each quasi-permanent structure, each Canon, something is clarified, codified and certified, and something else is relativised, overlooked and repressed.

Only God is the absolute truth and only Jesus Christ is the incarnated truth. The Creed reminds us that we 'believe the church' but we do not believe 'in' the church: we believe 'in' the Triune God. In the apparent strength of the pre-Vatican II church – which is not a figment of the past but is being actively restored throughout the world – was there not a great unacknowledged weakness because so much had been relativised, overlooked and repressed?

Did not a patriarchal church repress the feminine; did not the effective limiting of salvation to the soul in the afterlife devalue the body and human communication; did not morality understood as observance, stifle creativity and self-expression; did not the internalisation of self-righteousness leave us prey to hypocrisy and guilt? One could continue this list at length. But it is important to see why the issues are being raised in the first place. It is not just another exercise in that mindless moaning so prevalent at the moment. It is not a debunking of the church, not a simplistic dismissal of something which in its deepest reality, the writer himself cherishes as wonderful, irreplaceable and enduring; as something worthy of commitment; as something inseparable from Christ.

Rather, it is a matter of being attentive to the historical moment in which we live. No individual or group attentive to its mission and the tasks and choices that mission entails, can possibly pay equal attention to all aspects of its life, especially when the issues it feels forced to deal with are often emerging from movements over which it has no control. The result is first one thing and then something else gets overlooked so that something else may be emphasised and when this continues over time there is a price to pay for recovering what has been lost. A period of renewal is one in which there is the kind of awareness of such issues that actually generates real assent to transformative action. Not to recognise this is to simply feed the anger, apathy and alienation from the church of which the Ballymun group speaks and which is altogether too evident in so many situations.

This can be a moment of healing and reconciliation as a precondition for the church to become in an effective, as distinct from some kind of theoretical sense, a community of healing, forgiveness and reconciliation for the world. The heart of this is a reconnection with our forgotten and undervalued selves. For the church, that means theologically valuing the experiences that are facilitating this. This represents a shift in consciousness for the church, requiring a deep level of humility and honesty. The fact of the matter is that the official form of celebrating reconciliation in the church, the sacrament of penance, is not mediating this experience for large numbers of people. There is a further problem because it is often perceived to represent the very form of religious experience from which people wish to free themselves, not because they wish to be less morally authentic and responsible, but because they can no longer square the desire to be reconciled to self, the world and God with an experience that is perceived to be essentially one of submission and control.

For Jesus, the question of the legal requirements of the Sabbath was ridiculously insignificant compared to the imperative to heal.

Aquinas held that confession as such was more important than to whom one confessed and hence one could in a case of necessity, confess to a lay person.[2] Today, healing, forgiveness, reconciliation and spiritual empowerment are happening in a variety of situations – as they probably always did. *Eckhart House* represents a whole current of ministry among the people of God where compassion is displayed and reconciliation experienced and celebrated scientifically and purposefully, as well as with compassion and effect, not least in respect of what our previous 'strength' repressed in ourselves.

Symbols and rituals emerge from patterns of lived narrative rooted in transformative – and for Christians, redemptive – praxis. When the symbols and rituals are fixed to the point of being frozen and cut off from lived narrative and praxis, they cease to be life-giving. Whatever their institutional solidity, they soon cease to mediate the power of God's redemptive love in a transformative way. Is there not a dreadful formalism and minimalism in much of the church's own official ministry of rconciliation and anointing the sick?

These experiences and the movement of renewal they represent need to be theologically appreciated and evaluated for what they are: genuine initiatives to be the on-going presence of the healing and reconciling ministry of Jesus in the post-modern world and therefore, albeit in an incomplete way, the sacraments of the church. This theological recognition requires liturgical celebration in the Christian community, not simply to validate the initiatives but to complete and perfect their sacramentality as well as to retrieve and liturgically express the real meaning of the sacraments of reconciliation and anointing themselves. In this way they may express once again the power of liberating and empowering reconciliation which our Lord intended them to have.

Attending Mass or celebrating the eucharist?

Liturgists like to remind us that the 'eucharist is the source and summit of the Christian life'. In practice what people seem to think is that Mass attendance is the minimum condition and maximum commitment of the Christian life. For if you want to know what people really believe then look at what they do. One cannot but be struck by the observation that the manner in which a lot of creative Christian groups seek to express and celebrate their commitment is not primarily eucharistic – at least in the sacramental sense. Something has happened to the Mass, and what it has become in existential and experiential terms, as distinct from what it is proclaimed to be in theoretical theological terms, no longer seems to express, empower and celebrate the faith and action of many groups who seek to take in this society the stance Jesus took in his.

The writer remembers vividly an occasion when at the end of a study-day on Faith and Justice, about half of the participants flatly refused to conclude the encounter with a celebration of the eucharist. The reason given was that here once again 'the church' was trying to take everything over. Evidently, these people although baptised, committed to gospel values, inspired by Jesus and building community, did not see themselves as 'the church'. Other reactions were equally interesting. Some argued for the necessity of 'a celebration' – choosing their terms carefully. This made the opposition of the first group even stronger; they now felt they were being conned into 'going to Mass'. For others, there was regret that there would not be a eucharist; in some cases, because of a desire for a more intimate and meaningful celebration, in others, because they would now have to 'go to Mass' the following day – a Sunday. For still others, there was indifference. For some of us, there was, as well as growing insight, a real sadness that the profound link between Christian action for the transformation of the world and the eucharistic mystery was being relativised and lost.

It would be too simple to use such experiences primarily to critique the Christian faith and commitment of such groups; we must look deeper. We might start by making a very rough working distinction between the 'eucharist' and 'Mass'. Obviously, I'm speaking in behavioural rather than strictly theological terms. The eucharist is what we aspire to; Mass is what is going on. The eucharist grows out of and in turn empowers Christian praxis in the world. Mass is the traditional religious ritual of our society. The eucharist is celebrated by the whole priestly people and the ordained presbyter presides. Mass is said, or even read, by the priest; the people participate primarily and sometimes solely, by their presence; there is an obligation to attend but mere attendance fulfils the obligation. The eucharist requires active and informed participation. At Mass, passivity is not a major problem.

We might go further and ask how is it that large numbers of people who support consumerism, individualism, class distinction and are not significantly moved by the issues of unemployment, patriarchy, injustice and the Third World seem to experience little difficulty in being regular Mass attenders. Then we need to return to our question about people with a committed Christian praxis who find little or no sustenance in eucharistic worship. When they go, they do so with genuine faith but out of loyalty, tradition, hope, even solidarity; but fewer and fewer expect to be moved, empowered or challenged by the experience. For yet others, Mass signifies not only boredom but control, duty, the fulfilment of an obligation; the very symbol of a way of perceiving and living from which – sometimes even for religious reasons – they wish to liberate themselves.

There never was a liturgical movement in Ireland. Because of what was termed 'Ireland's loyalty to the Mass' it seemed there didn't need to be. For those who, in days gone by, wished to destroy our culture and identity, and then for ourselves as well, it was, as Cromwell wrote to Ireton, 'the Mass that matters'. It became a symbol of what we were – and that certainly included a deep religiosity and a Christian faith. But today this has ceased to be the case.

Just as Irish identity itself is no longer a clear concept about which there is consensus, so neither can 'the Mass' function as a core symbol of that identity. Ireland has chosen to stake its future on the consumerist political economy of advanced capitalism and not on a transcendent vision of the human person in community. In doing so, it is in danger of becoming a fragmented community with a heart of stone. It would be an obscenity to legitimate this in purely pietistic apolitical Mass attendance. It demands that the eucharist become a counter-cultural celebration for those who wish to work for personal and social transformation in the light of the gospel.

Instead, because of inertia and a lack of imagination, it may well remain a relic of the way things used to be – increasingly ineffectual and irrelevant. Yet large numbers continue to come and the numbers are by no means understated in surveys, a residue perhaps of the strong guilt feelings people may still have about missing it. In urban areas, attendance – one can hardly say participation – is highest among people in mortgaged private houses, with secondary school-going children. Such communities are trapped in the classic middle-class dilemma of aspiring towards greater upward social mobility within an ever-narrowing range of options because of taxation and mortgages, and seeking to be somehow open to a religious obligation to the underprivileged with whom they don't really identify.

As a social class – and prescinding from the numerous examples of individual sincerity and generosity – such communities feel the need for order, continuity, stability and respectability and they expect the church to be a guarantor of such values. In Ireland today, such communities are also victims of the system, though in a less extreme way than the poor. Through their skills they operate the economy which makes a minority much wealthier than themselves and through their PAYE, they and not the wealthy, pay for social welfare. They are a highly pressurised and increasingly insecure social class. Their church-going includes the expectation that the church will help to provide them with motivation, encouragement and consolation, but not question the moral basis of the economic options in which they have invested so much, but which keep them pressurised and many others poor.

A religious and sacramental practice tied more strongly to such aspirations rather than those of the poor, quickly becomes a legitimation of the dominant system, coupled with a means of consolation for those whose support for and participation in the system is a source of insecurity. The problems raised here go deeper than merely finding more meaningful ways of celebrating the liturgy, though quite obviously better preparation, more prayerful presidency and greater lay participation are essential and sorely needed. But such modifications, important as they are, still leave the real link between life and liturgy unexamined.

'When we eat this bread and drink this cup, we proclaim the death of the Lord until he comes.' There can be no celebration of the eucharist that is not linked to a communitarian attempt to engage in the kind of praxis which for Jesus, led to his saving death. The death we proclaim has a divine significance but it occurred as an historical event and as a consequence of fidelity to a radical option. To 'proclaim the death' in the eucharist means first to make the same option in relation to contemporary reality.

Jesus was not crucified in a house of worship between two candles but outside the city – symbolising rejection – between two thieves. 'Do this in memory of me' must not be reduced to the mere repetition of a religious rite. It must be reappropriated as an

invitation to be the presence of Jesus within the hopes and contradictions of our own society. Only then can it be rediscovered as an
invitation to celebrate the sacrament of the one and eternal sacrifice.

When Moehler was laying the foundations for the liturgical
movement in Germany well over a century ago, he was doing so
out of a pastoral context and specifically to develop and focus a
form of Christian resistance to the encroaching power of the State.
In developing his ideas and praxis, he was fascinated by the
world of the patristic church where he found a sharing, worshipping community developing itself in opposition to the dominant
pagan power. It is an image of undoubted relevance to today and
readily intelligible to people with a history such as ours. Liturgical renewal in this country need not worry too much about having
been somewhat bypassed by a phase of its development which
was always missing the real point anyway. We can leap over it
and get to the heart of the matter.

CHAPTER TWO

Theological issues

The foregoing theological appreciation of the pastoral initiatives which form the seedbed of a new and more adequate model of church in this country, invites further theological reflection on a number of issues. These include the inculturation of the gospel in a secularised society, the preferential option for the poor, the centrality of the person of Christ, the ministry of women, the reformation and holiness of the church, the consent of the faithful as co-constitutive of the 'tradition', the creation of community through reconciliation and dialogue and historical responsibility in the world of today. A reflection on these issues as emerging from a consideration of the church in this country at this time, as illustrated in what has been said above, will hopefully contribute to laying the foundations of a truly local theology which will be faithful both to the tradition of the Apostles as lived in the universal church as well as to the exigencies of the social reality it seeks to evangelise.

Inculturation in a secularised world

The somewhat exaggerated and long-standing emphasis on individual salvation in the afterlife as the primary goal of Christian existence has contributed to a distortion of the memory of Jesus and what he offered the world. This has been compounded by the impression that this salvation was limited to a certain number, however large. The roots of this probably lie in St Augustine's apparent failure to appreciate that the grace of God could be both gratuitous and universal. It is obviously true, as St Paul wrote, that it is not for this life only that our hope is in Christ. Nonetheless, the devaluing of history in the preaching of the church has had costly consequences. It certainly diluted the church's passion for the rights of the poor and made it suspicious of the scientific revolution, the Enlightenment and modernity. When theology finally began to come to terms with these developments, it usually provoked a quite authoritarian response, more often that not condemnatory. We need only reflect on what became known as the

Modernist crisis. With Vatican II's *Gaudium et Spes*, the church formally re-embraced the world and accepted the concerns of today as her own. The church rediscovered its commitment to and participation in the struggles of history and the intimate relationship between Christian salvation and historical liberation.

Religion in general, and the Irish church in particular, fear the secularisation process. I am not speaking here of secularism as a philosophical position which denies the reality of the spiritual and the transcendent. It is rather the process of giving the human sciences and human socio-political structures their proper autonomy and then finding God in the authentic pursuit of the human vocation of the transformation of this world that views both the autonomy and the transformation in the light of the gospel.

Secularisation began the day religion stopped being just magic. In a very particular way, it has arisen not in opposition to Christianity but because of it. For the heart of the Christian religion is the divine Word made flesh: the invisible becomes visible; the transcendent becomes historical; God becomes human; the religious becomes secular. The consequence is that it is in our flesh, in our visible human secular commitment to history that we find God at the heart of every moment, every situation, every struggle.

In a pre-scientific sacral world, God is not only the final cause but the immediate cause as well. Christendom, the Lutheran theory of the two kingdoms, the separation of church and State and concordats are all failed attempts to divide up space and time between Christ and Caesar. In a secularised world, god – not God, for in truth, it is merely the god of civil religion and not the one Jesus called Abba – is pushed out onto the margins. Bonhoeffer was the first to realise this clearly and we have yet to understand him. There is less and less space, whether physical, psychological or political which is categorically God's. The autonomy of human experience and institutions pushes God further and further out until God is found not so much in a specifically religious domain – as if to suggest that God is found outside this domain in a lesser way, if indeed God may be found there at all – but as the deepest and truest dimension of all that is authentic.

Yet this apparently autonomous world is shot through with fundamental contradictions for it implicitly favours the strong and the successful. God is thus pushed further out onto the margins; for the kingdom of compassion God seeks to inaugurate can now only be glimpsed from the standpoint of the excluded. How can the people of God address this world to transform and bless it?

A change in culture brings with it a change in values, relationships and language and arises in the first place because of a different understanding and organisation of human needs. When such change arises, the only way to say the same thing is to say it differently. Jesus spoke in the language and imagery of Jewish apocalyptic. The *Logos* christology of St John's gospel would have been unintelligible to the fishermen on the shores of Lake Galilee and, most likely, even to the historical Jesus himself. Yet in a Hellenistic world, it communicated the meaning of his person and praxis as truly as his parables and wonders did in Palestine.

The irony of trying to merely repeat what the New Testament itself says or indeed the language of any particular stage in the development of Christian doctrine, however classical, is to forget that this is the very thing both the New Testament and the great theologians themselves refrained from doing. The new culture necessitates the construction of a new religious discourse rooted in a new praxis. Historically, this has been the whole purpose of ecumenical councils and the reason for all the important developments in the history of theology.

There are few if any words that are originally and specifically religious. There is rather an original and specific religious use of language. That is perfectly valid. Language grows out of experience and reflection – in a certain sense it is experience – and its meaning can never be frozen once and for all. Language expresses and at the same time fails to express and not only because 'words strain, crack and sometimes break under the burden'. For as originating experiences are reconsidered in the light of events to which they gave rise, the spheres of the unexpressed around original terms get filled in. Language carries more and more meaning. There is religious language because there is human religious experience. Theologians do with language what everyone else does, except that they do it specifically in function of the experience of God's self-communication to the world as unconditional love; and the need of the community which shares this experience to pass it on in the form of a tradition.

All religious experience is human experience: firstly, because it is the experience of humans; secondly, because God has disclosed Godself fully and not just figuratively in human flesh. As Rahner might put it, the economic Trinity is the immanent Trinity. Even that most specifically religious experience – to know and love God in prayer – is coextensively a human experience. Not only because it is we humans who pray, but because coming to know and love God is ineluctably a process of coming to know and accept oneself.

If faith is to address a secularised world then it has to address a world which through economic analysis, psychology, sociology and all other forms of human science has its own ways of talking about itself. In a secularised world an important theological truth becomes clear: theology does not understand the world in a direct and immediate way. Rather, it struggles for a deeper level of meaning with the strata of truth disclosed by all other branches of human science. Theology can influence these human sciences by influencing the people who practise them. For their presuppositions are not value-free and different economic or psychological or biological models can be chosen partly as a consequence of different value systems. And these values must be clarified in the light of faith.

Yet if there is to be a religious discourse about all the various aspects of human experience, then it will take the form of a theological re-reading of the fruits of the human sciences. But the church must not baulk at the inevitable consequence of this process: namely, that theology itself and the religious discourse of the church will be internally reconstructed. With this will come a reconstruction of church structures as well as of its liturgy, ethics and catechesis. Here will be realised the promise of John XXIII's wonderful opening address to the second Vatican Council and especially its most ground-breaking sentence: 'The substance of the ancient doctrine of the deposit of faith is one thing, and the way in which it is presented in another'. [3]

If this seems strange then consider Aquinas. He reconstructed theology and indirectly a huge part of church life, by basing his theology on Aristotle. He chose Aristotle not because he was a better theologian than the preferred philosophers of the Fathers. No more than them, he wasn't a theologian at all. Aristotle was chosen because his philosophical-scientific worldview and discourse seemed more adequate to the complexities of human experience, as St Thomas understood them, than any other reading available to him. What a contradiction of his method it would be to seek to give the terminology of his or any other synthesis, permanent validity!

The notion of 'tradition' – in the active sense – is fundamental to the identity of the Catholic understanding of church. But the tradition of the church is not simply something fixed into which we come. By grasping and living and articulating it, we contribute to it and co-determine it. Tradition, the actual 'handing on' (*para-dosis*) of what the apostles handed on, teaches us that it is not a fixed and frozen object of study from the past but a living resource of many depths of meaning for the present. A moment's reflection on our own participation in this process of 'handing on' is enough to make us realise that after us will come others who will do so not only differently, but hopefully, even better.

Preferential option for the poor

There are limits to inculturation, but these arise not because the church possesses some supra-cultural or acultural language but rather because all cultures, being human achievements, implicitly or explicitly give priority to some groups and marginalise others. All give legitimation to some or other power structure. A cultural shift retraces the parameters of identity but, in so doing, retraces the parameters of poverty and exclusion. These days a new world order is spoken of but it is a semblance of order that disguises massive suffering and poverty throughout the world. The new Europe, for which our people so enthusiastically voted, plans its economic strength in alliance with the international structures of inequality. The North grows rich because the South grows poor; and becoming post-Maastricht Europeans makes us more a part of the process. But this process is visible at home. The same economic model that brings wealth to some brings unemployment and marginalisation to others. What does it mean to pretend that we are all members of the one body of Christ in such a world?

There is such a basic and intimate link between the liberation of the oppressed and the gospel message that a radical solidarity with the poor must always be a fundamental and unnegotiable element of Christian identity. The key theological principle at issue here is that only a solidarity which privileges the excluded can hope to be truly universal, as only thereby can communion (*koinonia*) be established. Only in and through such an inclusive quality of solidarity can the Kingdom of God break through and humankind be allowed to live in the image and likeness of God's total solidarity through complete self-donation and acceptance which is the Trinitarian community.

The scriptures are a sustained testimony to the disturbing and even shocking truth that God is not neutral but is on the side of the poor. God's limitless compassion extends to all people but the justice it requires is partisan in favour of the oppressed. God calls to community from the perspective of slaves, the disinherited, exiles, the brokenhearted, the persecuted, the crucified, the vulnerable. The Hebrews first came to know Yahweh through his fidelity to the process of their emancipation and the theology of Exodus thus becomes the principal interpretative key to the Old Testament. The Deuteronomic reform seeks a restoration of the purity of the original covenant with God which is real only if it can sustain a society of fraternity/sorority and equality in which there are no poor. Prophesy is always both a revindication of the holiness and uniqueness of the one God and a revindication of the rights of the poor.

When Jesus fulfils the messianic hope, the inclusiveness of God's reign is totally present in his person and praxis. It is symbolised in his table fellowship with the excluded, the element of eucharistic celebration overlooked in even the most progressive theories of liturgy. From fellowship with the impure, he critiques purity; from companionship with women, he unmasks patriarchy; from empathy with Samaritans, he questions orthodoxy; from compassion with sinners, he demystifies righteousness. Finally, on the cross and specifically as a victim of the violent exercise of power legitimated by a repressive form of institutionalised religion, the utterly excluded becomes the source of universal inclusion.

The apostolic church struggled to be faithful to this sacred and subversive memory. There is a permanent tension between the divine privilege of the poor and dispossessed and the growing organisational needs of a church rooting itself in Hellenistic urban culture. We see the tension in St Paul's reflection on class structure in the Corinthian agape and also in St James' sharp denunciation of class distinction in the Jerusalem church; we see it in the spiritualisation of the beatitudes and the growing emphasis on respectability in the pastoral epistles. For all that, the privilege of the poor remains intact and emerges as a cornerstone of Christian identity.

But the church payed a huge price for the supposed benefits of the Constantinian peace because from then on its priorities and identity could never be quite free from the lure of temporal power. Kept alive by the social teaching of the Fathers – a chapter often omitted from Patrology – the Franciscan and Vincentian movements as well as by the lives of countless unremembered Christians, it has re-emerged as the central theological issue of our times. Despite a thousand bureaucratic attempts to qualify, spiritualise or even remove it from the church's agenda, it has been repeatedly endorsed by theologians, episcopal conferences and John Paul II. More importantly, it has been endorsed by the Holy Spirit in the witness and even the martyrdom of many committed Christians.

The option for the poor is an option for justice. There is a rather smooth kind of theology which argues that justice is a merely natural virtue and that the Christian religion is about mercy, forgiveness and reconciliation. But there is a whole world of difference between, on the one hand, a church scrupulously just in its own doings and unambiguously promoting justice in society which goes beyond that justice to display compassion and mercy and offer reconciliation even to those who wrong it, and, on the other hand, a church less than passionate about justice, because its strongest links are with the status quo, which wishes to show a certain kind of mercy to the disadvantaged without examining the structures which keep them disadvantaged.

The Synod of Bishops in 1971 – which was the most significant exercise of collegiality outside an ecumenical council for centuries – taught that 'action (*actio*) for justice was constitutive of the preaching of the gospel'. Up to the last draft of the text, the wording had been 'struggle – or fight – (*pugna*) for justice' which gives some idea of the quality of action envisaged. Indeed for some years afterwards, the French Bishops continued to translate this part of the text as *Le combat pour la justice*.[4] The notion of 'struggle' returns in John Paul II's *Laborem Exercens*, as does a remarkably clear statement about the priority of labour over capital as well as an unambiguous statement that the right to private property is a strictly subordinate one. More fundamental is the right of all people to share in the goods of the earth. What our left-wing political parties have to say about capitalism and monetarism is hardly strong stuff relative to what Paul VI said in *Populorum Progressio*![5]

More recently, the Irish Bishops have produced a really worthwhile pastoral on work as the key to the social question. It is truly a sign of hope to find a stockbroker-politician criticising a homily of Cardinal Daly's on the right of the poor to work and dignity. The texts, the principles, the aspirations; they are all there. All that's missing is sustained action. Somehow, a moral passion for a

just society does not sufficiently pervade the psyche and imagination of organised Catholicism to truly shift the energies and priorities of the church.

Such a shift would be costly, both in personal and institutional
terms. Perhaps the road to change begins by recognising where it
is that we have already forged the strongest links. Then we need
the reality of poverty to irrupt into our collective consciousness
both as a social and then as a theological reality. This would then
need to be focused by a social analysis of the structures that keep
people poor as well as the church's own institutional linkage to
them. The grace of conversion is costly grace indeed!

The sacred and subversive memory of Jesus

At the centre and heart of any discourse on the church stands
Jesus Christ. The church is essentially a symbolic community
pointing us to a more primordial reality and constantly refining
and reforming itself to express that reality more adequately. A
community that does not unmistakeably and unapologetically
proclaim the irreducible significance of Jesus Christ for all of
humanity and all of history, is no longer the church. Here we may
have something to learn from evangelicals, for the church does
not proclaim itself but God in Jesus Christ and in the Holy Spirit,
in whom the kingdom of compassion and solidarity have as
gracious gift, definitively broken through into our threatened
existence.

Yet we may also have something to teach the evangelicals. For
unless we de-ideologise our minds, the Christ we proclaim may
simply be the reflection of ourselves. That is why the contemplation of Jesus must always be accompanied by the option for the
poor. Together they are the reciprocal essentials of discipleship.
Because unless we are on the side of the oppressed, what we contemplate may be a caricature of Jesus; but unless we are rooted in
Christ, the struggle for liberation may degenerate into pragma-
tism and self-justification.

It is perhaps a hopeful sign that the scandalous nature of the proclamation of Jesus Christ is being experienced again in our own
time. The range of contemporary experience can defamiliarise
Christ and that, in turn, can permit us to overcome the manner in
which we have domesticated him. 'To the Jews a scandal and to
the Greeks foolishness': not just a time-bound experience of St
Paul, but an intrinsic moment in the kerygma; a different logic to

that of worldly success and the ideology which legitimates it. Everything is pulled up short in front of the memory of Jesus. The world always crucifies him and then is appraised, forgiven and transformed by its tremendous lover. All our ideologies fall short before the one in whom 'the fullness of the Godhead was pleased to dwell'. Yet only within our ideologies, self-correcting and reconstructing, can we ever begin to grasp him – though perhaps it is he who grasps us. There simply is no other way; no way to simply leap over our experience and the way we interpret it. His own experience was the same; expressing 'the All' within the limitations of small country, particular language, short life, strange friends and scandalous death.

Speaking of Christ today must face up to a triple 'scandal'. A commercialised media industry in a capitalist economy proposes wealth and success as the human paradigm but Christ is poor and crucified. With a virtually exponential increase in the varieties of religious and transpersonal experience and supposed manifestations of the divine, the Christian community proposes the unsurpassable uniqueness of the revelation in Jesus. In the face of the emancipation of women and the social and religious revindication of the feminine, Jesus is male.

But there is a difference between the scandal of obscurantism and the inescapable scandal that the wisdom of the cross is not the wisdom of the world. The Christian project of the transformation of the world from the perspective of the oppressed, has to become credible both as a social project and as a religious project, even if it be the credibility of an Oscar Romero. If the man Jesus is proposed as universal redeemer, then in himself, he must redeem the split between the masculine and the feminine and in the priestly act of the Paschal mystery, transcend his own maleness to empower the church to do the same.

The uniqueness and unsurpassibility of Christ must be explored in terms which are post-triumphalist, post-colonialist, post-patriarchal, post-authoritarian and rooted in a dialogue of love. This in turn, means that a dialogical praxis proceeding from the perspective of the poor which values all authentic human experience and which in particular, incorporates the integration of the masculine and the feminine, both in oneself and in society, is so fundamental to the nature of Christian identity, that without reference to it, no adequate view of Christ or the church can be constructed.

The memory of Jesus is a sacred and subversive memory. The church contributes to the future of the world out of the memory both of God's infinitely gracious self-emptying into creation as well as out of the memory of the poor. In historical terms, these become one and the same memory because in the cross of Jesus, a limitless divine compassion draws all of humanity into the heart of God. In that same cross, the world of the powerful and the successful is subverted. The 'otherness' of God is revealed in the 'otherness' of the oppressed and the poor are disclosed as the primary architects of human community.

Discipleship, a personal and communitarian participation in the resurrected life of the crucified Jesus, is inseparably a participation in God and a participation in the struggles of the broken for a reconciled world. This discipleship is not primarily a morality but rather a mysticism of forgiveness empowering a morality that surpasses observance. It is a mystical communion with and participation in the life of the one who in loving the world and each of us, already bears within himself the consequences of our inability to return that love. Our incorporation into God opens out into a participation in God's unconditional fidelity to the world, the foundation of all Christian moral purpose. But because this limitless compassion of God is historically focused in Jesus' preference for the poor, the contemplation of the crucified Christ always translates into a political theology of the cross. The sacred becomes the subversive and the subversive, the sacred.

Over twenty years ago, Daniel Berrigan said that the time was coming soon when the pursuit of contemplation would be a strictly subversive activity. The seemingly all-encompassing power of transnational capitalism grinds down upon all efforts to construct a compassionate human community. Whether to desensitise the middle-classes or to distract the poor, an endless stream of superficially stimulating images and sounds threatens to crowd out the very possibility of sustained spiritual experience. Under these conditions, attention to the sacred becomes an act of contestation explicitly subversive. Correspondingly, action for transformation which contests the violence and superficiality of the system will almost certainly find its reservoir of hope in contemplation. The option for fidelity to the crushed will always return the Christian to the contemplation of God's fidelity in Christ.

Whatever the future shape of the church, I am convinced that in this era, the core values must be (i) a return to the contemplative spirit as a participation in the unconditioned holiness of the Mother-Father – the well-spring of that limitless compassion which alone can heal the brokeness of the world; (ii) an unambig-uous commitment to justice – as the on-going expression of the incarnation of the Word; (iii) commitment to structures of solidar-ity, participation and inclusiveness – to bear witness to having re-ceived the Spirit which is poured out on all flesh. The heart of the matter is the contemplation of Christ; for then the church will nev-er make the mistake of confusing itself with the reign of God but will experience the constant call to be the facilitator of the king-dom of compassion and universal solidarity and to embody these values in its own life.

Male and female in the image of God

The final draft document of the recent CELAM conference in Santo Domingo, when dealing with the question of women in the Christ-ian community, proposed 'a rethinking of the role of women in the church and in pastoral work', and stated that women could participate in seminary education as 'fellow disciples and pas-tors'. In relation to scripture, it wanted to 'abandon anachronistic interpretations that demean women' and also to 'develop a read-ing of the Word of God, which in the light of women's own exper-ience, reveals the characteristics which woman's own vocation contribute to the plan of salvation'. The conference secretariat was prevailed upon to change all these texts, which do not appear in the 'approved version' of the document. [6]

This censorship is disturbing. Apart altogether from the disres-pect it shows to the churches of Latin America, it exhibits a deep suspicion, if not to say hostility, to any re-examination of the role and ministry of women in the church and to valuing their experi-ence as a *locus theologicus* for fathoming the mystery of Christ. Ab-solutely nothing in these texts is even mildly erroneous, or even out of step with what John Paul II wrote in his encyclical on *The Dignity of Women*. Their rejection has nothing to do with theology but with a most unspiritual fear, linked to power-play, that leav-ing open one door, which should never have been closed in the first place, might lead to having to unlock another.

There is deep and systematic resistance to any suggestion that a reading of the Word in the light of women's experience, the ac-knowledging of the feminine in males, and the interdependence

of the sexes, might reveal levels of meaning of the Word as yet un-
disclosed, which could develop our understanding of salvation
and of the church which is its sign. In passing, we may note a par-
allelism with the debate on liberation. In his seminal work, Gutierrez had argued that there were nuances of the Word accessible
only to those committed to the praxis of liberation. His views
were strongly resisted. Most of his adversaries wanted a theology
derived from previously agreed principles, forgetting that these
principles and the terminology which expressed them, far from
being absolute and immutable, had themselves emerged from involvement in some or other form of praxis. Everyone is standing
somewhere. Fifteen years later, the Vatican document *Libertatis
Conscientiae*, implicitly endorsed the position of Gutierrez. The
same thing, one feels, will eventually happen in the feminist debate.[7]

While the issue, as already stated, is more fundamental and far-
reaching than that of the ordination of women, it is usually
focused here. It is only fair to point out that the position of the
church on this question is not a directly fundamentalist one: e.g.,
Jesus chose only men so the church will do likewise. Catholic
theology has long realised that the institution of the sacraments is
not something totally reducible to certain words and actions of
the historical Jesus at a given place and time. It recognises the
presence of the risen Christ in the on-going consciousness of the
church. This in turn, means that the church can develop and mod-
ify, as indeed it has, its understanding of the sacraments, something not without relevance to women's ordination. Indeed, reflective Anglican theologians are increasingly locating the
problems surrounding this question in the context of the authentic development of doctrine.[8]

By the same token, the choice of the Twelve should be seen firstly
against its eschatological background and symbolism whereby
the choice of men as distinct from women, and Jews as distinct
from Samaritans or Gentiles, was fitting. No valid conclusion can
be drawn from this about the intentions of the historical Jesus in
regard to the ministry of women in the historical church and any
exegesis of a solely historical kind cannot come up with binding
conclusions. The Pontifical Biblical Commission had already
agreed on this.[9]

Before examining the state of the question, some contextual clarification is called for. Jesus, and Paul too, were by the standards of their time, quite radical feminists. In the immediately post-apostolic churches, we can see a rapid repatriarchalisation process. This is culturally conditioned and occurs both in Jewish and Hellenistic communities. In essence, this represents an adaptation following on a felt need for a culturally intelligible catechesis and ministry, without necessarily giving a theological endorsement of those cultural values. What Paul tolerated in a world which was 'passing away' was not necessarily acceptable to those who 'live in Christ'. Ironically, in a post-androcentric culture, the same process might easily demand the reverse![10] John Paul II's *Mulieris Dignitatem* has implicitly accepted the end of androcentrism in the church: but the implications have yet to be thought through and implemented.

One of the reasons is the systematically distorted theological communication that arises out of long internalised patterns of thinking about the relationship between men and women that have no basis in revelation. Nowadays, a male theologian may well squirm in embarrassment when he re-reads what the Fathers of the church and even Aquinas, said about the status of women. Yet many of these were liberals and humanists by the standards of their times. We think St Augustine had narrow views until we remember he is debating with Manicheans. But this, in turn, goes to show the deeply ingrained prejudices and distortions there are about women, that are internalised and transmitted in all patriarchal societies and, therefore, almost certainly in the church as well. Not to recognise that these are still at the very least, peripherally and unconsciously present in much theological discourse, is to risk simply consolidating them.

I think we can distinguish three levels in the manner in which the Congregation for the Doctrine of the Faith (1977)[11] argues its case against women's ordination. At the first level, it suggests that the church has never admitted that it could be validly done and that this practice is normative. At a second level, it seeks to argue this theologically. It claims that those who would take the role of Christ must have a natural resemblance to him and therefore be male. At a third level, it points out that it is not committing the magisterium to any position concerning symbolism, not even when this concerns the priest acting in the person of Christ – *in persona Christi* – during the Mass.

Interestingly, most of the discussion centres around levels two and three. But the core argument is at level one – an attempted appeal to tradition that may, in fact, be only an appeal to a time-bound historical fact. It is true, of course, that the document is not irrevocable, though that of itself neither disproves nor proves its case. However, given that feminism is a relatively new item on the agenda of the church leadership, as well as the fact that this document is not of pontifical status and even asked for further research – an implicit admission that the last word has not been written – it is reasonable to conclude that it cannot be construed as the definitive teaching of the magisterium.

For St Thomas,[12] the reason a woman could not be ordained seems to be that because of 'her nature' she cannot rule men. When arguing that a woman can baptise in cases of necessity as a 'minister of Christ', he does not use the term *in persona Christi*, but explains it in terms of instrumental causality. However, while he does speak of the priest acting *in persona Christi* in the eucharist, St Thomas also explains this – very explicitly – in terms of instrumental causality and never speaks in terms of an immediate natural symbolism. Therefore on the basis of Thomas, or on the basis of texts derived from him, one cannot argue either for or against the ordination of women unless one accepts his rather uncritical androcentrism as theological truth rather than socio-cultural assumption.

In fact, women administer both baptism and matrimony *in persona Christi*; they are Christ's ministers, instruments and representatives. In the eucharist however, the priest, as well as being Christ's representative, is in some sense Christ's representation, firstly, through Holy Orders and secondly, because in the eucharist, Christ actually offers himself. But even if this did not risk overemphasising the priest himself as a sacrament, it would only establish that there is a real distinction between the priesthood of all believers and the ministry of presbyterate. Of itself, it cannot establish the inadmissability of women to Holy Orders unless one is prepared to argue that, in the Christian community, maleness represents Christ and the female, the church.

Apart from overlooking the fact that there are men in the church who are not ordained, this overlooks the fact that all sacramental ministry is the ministry of the church. In particular, it mistakenly views the priesthood as over against the community of the church and not first of all in it. As St Augustine said in the famous homily on the anniversary of his ordination: 'For you I am a bishop; but with you I am a Christian'.[13] Long before the privatisation of ministry in the medieval period, the Council of Chalcedon had declared ordination without reference to a community to be invalid.[14] When the Christian community gathers for the eucharist, the priest acts in the person of the church – *in persona ecclesiae* – because it is the priestly people which celebrates and not just the priest on behalf of it, much less for it. To act *in persona Christi*, a minister, ordained or not, must always act *in persona ecclesiae*. If it were true that the female symbolises the church, then this might well argue for and not against the ordination of women.

For the same reason, the symbol of the bridegroom, while widely attested in scripture, cannot be used to argue for an exclusively male priesthood. Christ is the mystical bridegroom in relation to the church as a whole, including its ordained ministers, and so this is something that cannot be symbolised in the ministry. When, in the medieval period, this symbol was applied to the bishop, it was always in relation to his fidelity to his diocese and not to his office and ministry as such. It was moral rather than sacramental.

Moreover, the priest, who is 'in the person of Christ', is not thereby necessarily in the image of the historical Jesus. Leaving aside for the moment that most imponderable of theological problems of what constitutes the person of Christ, it needs to be stressed that the maleness of Jesus is not central to his own priestly act. Jesus was not a Levitical priest. As Hebrews recounts so beautifully, it is in offering his own self in the Paschal mystery that Christ is the eternal high-priest and Catholic theology has never understood the Last Supper except in relation to this.

In the offering of the one and eternal sacrifice, Jesus enters into a resurrected existence in which 'they neither marry nor are given in marriage'. One has to pose the question as to whether in this pneumatised bodily existence, his historical gender has a perduring significance in any exclusive sense. Certainly, his humanity is of eternal salvific significance but hardly its maleness as such, when that is viewed over and against the female. Moreover as the exemplar, as well as the efficacious cause, of the salvation of all people, including females, and of the whole of our humanity including the feminine, Jesus himself must first exemplify not only the integration of the female and the male in the order of salvation, but also the integration of the feminine and the masculine within himself. This, the Jesus of the gospels, in his ministry and in the Paschal mystery, most certainly does. [15]

As advances in the human sciences disclose that more and more aspects of the role of women thought to be natural, are in fact cultural, it becomes increasingly difficult to sustain the view – explicitly held by St Thomas – that there is a natural or revealed anthropology assigning different status to men and women in the orders of creation and redemption. Apart from literalist and fundamentalist readings of Genesis and the Pauline corpus, which in fairness, it must be said, do not form part of Catholic theology, most attempts to do so proceed from trying to construct an anthropology by extrapolation from the distinct and different psychobiology of the male and the female.

To this way of seeing things, male sexual activity discloses that the man is orientated towards something beyond or outside himself and, in relationship to it, has an essentially representative role. By contrast, that towards which the man is oriented actually reposes within the woman as part of her own being. Consequently, so the argument might go, the one is representative (and can 'represent' Christ!), and the other is receptive and self-contained (and cannot 'represent' Christ!).

Apart from the rather arbitrary and unverifiable nature of this speculation, it seems to ignore that the distinct way in which men and women possess their common humanity is actually ordered towards interdependence and integration. Otherwise marriage could not be a sacrament. The oneness that is symbolised in sexual union and procreation, is also achieved in personal individuation. What is more, even if this typology were sustainable, it is equally open to the conclusion that the female, through her containing within her own being the new life that she will nurture, is, in fact, more naturally an icon of the divinity than the male, whose sexuality is more externalised and intermittent.

It is difficult not to conclude that all such typologies of the divine-human relationship in andromorphous-gynomorphous terms, lose their significance once the historical subordination of women is acknowledged and surpassed. Once that is done, the practice of the church through its history, is disclosed as a – culturally conditioned – tradition from the sub-apostolic period and not a normative part of 'the tradition of the apostles' in the strong and strict sense of the term. It is therefore custom – albeit a venerable one –

but not a norm. As such it can and – given our contemporary insights – should be changed.

This in turn, invites us to see for the first time as it were, that male and female are in the image of God. Then the interdependence of the sexes, as well as the process of each person integrating the masculine and feminine in her/himself, is disclosed as a privileged locus for experiencing the presence and redemption of God. With this will come a reconstruction of so many aspects of the life of the church that it would require a full study to even begin to spell them out. The single most important condition for this most necessary development is the participation of women in theology and in decision-making in the church.

By contrast, a refusal to acknowledge this as an essential part of the agenda for the renewal and reformation of the church will only widen the split between the male-masculine and the female-feminine. A community that would do so, even by default, would be a sign not of salvation, but of division and disintegration. It would be constructing an ideology which, despite its religious vocabulary, would no longer be the Christian faith.

Celebrating reconciliation

The present atrocities in the Balkans are an ugly reminder that religion is not always an instrument of reconciliation. We do not have to look beyond our own shores to reach the same conclusion. Whether we look at the war in the North, the social apartheid in our cities, the growing brittleness in communication between the sexes, the increasing breakdown in relationships or even, perhaps one should say especially, into our own hearts, we see division and alienation. We need to feel this deeply lest we accept too flippantly St Paul's words that God has entrusted to us, the people of God, the news that God has reconciled the world to Godself and even more flippantly, Christ's gift to the church of the sacrament of forgiveness and reconciliation. Only a reconciling church can be a credible church or even a Christian church.

In reflecting on reconciliation, we must not allow ourselves to be domesticated, for any apparent shortcut to reconciliation only deepens the divisions by repressing the pain. Injustice persists not only because of our hearts of darkness, but because it is perpetuated in structures of oppression from which some, usually a powerful minority, gain at the expense of others. To forgive your enemies, you have to know who they are. Love, if real and concretised, is always conflictual; the first thing conflict resolution does is to recognise the reality of conflict and to seek its roots. There is an insipid form of bourgeois Christianity which implicitly proposes a conflict-free life to us and actually increases our alienation. The gospel proposes to us a passion for the transformation of oppressive structures and institutions, but not the destruction of the people who support them. It discloses a quality of love which will fight for justice for the oppressed, but will show compassion for the oppressor.

Meister Eckhart tells us that this compassion for the world begins with compassion for ourselves: and certainly the two go together. This compassion for self at the personal level and also at the wider levels of community and the church itself, is quite different from self-love in the sense of *amour propre*. The latter is rooted in self-importance and pretence; compassion – for the world and for self – is rooted in a love that stares unblinkingly into fragility, limitation and sinfulness.

The church is constituted by Christ as the community that realises and celebrates the unconditional forgiveness of God for humanity and the reconciliation that it brings. As such, it is the sign and servant of universal salvation; otherwise, despite any amount of orthodoxy, it cannot be that sign. It has the means to be the sign of the world's reconciliation only if it can so experience that reconciliation within itself, as to be demonstrably a sign of it. The condition for this is an on-going experience of God's compassion which expresses itself in compassion for self, each other and the world. The condition for that is to sit in and not to flee the vulnerability and sinfulness of self, our groups and our movements. The church does not forgive and reconcile out of its own moral self-sufficiency. Its compassion for the world is the repercussion of its never-ending experience of God's compassion for itself.

Groups and institutions that, consciously or unconsciously, operate out of an unreconstructed desire to legitimate a power-structure are most unlikely to be instruments of reconciliation. Whether we are in dialogue with our opponents, our separated brothers and sisters or our own divided hearts, as long the real agenda is reconstituting some kind of moral order in virtue of a previously constituted view of how things ought to be, we may be something other than ministers of reconciliation. For that view of how things should be may itself be, to a significant degree, merely the internalisation of an ideology constructed to give moral endorsement to a power structure.

Change in others probably occurs or fails to occur more or less as it does, or does not, in ourselves. Paradoxically, change in self, when it does happen, seems to begin with a liberating form of self-acceptance. I recognise something that needs to change and I experience that condition so classically described by St Paul, of wanting and yet not wanting that change. I learn through reflection on previous experience, the futility of denying it, simply shaking it off through will-power or even making 'firm purposes of amendment'. Realism invites me to learn the art of what I can only describe as sitting in this vulnerability, either in dialogue with an *anamchara* or before the gentle – though sometimes terrifying – silence of God's infinite compassion for all creatures and for me.

Reconciliation happens when I begin to glimpse God's unconditioned and unconditional acceptance of me through my glimpsing God's acceptance of that part of me which for whatever reason, I cannot easily accept myself. I begin to grasp what the Apostle meant when he wrote that 'God has consigned all people to disobedience so that he may show mercy to all'. The ethical base of one's existence begins to shift from observance, with its inevitable propensity towards a mixture of self-righteousness and guilt, to an existence within and out of God's mercy.

Needless to say, this doesn't happen just once and it is probably never complete. But the realisation that I am never more than a forgiven sinner, roots my moral striving first of all in the love that must always express itself as forgiveness to a broken and divided world (grace), and not primarily in some supposedly attainable individual moral standard in relation to an external norm (law). This in turn, is the condition for being led not solely by previously internalised extrinsic ethical norms, but by the Holy Spirit; and that is a foundational dimension of Christian existence. It is the ground of 'that joy which no one can take from you'.

Only a church existing and acting out of God's mercy can be a sacrament of reconciliation to its own members and to the world. Such a church will be in touch with its own weakness, bearing witness to the paradoxical weakness of God. The weakness of God, stronger than human strength, is a powerful theme in the New Testament.

Part of the price paid for the Constantinian peace was a reinterpretation of the power of God – and therefore of the church –

in imperialist terms. The symbolism and even the theology of the church, not least in the areas of ordination, penance, forgiveness and reconciliation, remain, to this day, bound up with the mindset and symbols of the feudal order. The enduring temptation for such a church is to misunderstand its holiness in terms of moral and spiritual self-sufficiency, instead of seeing it as God's self-gift in forgiveness. This leads to the danger of penance and reconciliation being seen in terms of submission to a morality totally encompassable within Canon Law. The consequence is moral immaturity for those who can accept it and a growing alienation, due to experiencing 'reconciliation' as domination and control, for those who cannot.

There is a crisis in the contemporary ministry of the church. On the one hand, the people of God have voted with their feet in relation to the official form of sacramental reconciliation. On the other, people are searching for and, to a greater or lesser degree, experiencing reconciliation and spiritual empowerment in a variety of different ways. Is this to be experienced as a threat or an invitation to broaden the horizons of how the church facilitates penance, forgiveness and reconciliation?

A church living in the spirit of the beatitudes is aspiring to the strength that comes from gentleness and not the strength that comes from institutional power. It is not that the Christian community should not seek to influence people and structures, to change minds and hearts, to give culture a spiritual soul and even to contribute to transforming socio-economic structures and laws, even when this involves conflict with the status quo. It most certainly should seek to do these things. The issue is what kind of power does it wish to exercise in seeking to do so, if it also wishes to be a servant of reconciliation.

As soon as we accept that we cannot bully people into goodness, we begin to see that proposing the gospel and wanting that gospel to be the heart of culture, can only be done in a manner that empowers people to cooperate freely and responsibly in this project, which Christians believe to be the project of God. But that also means accepting that some or many may not wish to do so. That in turn, means resisting the temptation to relate to such groups primarily in terms of political power and, instead, risking the vulnerability of trusting in the power of the truth lived out in a service of love.

The people of God, and especially their leaders, need to take seriously the possibility that the Holy Spirit may be leading the church in this direction. As society becomes more secularised and God is pushed further out onto the margins, as the church forges its primary social links with the dispossessed and the crushed, as the implications of a new and radical acknowledgement of the feminine are accepted, the church will experience a new depth of vulnerability and spiritual poverty allowing it to root itself anew in the spirit of the beatitudes. To some, this may appear to be a loss but, in fact, it is a gain. In particular, it is the only possible experiential base out of which the church can be a community and servant of reconciliation. For reconciliation and forgiveness do not come about through compromises made by the powerful but from the mutual compassion derived from shared vulnerability.

There is, nonetheless, a huge problem about how the people of God may celebrate the sacrament of reconciliation in a post-psychoanalytic world. This problem cannot be tackled simply by a theoretical theological justification of the status quo. It is not the fundamental theological principles that are at issue. Rather, it is how they may be understood and made pastorally meaningful in a new epoch of human consciousness. A sacrament is after all a visible sign; the sacrament of reconciliation has to be a tangible experience of reconciliation and actually celebrated as such. Yet people are nowadays celebrating that experience outside the official sacrament and hardly even expecting to experience it in the sacrament itself.

A sacrament is a human experience as well as a theological formality; it truly effects the grace it signifies only when it empowers. This certainly has implications for the penitent but no less for the minister. Simply steering the discussion back to the question of power and jurisdiction is sterile. It is not that *ex opere operato* is false; it's just far from the whole truth. Scotus came nearest to a purely formalistic-mechanistic understanding of penance and reconciliation but it was a view that never won acceptance. Something has to happen within the person seeking reconciliation and restoration. But, in a secularised post-psychoanalytic world, who in fact should be ordained to facilitate this?

This problem is not lessened by the fact that some of the principal places in which reconciliation needs to take place, even within the church, are between the clergy and the laity as such, between its rather comfortable leadership and the church of the poor, and between men and women. Who can be the minister and how can it be liturgically celebrated when one of the parties to the reconciliation is the one who will presume to preside? The Tridentine understanding, followed in Canon Law, of exactly how the presbyter can be the only minister of this sacrament needs careful re-examination, leaving aside for the moment the equally important question of the liturgical and communitarian dimension of reconciliation. St Thomas, after all, held that in cases of necessity one could confess to a layperson[16] and his is but one voice in a current of thought that spanned eight centuries. [17]

There will be resistance to this, but how can we so clearly eschew biblical fundamentalism yet cling obdurately to dogmatic fundamentalism? Clearly a huge amount of research and reflection is needed here and it may well be that the essence of the Tridentine position will be vindicated. But even if that were to be the case, the question would then arise as to who might be suitable candidates for the ministry of reconciliation and therefore for the priesthood itself. It is most unlikely that such an issue could ever be adequately faced within the present system of recruiting and training priests. One possible way forward might be to restore the communitarian dimension of penance and reconciliation and develop its liturgical celebration, by inviting all those who are experiencing reconciliation, in whatever way, together with those who are facilitating the experience, to participate in a liturgical celebration of the new life they are discovering and living out.

Reformation as well as renewal

Ecclesia semper reformanda runs the classic expression of everything we are seeking to express in these pages; the church must always be reformed! Although reform comes side by side with 'renewal', which can also point towards the on-going conversion which is the motor of all reformation, it is important to speak explicitly of reformation in order to communicate that what is needed is not merely what we already have lived out with a greater spiritual intensity. 'Reformation' implies the experience of renewal expressed in visibly different structures and priorities.

'Reformation' also implies accepting the reality of the sinfulness of the church, concretely focused in the imperative to reform. It is only since Vatican II that mainline theology has been able to re-appropriate this teaching. Indeed, even the council, presumably because of supposed Protestant resonances in the term, did not use it but preferred *perennis reformatio* instead. In fact, it is an ancient Catholic idea. Popes, councils and theologians of the Middle Ages used the expression quite naturally and so did the Council of Trent.

The sinfulness of the church is a practical existential doctrine of Christian faith implicit in the liturgical praying of the 'Our Father'. But so also is the holiness of the church. Yet the church is holy only in its indissoluble union with Christ in the Holy Spirit. Trying to claim that holiness as its own, as evidenced in its institutions, sacraments and saints, would necessarily imply claiming sinfulness as its own in its power structures, abuses and sinners. It is certainly true that the church possesses the holiness of Christ as its own in him, but the church does not possess this holiness of itself.

On the one hand, the visible historical church has too easily sought to collapse the distinction between the eschatological church (its final sanctified state at the end of history) and the institutional church (its complex of socio-cultural forms in the here-and-now) and claim the holiness of Christ for its own historically-conditioned institutions. On the other hand, we cannot simply juxtapose Christ and the church-in-history. The New Testament metaphors describing the relationship between the two are predominantly organic: vine, branch; bridegroom, spouse; head, members. The historical visible church, even in its sinfulness, remains indissolubly linked to the holiness of Christ and so is holy.

Yet the church's sinfulness cannot be just explained away, for example, by simplistic, even if convenient, explanations like the objective holiness of the institution linked to the subjective sinfulness of the members. That is quite simply to deny that the church is the people of God, as if somewhere behind the people there exists a sinless institution. On the contrary, as soon as the visible, institutional church is viewed concretely and historically, the view that the sacraments, institutions, teachings and laws do not share in the objective and concrete sinfulness of the people of God becomes unsustainable. It may well be that a sinful act as such can be attributed only to a person and not to an institution, but it is certain that all the shortcomings, blindnesses, contradictions and impoverishments that follow from the sins of the members may be attributed to the institution and, in a very particular way, to those who exercise power within it.

In ecclesial terms, the most pertinent example of the sinfulness of the church today consists in the implicit policy of blocking the implementation of the reforms of the Second Vatican Council and refusing to see the work of the Holy Spirit in the 'reception' of the council, especially in the lives of committed laypeople actively involved in living them out. One need only reflect on the removal of the language of 'collegiality', 'people of God', 'dialogue', and then the theological realities they represent, from the official agenda. If that is not sufficient then reflection on the emasculation of the local church, consolidated by a crudely authoritarian policy on the appointment of local bishops, will surely make the point. Whether it is done by controlling the agenda and the final document of the Extraordinary Synod, or repudiating the ARCIC agreement on ministry, or holding an African Synod in the Vatican, reintroducing the Tridentine rite over the head of the Congregation for Worship, or silencing and marginalising any voice that questions these retrograde steps – or, as a local church here in Ireland, simply going along uncritically with all of this – there is ample evidence that the church is living through a time of terrible temptation – the temptation to implicitly repudiate an ecumenical council in the name of a call to order and identity which may well mask an unconscious love of power.

Seeds of a new church

In one of his classic works, Newman wrote that: 'The episcopate, whose action was so prompt and concordant at Nicea on the rise of Arianism, did not, as a class or order of men, play a good part in the troubles consequent upon the council, and the laity did. The Catholic people, in the length and breadth of Christendom, were the obstinate champions of Catholic truth, and the bishops were not ... on the whole, taking a wide view of the history, we are obliged to say that the governing body of the church came short, and the governed were pre-eminent in faith, zeal, courage and constancy'.[18] He goes on to suggest that this remarkable fact was permitted by God precisely at the time when the church was passing to her long temporal ascendancy, in order that the church might never forget where her real identity lay.

Now as the church – and especially in this country – passes out of that period of temporal ascendancy, something similar is unfolding before our very eyes, even though it will take the passage of history to see it clearly. It is the ordinary people of God as exemplified in the pastoral initiatives described in Part Two of the present work, who are receiving and implementing the ecumenical council and fulfilling the dreams of John XXIII and Paul VI, no less than the people of whom Newman wrote received and implemented the Council of Nicea and fulfilled the dream of St Athanasius.

Catholicism is distinguishable from fundamentalism not least because it is not founded on a single interpretation of a single text frozen in time. It is rather a living tradition to which every generation of believers contributes. An ecumenical council, no more than the scriptures themselves, does not yield its meaning entirely by itself. It requires tradition, which is the active presence of revelation in living subjects by the power of the Holy Spirit. 'Reception' by living subjects can never be reduced to mere passive acceptance; for only in the reception, concretised in a lived implementation, does the text have real ecclesial existence and become part of 'the tradition'. In this way, the recipients of the council become co-creators of its meaning.

It is hardly convincing to argue that the council has been received by pointing to the gradual introduction of some of the changes it proposed such as vernacular Mass, married deacons, communion under both species and new rites. Apart altogether from the somewhat piecemeal and intermittent way in which these things have been implemented and the manner in which the effectiveness of the various council documents has been reduced, all too often the changes have been superficial and extrinsic. In reality, they have been superimposed on a pre-Vatican II mind-set and ecclesiology which remains unreconstructed, and scarcely represent an expression and implementation of the renewal which the great event of the council sought to inaugurate.

What we have seen is that in Ireland today there are many groups led by the Holy Spirit who in their lives and actions, are a new and renewed presence of the church in this country. Through them the presence of Christ in prophecy, service and blessing is addressing the hopes, promises, contradictions and absurdities of contemporary Irish life. In some of them, we see the unmasking of the structures and value systems that increasingly enslave us. In others, we see Christ's identification with the excluded. We see groups trying to empower the poor so as to articulate a truly inclusive and therefore Christian concept of the human person in community and we see groups elaborating an adult catechesis which is empowering and rooted in experience. The feminine is finding its own theological voice, holding out the promise of a deepened and enriched experience of Christian community. Models of work and enterprise celebrating the primacy of human purposefulness over mere profit are in successful operation. Healing and reconciliation of the individual, the group and the community is happening in ever more liberating and empowering ways. Consumerism is being surpassed and we are re-linking with the spiritual depths that are deep within us. Through all of this, Christ is being formed in us, and the church, ever ancient and ever new, is being born again.

One of the most threatening aspects of sustained prayer is the fear that God might take us seriously. This, we were told, was to be the age of the laity and a new Pentecost. The church prayed for this and God heard our prayer. We can all be blessed in building upon what has begun.

CHAPTER THREE

Ways forward: action for renewal

As a community of hope, the church is energised at the prospect of co-creating the future out of the memory of the poor and the power of the gospel. By contrast, a pre-occupation with the past that fears any move forward into the unknown, spells death and disintegration. The renewed and reformed church, offering hope for a transformed future, already exists in the lives and actions of groups such as those presented in Part Two of this present work, as well as in many other situations. The one who 'makes all things new' calls us forward to build on what has been begun and to allow him to be among us to empower us on the way.

Free from fear...

Throughout the gospels, Jesus is telling his disciples not to be afraid. The presence of the risen Christ among us is one that drives out all fear. Yet fear is the capital sin of the church in this country, fear of things being different, fear of a loss of status and influence, fear that an informed laity will demand its rights as the people of God, fear of open communication and the obligation to communicate on an equal basis, fear of freedom and fear that people will use/abuse that freedom to choose things the church leadership doesn't want, fear of genuine dialogue and of hearing hard truths, fear of change, of becoming small or vulnerable, fear of having to rely primarily on the grace of God. It is this fear, and not the changes in Irish society as such, that is crippling the church. It is this fear, and not secularisation, feminism or the autonomy of experience, which is the real enemy – the enemy within that blocks all serious attempts at renewal, stifles the Spirit and dilutes the gospel's transforming power. We need to give a new urgency to our prayer to be freed from this fear.

Part of this process may involve a time of grieving for what is lost and gone. At the very least, it would be more realistic than denying it, defending the remnants of it and wasting energy and good-will in trying to restore a caricature of it. Certainly, it will be a process leading us to a new poverty of spirit, uncomfortable and vulnerable, but the condition *sine qua non* for God to work through us and therefore a gift to be welcomed.

There was a moment of deep symbolic significance during the first session of Vatican II when the draft constitution on the church was effectively rejected by the council Fathers. The turning point was the sensational intervention of Bishop de Smedt of Belgium who insisted that in speaking of its mission, the church had to avoid 'triumphalism, clericalism and juridicalism'. What this intervention represented was an opening towards a new style of being church, a real shift relative to the immediate past: a major break – albeit within a deeper continuity and tradition – but a break nonetheless.

Its first fruits was Cardinal Suenens' amendment of the second draft which made way for a full chapter on the 'People of God' to precede the discussion on the hierarchy and following immediately on the discussion of the mystery of the church. In this development, in the very structure of the text as it were, a new model of church was born; not new really, but the ancient apostolic, patristic church in contemporary idiom, incorporating the genuine developments of the ages and relativising the secondary ones. It highlighted that the mystery of the church is made visible first of all in the faith-life of the people of God as a whole rather than primarily in the hierarchy. Communion (*koinonia*) is disclosed as being more fundamental than the authority structure which exists to serve it. In principle, all the baptised are of equal dignity in building up this communion. Can we doubt that the council fulfilled John XXIII's prayer for a new Pentecost? Or shall we hide behind that most unworthy suggestion – proposed with increasing confidence in reactionary circles – that while the council itself was a good thing, its reception and implementation were not? [19]

The texts of the council were not written just for libraries but to be received and implemented by the people of God and in a special way by those committed to and active in the very forms of ministry which the council called for. In a very real sense, the council documents have a real existence only in their reception and implementation. The church of to-day is not merely the church of yesterday armed with a new batch of documents. It is called to be a renewed and in that sense, a new church. It seems pathetic to have to repeat all this almost thirty years after the ending of the council. But it is vitally necessary to do so because there is a struggle going on now in the church between those who wish to implement the council and those who, in their heart of hearts, fear what it represents, often wish it had never happened and in various ways seek to repudiate it.

Consulting the faithful

For the church to be communion, there has to be a sharing of faith among the people of God. Certainly, there are in the church, according to both the Pauline lists of charisms and the church's own developing self-understanding, some who have the ministry of teaching. But they do not possess this gift in such a way as to effectively deny the people of God as a whole, any substantial participation or constitutive role in the articulation of the faith which, in principle, they possess and live out no less completely than either bishops or theologians. It is time in this country for a far-reaching, wide-ranging and most importantly, open and honest consultation of all the faithful in relation to the options we must take to effectively live out our common Christian and ecclesial vocation in the Ireland of to-day.

The reactionary voice will immediately cry 'Foul!' 'The church is a *mysterium* and a hierarchy: you cannot make it a democracy; that is to confuse the theological and the political'! But apparently, it is alright to make it a monarchy or an oligarchy, as if such things were not only political but, in the eyes of many serious and sincere Christians, a countersign to the gospel in an era which has espoused human rights and participative organisation. Since Pius XII's Christmas address of 1944, the church has emphasised a clear preference for democratic structures in social and political life. Does it want such structures everywhere except in the organisational aspects of its own life? The question becomes all the more pressing since John Paul II, in *Centesimus Annus*, has sought to go beyond a stated preference for democracy and to invest it with a moral content not found in other systems. Can this moral content not contribute to expressing those concrete and incarnated dimensions of the 'mystery' of the church which are visible and therefore socio-political as well?

Unless the church leadership consults and listens to the faithful, it will simply bore the passive and alienate the reflective while reassuring only the reactionary. There needs to be a comprehensive and systematic sounding out and surveying of all the Christian people in relation to the structures and mission of the church in the Ireland of to-day. The point is not that the truth of Jesus Christ can or cannot be determined on a show of hands but rather that the transforming power of that truth cannot be spoken as good news for growth, conversion, reconciliation and community without the consent and participation of those it seeks to address. It cannot be spoken to a situation whose hopes and aspirations those who would speak it seem to have taken all too little effort to understand or appreciate.

The surveying of the people of God is not to be confused with getting selected groups to fill out a questionnaire designed by an unrepresentative minority. Before a questionnaire stage is reached there has to be a less formal but deeper kind of listening to the joys and hopes and struggles and anxieties of the people of God. For this kind of listening and surveying, a specific kind of expertise is needed – in particular, the capacity to discern the really generative themes in the various communities of the country, coupled with a genuine commitment to the person of Christ and the community of the church. The fruits of this listening and surveying need to be interpreted theologically and for this a team with expertise in theology, adult religious education and communication skills is needed. From this theological reading, a truly representative and detailed questionnaire could be designed to survey the people. All of this together could form the initial stage in constituting a church synod for the whole country.

But this process of listening would have another and equally important significance. It would be an act of repentance for the sins of 'clericalism, triumphalism and juridicalism', not a wallowing in a paralysing guilt, but an honest recognition that all is not well and that much of the malaise is of the church's own making. There is much anger and alienation about and, if it is not acknowledged and expressed, it will quickly translate into even greater apathy and disaffection. Not that preserving the institution is the most important point of the exercise; it is demanded by the nature of the church itself. For how can the church leadership offer reconciliation and invite conversion and the vulnerability they entail, without being open itself to participate in a similar process?

Listening to the faithful and consulting them – in the strong sense of 'taking counsel' from them – should not be thought of as a kind of condescension on the part of the 'teaching' church; a sort of surrender to the spirit of the times. On the contrary, not to do so is to become something other than the church. Faith is first and foremost, the 'faith by which we believe' (*fides qua creditur*) and in the main, it is the laity who are God's instruments in passing it on. But even the 'faith which we believe' (*fides quae creditur*) and the praxis out of which it grows and to which it is referred, as well as the liturgy which celebrates and deepens it, cannot be elaborated without reference to the People of God as a whole. The Holy Spirit, active in the lives of the faithful, gives them an instinct for the faith and for how it is to be lived, articulated and handed on in different eras. This is the subjective pole of tradition; as conciliar decrees and collegial statements are its objective pole. These are inseparable, just as the sense of the faith expressed in the consent of the faithful, is intrinsic to the teaching authority of the church.

Synod

These theological principles, somewhat relativised in an era of growing centralisation, are not new but are the common currency of the consciousness of the church from the beginning. The church, while including, as an integral element, an episcopacy in communion with the successor of Peter, as something it has received from the Lord, is not simply constituted by this hierarchy over and against the faithful, as if the latter could belong to 'the church' somehow existing prior to and quasi-independently from them.

More fundamentally, the church is the People of God as a whole. All of us together are the Body of Christ, the priestly people which not only offers the 'spiritual sacrifice' of lives of faith, hope and love but the eucharist itself. This was 'retrieved' by Vatican II as a grace of renewal for the whole church: not simply as a sort of academic exercise to be pored over by historians of theology, but as the voice of the Holy Spirit calling forth a more communitarian church in the service of the transformation of an utterly changed world.

These theological truths and to a large extent the council itself, have been 'received' and implemented by individuals and groups in this country but not – may one venture to say – in an unmistakeable way, by the church as a whole. We need to give them new expression in a synod for the whole country whose preparation, structure and implementation would reflect and express the real nature of the Body of Christ.

The first question to be tackled in preparing such a synod is representation. We could do worse than use the Church of England's model as a starting-point in planning the mode of representation, with its houses of bishops, clergy and laity, and consensus in and between all three as the norm for decision-making. A synod can hardly know the mind and heart of a local church unless it is itself a celebration of the communion (*koinonia*) which the Holy Spirit has raised up that church to be. Attention would also have to be given to the participation of religious as well as missionaries sent by this local church. It hardly bears repetition that a particular effort would need to be made to include the voice of Christian women and most important of all, that of the poor, as an expression of Christ's and the church's preferential option for the oppressed which, far from being sectional or exclusive, is crucial to expressing the catholicity of the faith.

The generative themes disclosed in the deep listening of the informal survey would be explored at parish and local community level. The preferred method of exploration would be that of a problem-posing pedagogy, employed by several of the groups presented in Part Two, including *Partners in Mission* and *Partners in Faith*, one in which all are participants and co-learners. This process would yield intermediate conclusions, priorities in relation to social and personal issues, possible courses of action and strategies for action, expressed shared needs for more specialised information, problems and possibilities of networking.

These, in turn, would propose a two-fold agenda to the church. At the level of 'action for God's kingdom', they would propose the basic agenda for the involvement and commitment of Christians as individuals, members of base communities and parishes in social action 'in the world'. At the level of the 'inner life of the church', they would propose in a concrete fashion, the 'joys and hopes, griefs and anxieties of the people of this age' which are to be re-read in the light of scripture and the living tradition of the church. In the light both of this reading and reflection on grassroots action – for the two go hand-in-hand – a more rooted and renewed pastoral theology and strategy could be elaborated. The elaboration of this would be the main on-going task of the synod.

This theological reading of the fruits of grassroots reflection proceeds from the perspective afforded by a preferential option for the poor.[20] As long as theological and pastoral readings of the fruits of consultation attempt to give equal weight and importance to all perspectives and worldviews, the result will always be an ineffectual compromise. God's view is the view from below.

God, in the incarnation, is not neutral; neither is an incarnated Christian theology.

In deciding on a method of procedure, it could learn a lot from the methodology of the ground-breaking experience of CELAM at Medellin in 1968, and take as its headline and task 'The transformation of contemporary Ireland in the light of the gospel'. The Catholic Church in this country must become synonymous in the public perception, not with slowing down the process of social transformation, but with promoting it, giving it a clearer focus, sustaining it with a humanising vision and spiritual depth, and refining its goals in terms of a more inclusive compassion and a more solid grasp of what is real and true.

This stage of the synod would aim to produce not simply a statement, but an invitation to participate in a process which sought both the transformation of the socio-cultural reality of the country in terms of the values of the gospel, as well as a deepening of the faith, expressed in the communitarian and liturgical life of the church. There would necessarily be a degree of openendedness in this process, for to be communitarian it needs to be dialogical and therefore open to self-correction.

This work would need to be accompanied by a sustained process of training and equipping pastoral workers, some though not all of whom would be ordained, to accompany and animate this process. This will involve a financial commitment, never a popular suggestion: but to baulk at it means we are not really serious. How much money is used on other things with little enough self-examination or accountability? One may wish, but hardly demand, that much or all this be done voluntarily. To so demand will inevitably result in unrepresentative participation. Nevertheless, there is the gospel call to simplicity and evangelical poverty – though not to penury. Yet those who would remind lay pastoral workers of this should first of all exemplify it in themselves.

The process of evaluating this on-going pastoral initiative would be concluded at another stage of the synod which would also produce a blueprint for the next stage. For the structures of animating, implementing and evaluating it would now be in place. This may seem like a very long-drawn-out process. It would in fact take a few years. Why not have the bishops meet for one week and hand down the decisions? But it is not as if the church is somehow suspended while all this is going on. For the church is not just a tiny minority making decisions, but a whole people living out the communion in and through which the Holy Spirit is fashioning them into the people of God.

Far from being already fully formed and needing occasional redirecting onto previously constructed and immutable tracks, the church is actually a mystical communion in the process of visibly and historically constituting itself as the leaven of a new humanity. It is, by the very nature of its historical existence, always within the process of self-constitution, always coming into a deeper Christian identity – which is its identity with Christ, crucified and risen – always reforming and correcting itself, always opening itself out to that fuller and deeper inspiration of the Holy Spirit. It is this process and not some past historically conditioned institutional expression of it, which is the true church: the whole people of God growing together towards the fullness of Christ. The process being described here is simply an attempt to do this more consciously and openly and therefore to become more openly and more consciously the church.

The Lord hears the cry of the poor

We can move forward to more adequately become the church of the poor only through allowing the aspirations of the poor for dignity, equality and inclusion to function as a structuring and focusing element in the consciousness and organisation of the church as a whole. This must become a reality both theologically and organisationally and therefore liturgically as well. All levels of ministry and leadership in the church must open their minds and hearts to an irruption of the reality of poverty – global, national and local – into their consciousness.

This must be focused by social analysis so that a compassion for the victims of injustice and marginalisation is informed by the capacity to recognise the structures of inequality and privilege that create and consolidate poverty. But a further step must be taken. The same principles and the same analysis must be applied to institutions and organisations in which church bodies have a significant input: schools, hospitals, seminaries, diocesan holdings, religious orders and even the church itself. With the gospel privilege of the poor in mind, we must ask of all such institutions, with honesty and openness: who owns them? who benefits from them and who is marginalised by them? what values and social structures and privileges do they uphold and defend? who is excluded from them and who is further exploited and marginalised by their manner of operating?

There is another step and it is this. The members of the church at all levels, but especially among the leadership, must display in their own lifestyles that simplicity and detachment from wealth and comfort which is a rejection of consumerism, a pointer towards an alternative society and a condition for real solidarity with the deprived.

There is a wonderful saying of Ghandiji which the church might do well to ponder at this historical moment of reappraisal and renewal which truly calls for changes of direction: 'I will give you a talisman. Whenever you are in doubt or when the self becomes too much with you, apply the following test. Recall the face of the poorest and the weakest man whom you may have seen and ask yourself if the step you contemplate is going to be of any use to him: will he gain anything by it, will it restore him to a control over his own life and destiny? In other words will it lead to *swaraj* for the hungry and spiritually starving millions? Then you will find your doubts and your self melting away.'

Every time a church group of whatever kind, operating at whatever level, including the diocesan, is exploring issues and making decisions, it should keep this question before them. In what way are our deliberations to-day going to affect the poor? Otherwise, the discussion can hardly be said to be Christian and from the perspective of the gospel.

One further step is necessary and that is to go beyond a feeling for the poor or even consulting the poor to give representative – and articulate – poor people a deliberative voice in decision-making bodies in the church. Until we actively aspire and plan for this we are still locked in paternalism – or maybe even indifference.

Training for ministry

The renewal of the church necessitates a reappraisal of selection and training for the ministry. In reality, far-reaching change and development is needed. The heart of the reform needed in this area, would be to base selection and training on the gifts the prospective minister has received from the Holy Spirit and not primarily on institutional requirements which have neither a scriptural foundation nor the consent of the faithful. However, as we work and pray for such changes, in the interim the church would benefit from developments within the existing model.

The seminary model of priestly formation – as distinct from some of the people who work in seminaries – is implicitly intended to be promoting a model of leadership which is authoritarian, exclusive, detached and self-contained. It assumes and consolidates a view of church with 'the few in charge of the many'. By effectively eliminating laypeople and especially women, from the staff and student bodies, the range of questions to be explored and the perspectives and sentient base from which they are explored are so narrowed as to risk becoming a caricature of contemporary historical and Christian experience.

The very idea of a seminary is, in fact, to deliberately create an artificial environment cut off from the everyday. The resultant sub-culture will almost inevitably give rise to irresponsibility and an absence of realism in people's attitudes, expectations and lifestyle. Even when the experience of lay men and women is allowed to impinge on the programme of study, it usually does so in a merely extrinsic and intermittent way. It is perceived as something requiring an answer from a perspective already agreed upon, rather than something co-constitutive of the questions and the perspective from which they are asked.

In the training of theology professors – who, according to the official line, must all be men – there is little or no attention to adult education principles or group-work methods, and those who have acquired such skills have had to do so off their own bat. Consequently, with honourable exceptions, the seminary discourse is in principle, entirely monological, based on hand-outs and examinations in which the primary demand is the repetition of lecture notes. This can hardly fail to orient the future priests to a similar monological form of discourse, less and less acceptable or even meaningful, in a society that increasingly values shared experience over traditional authority.

Given the concept of church as People of God and the forms of communicative competence required in a secularised and increasingly educated world, the very concept of a seminary is suspect. Since the bishops, for the present at least and for a variety of reasons, are unlikely to want to entertain far-reaching change in relation to these issues, an attempt must be made to move forward within the limited room for manoeuvre available. It is however, interesting and somewhat ironic, to note in passing, that neither Paul VI nor John Paul II received their theological formation in a seminary!

The school of theology should be one where seminarians, religious and lay men and women all study together as equals. Together with the staff – or leading learners – they would seek to form a community of learning, itself an embodiment of communion and shared Christian praxis. The teaching methods must incorporate adult education principles and group-work methods as reflection on lived faith experience, as well as problem-posing education. Teaching theology by a primarily banking method will produce a clergy which can only sermonise and promulgate. To enable the People of God to interpret their own experience in the light of faith – something essential to the development of an adult church – demands that candidates for the priesthood must themselves be trained to examine their own experience in the light of faith – and that must include both the personal dimension and the dimension of shared reflection on praxis – for otherwise they can never be able to facilitate such a process for others.

The teaching and study of theology must also be rooted in the pastoral praxis of the learning community, both staff and students, and this pastoral practice must be rooted in a preferential option for the poor. This could be concretised by members of staff living with students in small communities in deprived areas, sharing the lives and struggles of the people and theologising out of that experience.

From the beginning, theology must be examined against the touchstone of its ability to enlighten, liberate and empower people in their everyday Christian life, especially in relation to action for the transformation of unjust social structures and dehumanising concepts of the human person in society, as well as the internalised ideologies that legitimate them. Otherwise, it will be just an intellectual exercise in the history of religious ideas; worthwhile and even enjoyable, but scarcely liberating and no longer the living word of God seeking contemporary transformative understanding.

It is time to question seriously whether students should be ordained at the end of the seminary course – even to the Diaconate. Seminaries are so sub-cultural that the seminarians, instead of learning how to serve in the ministry, principally learn how to survive the seminary system. Even after a seminary programme rooted in pastoral practice, the student on completion of his – regrettably, one cannot yet add 'or her' – theological studies, might be better advised to spend at least two years as a full-time lay pastoral assistant in a parish; working and residing – and being remunerated – as a full member of the parish team before being ordained deacon. He might then spend a similar period of time in full-time ministry in another parish before being ordained to the presbyterate. In addition to pastorally rooting his future priestly ministry, this process might also honour the need for the call from God to that ministry to be mediated by the people of God as a whole.

The (no longer) silent majority

The question of the participation of women in the ministry of the church in a post-feminist age, cannot be tackled simply by token adjustments aimed at papering over the cracks in the system or by a verbal acknowledgement of the issues without repentance and reconstruction in the life and structures of the church. Incorporating the Christian feminist agenda is likely to have far-reaching effects on many aspects of church life – as indeed it should. Here, as in so many of the areas under discussion in the present work, an intellectual conversion is called for: a recognition that most of the factors slowing and stopping change are not theological at all.

In practical terms, this can only become real in an active promotion and appreciation of the participation of women in ministry and theology, and in reflection and decision-making at all levels of church life. This must not simply be a matter of letting 'them' join the 'the club' for fear they might simply go off and form their own. In this new form of shared Christian praxis and reflection, men and women will be drawn into a new communion, something new will come to be; neither the patriarchal status quo nor its feminist deconstruction, but a richer and mutually enriching synthesis of what it is to be the church. It must flow from a realisation that unless women and men together articulate the exigencies of the Christian faith, that faith will no longer be capable of addressing a post-feminist culture.

One way of concretising these aspirations and demonstrating the sincerity of those who consider them, would be to take immediate steps to give women substantial representation on all decision-making bodies at every level of the church in this country; something already possible within an imaginative though entirely admissible, interpretation of even the existing code of Canon Law.

(A woman, Ludmilla Javarova, was vicar-general in a Czech diocese from 1967-1988). Whether at the level of base community, parish council, diocesan or national synod, the theological voice of women needs to be heard in a direct and immediate way. There is no point in hiding behind the familiar practices. For the time being, strictly defining the official canonical status of such developments or the language used to describe them, is far less important than the real option to initiate them and to make the process of decision-making in the church a genuine reflection of the true nature and composition of the church itself.

In selecting and electing women, care must be taken that they are truly representative. If there is to be a preference, it should not automatically be for women members of restorationist movements, but for theologically articulate women who have made an unambiguous option for the poor or, better still, for women who themselves are poor and whose articulation of the faith is linked to working-class movements active in confronting oppression and marginalisation. This would represent a clear sign and recognition of the right of the poor – who are more than half of the church in this country – to think theologically, and of the constitutive importance of this dimension of Christian life for the self-constitution of the church.

If there is one area which badly needs such a development, it is the Christian reflection on human sexuality. Having attempted to give all the answers to all predicaments under all circumstances, the church leadership finds itself taken less and less seriously in anything relating to sexuality. Having proclaimed the silly and the serious with equal emphasis, it now finds that the relativisation of one brings with it the downgrading of the other. People long for sexual liberation and the media moguls grow rich reminding them of that longing. While for some this quest for sexual liberation may lead to growth and freedom, many of the socio-cultural forms this alleged liberation takes seem to lead only to greater exploitation, unhappiness and confusion.

In this area, no less than any other, the values of the gospel – responsibility, truthfulness, mutuality, tenderness, fidelity, forgiveness, self-control, respect for life and realism – remain valid and essential, but somehow the church leadership seems no longer capable of communicating them in a credible and life-giving way. It's as if the church has the right principles but lacks the communicative competence to share them. But this cannot be solved merely

by greater access to and more competent use of the media, important as that might be: the problem goes deeper.

The manner in which the Christian experience needs to impact
upon the world of contemporary experience requires a form of
communicative competence which, unfortunately, is the very one
that is often weakest in the church's own deliberations. The manner in which a truth of Christian existence is appropriated,
shared, explored and communicated is not wholly extrinsic to the
truth itself; perspective, context and shared Christian praxis enter
into formulation. Because the church's own deliberations on
sexuality are, or are perceived to be, monological, deductive and
unrepresentative, they have difficulty in dialoguing with and enlightening the contemporary situation which expects an inductive
method based on shared experience. The single most important
step in beginning to deal with this situation is the inclusion of
women at all levels of theological reflection and decision-making
in the church.

Pastoral pathways

One of the most pressing shifts in orientation that a reformed and
renewed church needs to make is from being an institution unconsciously bent on preserving the past to a movement energised
at the prospect of co-creating the future. Given the accelerating
rate of socio-cultural change, anything less will consign the
church to be a relic of the past.

As a consequence, pastoral work will become more a matter of
evangelisation than of preserving a given model of church in continuity with the recent past. Increasingly, the faith will no longer
be automatically 'handed on' because the means and structures
and traditions of 'handing it on' are themselves undergoing such
rapid transformation. Furthermore, the socio-cultural context
within which the tradition was 'handed on' and which gave the
means of 'handing it on' such wide recognition and acceptance,
has already been irreversibly changed. If this is not recognised, religion will become increasingly relativised and privatised – a set
of innocuous rituals for children, a source of consolation for the
elderly, a manner of summoning up memories of things past.

One already notices how, not only in the media, but even at the
Christmas liturgy in middle class parishes, instead of proclaiming
the revolutionary story of the birth of Jesus and the manner in
which it calls into question our consumerist culture and invites a

more inclusive compassion, we are treated to tales of how Christmas used to be celebrated in rural Ireland 'long ago', i.e., within living memory! The vindication of autonomy and personal freedom has not turned religious practice from obligation to conviction and celebration. Instead, religion has simply been adjusted from being the legitimation of an authoritarian society to being the legitimation of middle-class culture. There is a place for God as long as it is a nice god and a place for the church as long as it preaches a god who sustains and consoles us in the lifestyle and pre-occupations already largely determined for us by our complicity in the operations of the financial institutions. No need to crucify such a god and so no need for him to rise from the dead and so no need to celebrate a eucharist to proclaim his death until he comes!

Unless we are prepared to pretend that this is the gospel, then it is clear that the emerging Ireland needs to be re-evangelised. Given the socio-cultural context as well as the nature of evangelisation, the form this must take is to proclaim and promote, and image in alternative structures, the ethical norms and human values upon which the new Ireland might be built. To some extent, the church already seeks to do this, but it often appears to fail to see that the enunciation of principles divorced from a critique of structures and the articulation of alternatives is often a barren exercise. For this reason, a central aspect of the evangelisation needed is to identify and address the emerging issues of Irish society in the light of the gospel, Christian tradition and from the perspective of the poor, with a view to empowering those who seek to construct more human alternatives.

The issuing of *Work is the Key* could be seen as a first step in this form of evangelisation in relation to the issue of unemployment. The point being that if as the bishops – correctly – state, unemployment is the single greatest social issue facing the Irish people to-day, then there can be no preaching of the gospel which does not proceed from a critique of the causes of this widespread injustice, as well as in the context of attempting to construct alternative economic models.

The publication of the document was a first step in two senses. Firstly, because, as the document itself pointed out, it is now over to laypeople to work out models and strategies to implement the values and principles it proposes. Secondly, because even in its present form, it needs to be followed up by study sessions at local community and parish level. This, in turn, needs to be linked to catechesis in schools and adult religious education. At another level, it needs to lead on to discussion in the public forum, preaching in the churches, as well as in songs and posters for the liturgical celebration of these initiatives. Finally, if it is for real, it must lead on to popular socio-political action – not necessarily party-based – for economic change on the basis of a shared vision inspired by the gospel. When it comes to action, however, guarded and even-handed listening to all sides will have to give way to choices with all the attendant risks implied. If our vision is that of the gospel, then the choices will have to favour the poor.

Each year a new theme could be chosen, following on from consultation similar to that which preceded *Work is the Key* and leading on to the same kind of action and reflection outlined above. 'Male and Female in the image of God'; 'The moral foundation of the political order'; 'Justice and reconciliation'; 'Human sexuality as gift and responsibility'; 'Communications as the service of truth'; 'Community for service: the common human vocation'; 'The integrity of creation'; these could serve as a first approximation to the pastoral agenda of the church for the next several years.

If this seems to be a sort of Christian equivalent to the United Nations' 'Year of the…', then that is nothing to make us hesitate. Christianity is a historical religion entrusted with the transformation of history and culture, and historical responsibility is all about creating the future out of the memory of the past and the contradictions and possibilities of the present. Theologically speaking, this is the meaning of eschatology: viewing the present in terms of the hope – concretised in the life of Christ and the lives of the saints – of that total salvation offered to humankind by God and then critiquing and transforming present reality in the light of that hope, with a view to empowering the construction of alternative models of human community. In practical terms, this is the only way we can 'give an account of the hope that is within us'.

In an immediate sense, the world sets the agenda for the church whether poverty, unemployment, reconciliation, ecology, gender, alienation, indoctrination, violence, oppression or whatever. The task of the Christian community is to mediate God's salvation, which breaks through these threats to our common humanity as the integral human liberation of human persons in community, from all that oppresses them. The fullness of redeemed existence offered by Christ and described by St Paul, can never be appropriated in detachment from confronting these issues, as if our spiritual selves dwelt in some privatised sphere of personal religiosity, but only in bringing the transforming power of the gospel to bear on these human conflicts and the dilemmas to be faced in tackling them. This is the lived experience and praxis out of which prayer and worship emerge, in order that, as individuals and communities, we might root ourselves even more deeply in God's infinite compassion for God's creation, the better to be part of its transformation and growth to wholeness.

The development of this kind of evangelisation and catechesis would require the kind of full-time team of theologians with interdisciplinary skills, including adult education, surveying, communications and liturgy already alluded to, linked to a group of consultants with the highest expertise in the human sciences, but operating out of a Christian and ecclesial perspective. Such a team could also function as a sort of 'think tank' for the episcopal conference, as well as a meeting point for structuring the interaction between contemporary experience and the riches of the Christian tradition. It would be a team with the same level of theological expertise as the present Theological Commissions that operate in various countries, but elaborating a theology that is organically linked to action for social and personal transformation.

Such a team might best operate as the core staff of a National Pastoral Institute to be set up by the bishops. The main aim of the Institute would be to devise and implement an overall pastoral plan for the renewal and reformation of the church in this country. The team would work in dialogue with the whole people of God, including the bishops. Since its theological method would be rooted in the praxis of the People of God – though no less scholarly for that – its composition, location, social linkage and mode of operation would bear careful clarification.

Leadership

If this kind of pastoral planning is to characterise the shape of the church of the future, then the episcopate must include people with a deep understanding of this evangelical imperative, who can support it, implement it and lead it forward. It is time that theological values took priority over purely organisational ones in the appointment of bishops and in the definition of their ministry. Perhaps the essential quality to be sought in future bishops is the charism of being able to discern the charisms of the Holy Spirit in others, to promote and empower them in the exercise of these spiritual gifts and, in this way, to preside in love over the community of communities. It is something far deeper and richer than an essentially administrative role and probably something fervently, even if silently, wished for by many bishops themselves.

While our bishops are certainly men of ability, piety and commitment, it would hardly be unfair to suggest that too many of them come to the episcopacy out of the same kind of background and experience; often diocesan school presidents or seminary or college professors. Unquestionably, men with such gifts are also needed in the episcopate but so are people with other kinds of ministerial expertise, notably parish ministry, communications, adult religious education and not least, a rootedness in the struggles of the poor. In a very particular way, the episcopate needs people with a proven track record in animating and accompanying people exercising a variety of ministries, ordained and nonordained, and who minster specifically in function of the kind of issues we have been discussing in this present book.

Sacramental practice

For a variety of reasons, notably the deep religiosity of the people, the externals of religious ritual continue to have considerable socio-cultural significance, even among individuals and groups where explicit Christian commitment and faith have declined close to zero. Infant baptism, confirmation and church weddings with Nuptial Mass are widely demanded and automatically expected, even by people who in real terms, have abandoned religious practice. Some, of course, may say that abandoning religious practice is one thing and losing the faith is another. It is an area of human experience notoriously difficult to evaluate in a hard and fast way. Yet there are unmistakeable signs indicating that simply letting the present situation continue will result in trivialising and cheapening the sacramental life of the church.

Here too, there is an element of intellectual conversion called for: a reappropriation of the ancient theological principle, lost sight of in the early modern period, that 'God has not tied his grace to the sacraments'. He certainly wishes to bless his people through them, but is not limited to them. Moreover, the theory of *ex opere operato* which, while certainly intended to emphasise the sovereignty of God and God's graciousness, as well as the Christian dignity of those who, however unformed their faith, were none-theless believers, was never meant to propose the sacraments as automatic channels of grace independent of the dispositions of the recipient. Inattention to these truths has, in an era of waning devotion and belief, produced an almost slot-machine sacramen-tal practice too often characterised by minimalism and near-empty ritualism. It easily degenerates into a mechanical form of worship which impoverishes both priest and people.

This is both contributing to and being exacerbated by the crisis of relevance for the clergy, evident in the still significant numbers – especially of reflective priests – leaving the ministry. This crisis cannot be resolved by the clergy seeking a new, even if more re-stricted, functional role in the emerging culture, for the crisis is one of meaning and not just of technique. It would be a great mis-take for the clergy to retreat into a sort of religious department of the consumerist society – all the more so because it would fit into and further legitimate the dominant ideology. A certain kind of relevance could be sought in supplying religious services on de-mand: but that would be to promote civil religion and not the Christian faith.

If the community of the church involves free and responsible commitment, then the church leadership will have to reckon with the possibility that, for better or worse, some or many people may not wish to belong to it. Where this has been unmistakeably indic-ated, prudence and honesty demand that such persons cannot assume automatic admission to the sacraments simply for socio-cultural or family reasons. There will be, of course, all kinds of borderline cases and quite clearly, these occasions can also be op-portunities for renewal and conversion. The 'clued-in' pastor will know what is going on and is best situated to make an informed judgement, especially when he is operating as part of a pastoral team in tune with the local reality. But such possibilities cannot be used as a cloak to cover up a real pastoral problem demanding ur-gent action. Losses there will be, but gains too; for the symbolising power of a sacrament is virtually lost when what it points to is so facilely universalised and diminished that it is no longer distin-guishable from what it points from.

Renewal of sacramental life has three aspects. Firstly, the re-linking of sacrament to faith community; secondly, the deepening of the faith life of the ministers and the communities so that they live what they celebrate; thirdly, a genuine inculturation of liturgy in the contemporary lived experience of the Christian community.

All of the gestures, symbols, materials and actions of the liturgy were originally, perfectly intelligible to the worshipping community as significant gestures and symbols of everyday life, being invested, through the outpouring of the Holy Spirit, with a deeper and divine significance. Because of a less polarised split between the sacred and the profane, prior to the modern era, there never was a sense of a totally secular sphere of reality, totally devoid of immanent divine presence and spiritual significance. Paradoxically, the virtual reification of the sacraments in the early modern period, coupled with their popular presentation as the only true resource of divine grace, may well have contributed to a loss of the sacred sense of all objects and actions.

This is a development quite foreign to our native religious sensibility. Reading through sources like Fr O Laoghaire's *Ár bPaidreacha Dúchais* or A. Carmichael's *Ortha nan Gaidheal*[21] provides a beautiful reminder of how, for the generations who went before us, all of life and every aspect of living was shot through with the glory of Christ's presence. Happily, all of this is being rediscovered and celebrated in a contemporary way, though its potential for liturgical renewal has scarcely been realised. Especially in a secularised world, it is crucial that we do so for, otherwise, the acceptance of the legitimate autonomy of the secular will easily slide into a thoroughgoing secularism which systematically eliminates the religious and the spiritual from every aspect of life.

If we celebrate baptism nearly always as infant baptism, then how does our celebration build on the experience of nurturing and welcoming infants and supporting the mothers and families who do so? How can the celebration of the sacrament of reconciliation incorporate the many ways people are seeking and experiencing reconciliation to-day? How is the relationship between bread and hunger and sharing and social apartheid addressed in the symbolism of the eucharistic bread and wine? If matrimony signifies and celebrates an indissoluble union, then how shall we organise ourselves to critique and replace the socio-economic structures that trivialise and commercialise all relationships? How can care for the body and the rediscovery of the healing powers of therapy with oils be re-incorporated into the sacrament of the sick? And how is it that Irish people working abroad can contribute so meaningfully to the exploration of these issues in other cultures but we cannot do so at home?

Communication

One of the principal characteristics of our emerging secularised culture and one with the most far-reaching consequences, is the fact that the church has little or no influence over the flow of information. In itself, this is a good thing. Vatican II stated clearly that access to information was a human right. No institution, least of all the church, should wish to control access to information in the sense of wanting to dictate to people how much or how little they should know about things that affect their lives.

In Ireland as elsewhere, the media, especially television, have replaced the church as the forum where public opinion is formed. Not only have the ideas which are being circulated, discussed and which form the public consciousness changed, but the idiom in which these ideas are explored has been profoundly and irreversibly altered. In theory, these changes have been in the direction of openness, truthfulness, accountability, democratisation, pluralism, the rights of the individual, tolerance and consensus, though the reality may be somewhat different. Increasingly, the media have to answer to market criteria rather than to social goals with an ethical basis shaped either by tradition or consensus.

To a significant degree, the selection of topics, the filtering of information and the pre-established boundaries to debate operate in parallel with the interests of dominant socio-economic groups. This would seem to be supported by an analysis of how policy, content and orientation change with ownership, all the more disturbing as single companies and even single individuals acquire more and more control of the media. Moreover, the power of advertising revenue tends to turn communications into semi-permanent diversion resulting in a terrible dulling of people's capacity for reflection. One need only reflect on the manner in which a thirty-second sound-bite can present an emotionally potent over-simplification as unassailable truth. Often, rather than reporting consensus, the media are actually manufacturing consent.

While the task of humanising and evangelising culture demands that the people of God pay attention to these issues, what is equally important is the manner in which they do so. In a certain sense, the world sets the agenda for the church. The spirit of the times, ephemeral as it often is, cannot determine the substance of the Christian gospel and catechesis, but it can determine the manner in which that gospel may be meaningfully communicated. The gospel is, above all, a truth to be communicated and the contemporary idiom of communication demands that this be, as far as possible, open, public, linked to experience, credible, consistent, creating space for freedom and participation, reasoned and justifiable as well as being broadly intelligible.

These issues cannot be tackled simply by having Christian mass media, even though there may be a place for these. The evangelisation of post-Christian culture has to be done in terms which are intelligible to that culture and the manner in which it creates meaning – even though there is also the important parallel task of critiquing the assumptions and methods according to which that meaning is created. The church must abandon the idea of being a 'perfect society' with all the means for its own life at its disposal – and one might add, under its control. Instead, it must conceive of itself in dynamic and creative terms as a movement or community in the process of self-constitution. We are not in the business of protecting the church – as if it already existed in some final, perfect and unalterable form – but rather in the process of making the church come about.

The media, as communications industry, unconsciously at least, broadly share the presuppositions and goals of advanced capitalism, though not unambiguously. The orientation of reflective self-critical journalists as well as the media industry's own need to uncover more and more information to feed the addictions it has itself created, means that the system is being both legitimated and undermined at the same time. Almost as if the church – as system – knows that the same thing will happen to itself, it is suspicious of the media. Yet that, as we have seen in recent years, simply makes it an easier and softer target. For better or worse – and on balance, it is probably for the better – the media have become the playing field where the game for the minds and hearts of the public is being played out.

The church must participate in this game as an equal; neither expecting nor demanding any privileges – it won't get any anyhow! Participation begins by so obviously living out the gospel that its lifestyle is permanently newsworthy. It is probably true – as Paul VI is reported to have once said of Le Monde – that the media are usually much more interested in the sensational and conflictual aspects of church life, than they are in the inner reality and truth of the church. Yet in a secular society, it is hardly the task of the media to promote the church as church, just as it is not their right to gratuitously undermine it. They are supposed to report the news: just as the Christian community is supposed to make news – by living out the gospel. If there are sensations and disagreements in church life, no service is done to the gospel by systematically hiding them. What distinguishes the church is not the absence of any falling-short of what it professes but rather the values manifested in the way it faces up to these shortcomings.

If there are aspects of the communications industry that are perceived to be indifferent or even hostile to the gospel, then these are to be confronted not by seeking to stay aloof from the media, but by participating on the media's own terms with an indisputable commitment to the truly human values the media claims to seek to promote – and which committed journalists certainly do promote – and in the name of which they often feel it necessary to criticise the church. If truthfulness, openness, a spirit of dialogue, reliability, accountability and access to information are the values to which the communications industry aspires, then the church should be transparently communicating with its own members and with the world at large, according to these same values. And not only to win the sympathy of the media, but because this is demanded by the very nature of the gospel which is above all, a truth to be communicated, to be communicated on the basis of its own inherent truthfulness.

Reconciliation and justice

The war in the North of Ireland is not a religious war but it certainly has a religious dimension. This is not the place to resume the virtually endless permutations of the political debate and commentary, yet neither can one simply side-step the issue as if the renewal of the church were not connected to justice and reconciliation in the North. In fact, just as in the case of unemployment, so too in relation to the Northern conflict: the acid test for the power of the gospel and the credibility of the church is the ability to contribute meaningfully to the elaboration of a just political solution.

The role of the church – of all the ecclesial communions – must extend far beyond the condemnation of atrocities and the consolation of victims, important as these ministries undoubtedly are. Everything both Protestants and Catholics say about the power of Christ and the truth of the gospel and the divine origins of the church, is called into question when the churches are perceived to be powerless to bring the power of the gospel they proclaim as the truth of human existence, to bear on the search for justice and reconciliation. The difficulty of the task can scarcely be underestimated nor should the sincerity of many individuals and bodies be doubted, but the question has to be asked both for the sake of reconciliation as well as for the credibility of the church.

In political and in cultural terms, different ecclesial communions may well want different things; but the ethical basis and the human values out of which their members articulate their different socio-political goals cannot be irreconcilably different if, in fact, they are both informed by the desire to live out the gospel of Jesus. Perhaps this is the great task – and also the great risk – that the churches must undertake: to examine the human values that lie at the base of their respective socio-political visions, in the light of the values of God's kingdom as revealed in the gospels. For, perhaps, only in this way can the people to whom and for whom they wish to speak begin the journey towards political consensus on a sure enough footing of ever getting there.

The role of the church is not political in a party-political sense but it certainly is in the deeper sense of clarifying the human values – informed by the gospel – which are the cornerstones and building-blocks of a just political order. The churches cannot avoid this even if they want to, because every theology is political, even one that does not speak or think in explicitly political terms. If we do not take the trouble to work out the political implications of our theologies as well as the theological implications of our politics, we may simply be consolidating and legitimating the existing divisions.

We can neither receive nor believe in the gospel except in the context of personal and communal decisions for transformation. The truth of Christ is not just a theoretical truth. Only insofar as the churches are formally and consistently engaged in a common project of mutually establishing the value system that stands at the base of a just society and political order, can they be said to really believe in the power of the gospel to transform society and the human heart. There is a great risk here calling for courage and the faith to live on the basis of the gospel and God's grace; and consequently, the readiness to change.

For the churches may discover that what they actually stand for, as distinct from what they would like to think they stand for, includes to a greater or lesser degree – in addition to many fine and noble things – a clinging to local socio-political power, a fear of truly encountering the other as sister or brother in Christ and of encountering their tradition as Christian, a desire to control people's lives, being wilfully sunk in a very selective memory and the abuse of religious categories to conceal any real desire for socio-political change for fear it might mean a loss of power. It is easy for all sides to see such shortcomings in other groups; not so easy to see them in one's own.

A possible starting-point might be the willingness to jointly examine whether in their statements and initiatives, they truly possess and express that parity of sympathy, protest and compassion suggested by one honourable protagonist. Jointly working on what must be appropriated and what must be jettisoned in their value-systems and hidden agenda to achieve that parity, would be a significant exercise in clarification and a condition for a new beginning.

The willingness to be political in this more basic sense applies not only to the church's ministry in the north but throughout the island of Ireland. The previous implicit church-state arrangement in the twenty-six counties is rapidly fading, but that does not mean either that we should be busy trying to restore it or lamely accepting to be closeted in a purely private sphere of the country's life. It would be shameful and cowardly for the church not to wish to publicly contribute to the new and more inclusive, just and participative notion of Irish identity that is sorely needed. Arguably, no other group is more equipped to do so.

Yet the present situation of relative liminality is not without its blessings. For it is obliging the church to make certain options about its apostolic priorities and internal organisation. The condition for the church proposing gospel values as the basis of a just society, is to be first radically converted to those values itself. Only then can it clarify its social goals – become clear not only about what it is against, but of what it is in favour – and then facilitate the nation in doing the same.

Initially, that may well take a critical or even negative form; critiquing the assumptions and results of the consumerism and dependency we have allowed our elected representatives to choose for us. That critique, sustained as it will need to be, must open out into the articulation of alternative models of socio-political organisation since the present one is not only not working, but is extremely destructive of our environment, our culture and our social fabric.

Articulating and implementing such alternatives as well as building the political movements which will attempt to make them come into being, is not the direct task and responsibility of the church leadership who will always do well to keep their distance from direct political power. Their task is to facilitate the process whereby the human values and ethical principles undergirding a just society can be clarified and articulated. But this articulation can take place only in the process of constructing alternatives or else it remains disembodied. This construction of alternative models of socio-political organisation is itself a process open to critique in the light of human experience informed by the gospel.

The gospel has political implications, even if we wished it didn't have, since there cannot be an active presence in the world which is apolitical. The church as church, does not seek political power but it must shoulder political responsibility in empowering its members to clarify the values implicit in their political culture. It is a matter of being at the heart of things without wishing to control them: of wishing to be a source of energy, clarification and direction without desiring privileges from the power thereby generated. It is an invitation to dwell in the space where politics and spirituality meet: neither disembodied spirituality nor worldly power; rather, a political love of the world that respects the world's autonomy.

The call to holiness

In the final analysis, the church exists to be the continuation in history of the mission of Jesus: to propose to humankind that its destiny lies in a loving communion with God, mediated by the process of constructing a compassionate society of equals. It proposes to the restless, searching and oftentimes divided human heart that it was made for God and that it will remain restless, searching and divided until it turns to God and finds its home in God's infinite compassion. It proposes to the human spirit that a rootedness in this divine compassion is the only sure foundation for a socio-political order incorporating the rights of the human person and justice for all. By contrast, it suggests that systematic inattention to this transcendant dimension of the human spirit and to its destiny in union with God, cuts off the quest of the human person for fullness of life from its very foundation and deepest resource. It claims that history demonstrates that the result will be either a heartless totalitarianism or a corrupting narcissism, both of which lead to even greater cruelty and exploitation of the poor and vulnerable.

Yet religious discourse must not be mere ideology. There are too many examples in history of religious language being abused to legitimate structures of power and privilege. To-day religious language has little enough significance unless it is the clear articulation of unmistakeable religious experience. If the church is to speak about God at all, it must do so out of a profound on-going experience of God. Religion, after all, is not the same thing as God. The church, especially in and through all those who exercise ministry in it, can only call people into a deep experience of God when that same experience is the context and rootedness of its own being and action. Only a church which is in love with God can invite the world to surrender its egoism in favour of that love. This cannot be concocted and it cannot be substituted in learning, culture or power. Its many imitations are eventually seen for what they are, bu,t when it is real, it is unmistakeable. More importantly perhaps, it is arresting and attractive and life-giving; for there is nothing so beautiful as God.

This historical moment then, is the occasion for an ever more profound journey into the heart of God. Just as the church expresses its mystical and divine reality in the praxis of a visible and historical community, so does this community disclose its mystical and divine heart in its daily exercise of historical responsibility. If and when it does, it is recognised for what it is; because the capacity to recognise these things is written in every human heart.

But this call to holiness of life must be contextualised. It must not be hived off into a call for more prayer and self-sacrifice without reference to the issues of the day. That would be alienation, not spirituality; and we have already had far too much of it. Christian holiness is always an incarnated holiness; a profound entry into the heart of God, within an immersion in the struggles of the present. For this is where God is: not 'in his heaven' but upon God's earth. Here, among the hopes and joys and conflicts of today, is this infinite compassion pouring itself out upon all creatures. Here and only here, is Christ crucified until the end of time: and, in that cross, in which even a sinful world is loved unconditionally, there shines forth the glory of his resurrection as he 'easters' in us and draws all things to himself.

The secularisation of society discloses that it is not the sociologically religious act which makes the Christian. It is rather, the conscious and freely chosen participation in God's redemptive suffering love for all creation in the real world. Only then may we worship. For God dwells neither in Jerusalem nor Mt Gerazim but only in the spiritual and truthful project of constructing what Paul VI called 'a civilisation of love'. The church expresses God's solidarity with humankind in an unambiguous solidarity with the people of our own time in their hopes and struggles.

To-day, this solidarity calls for an unambiguous option for the oppressed, even an identification with them, that allows their struggle to be the aperture that illuminates the very nature of the church. In a particular way, it demands a new sensitivity and openness to the feminine and radically transformed structures of dialogue and participation within the Christian community itself.

But not even conversion is a recipe for worldly success. Christ guarantees not success but fidelity and asks the same of us. In that struggle to be faithful, selfishness, illusion and discouragement trespass and all too easily impose themselves. Only the shadow of the cross prevents us from being blinded by the glare of our failures. But our very weakness forces us to 'cast ourselves upon the Lord' to discover that God always sustains us. And in that deeper dependence upon God, we glimpse the joy and wholeness of an even deeper rootedness in this divine compassion.

We are witnessing what is perhaps the greatest ever watershed in the self-constitution of the church; perhaps only three or four other periods in its history are even comparable. Potentially, it is a moment of monumental significance in the religious history of humankind. To be worthy of it, we must seek our identity in Jesus Christ and nowhere else. We are being called to a profound conversion; an openness of mind and heart to the Holy Spirit; an invitation to become the poor in spirit to whom the kingdom is given; the pure in heart who see God.

1. See pp. 179-185 below.

2. S.T. Suppl., q.8. a.2, SC., ad1 and ad2; a.3, SC.

3. I have given the text as translated in W.M. Abbott ed., *The Documents of Vatican II* (Dublin, 1966) p. 715, which is the standard work in English. The original read: *Altera e la sostanza dell'antica doctrina del depositum fidei, ed altera e la formulazione del suo rivestimento*. There has been much controversy about this sentence. Pope John XXIII composed the speech himself in Italian, but it was delivered in a Latin translation to which the words *eodem tamen sensu eademque sententia* (with nevertheless the same sense and the same meaning) were added by others. This addition, with resonances of the anti-Modernist oath, was presumably intended to uphold a fixed view of doctrinal formulation, but it qualifies the meaning of the Italian text. (The preceding two sentences in the speech were also changed and their open and forthright tone neutralised). It is the edited version that appears in official documents. P. Hebblethwaite in *John XXIII: Pope of the Council*, (London, 1984), argues that a Latin version of the original speech can be found in the transcript provided by Vatican radio and that the version published in the official documents (A.A.S.) contains the alterations, which only became known to the Pope some weeks later. However, in the *Tablet*, 25/1/1992. p.108, he seems to say that this phrase was used in the Latin text of the Pope's opening address to the council, while still arguing for a difference between the Italian text prepared by the Pope and the 'official' text prepared by someone else (probably Mgr Zannoni). Perhaps the most telling point, as F. Sullivan argues in *Tablet* 1/2/1992, and the clue to the Pope's real intent, is that Pope John gave instructions to his secretary, Mgr Loris Capovilla, to publish the Italian version, without the amendments and that subsequently it was always this version that the Pope quoted. (cf. Fr Sullivan's letter for references.) (Because of its colloquial style, I have given Hebblethwaite's translation of this text on the opening page.)

4. *Documentation Catholique*, 56, 71 (1974). p.163, c.2.

5. '...certain concepts have somehow arisen out of these new conditions and insinuated themselves into the fabric of human society. These concepts present profit as the chief spur to economic progress, free competition as the guiding norm of economics, and private ownership of the means of production as an absolute right, having no limits nor concomitant social obligations.

This unbridled 'liberalism' paves the way for a particular type of tyranny rightly condemned by our predecessor Pius XI, for it results in the 'international imperialism of money'.

Such improper manipulations of economic forces 'can never be condemned enough'; let it be said once again that economics is supposed to be in the service of the human person.' *A.A.S.* 59 (1967), 257-299, no. 26.

6. F. Mc Donogh in 'Saving Santo Domingo' in the *Tablet* 30/1/93, pp. 128-129 says that the changes were ordered by the Vatican.

7. Compare G.Gutierrez, *A Theology of Liberation*, (New York, 1973) p. 49, with *Libertatis Conscientiae*, (C.D.F., Vatican City, 22/3/86) No. 74.

8. R. Greenacre, 'Epistola ad Romanos' in *The Month*, No. 1503, March 1993, pp. 88-96, esp. p. 90.

9. Text published in *Origins* 1, July 1976, pp 92-96.

10. J. O'Brien, 'St Paul's attitude to women' in *Al-Mushir*, Summer 1992, pp. 3-12.

11. *Inter Insigniores*, C.D.F., *A.A.S.* (1977) 98-196.

12. *Summa Theologiae*, IIa IIae 177, a.2, SC and R; IIa IIae 164, a.2, R and ad1: III, 67, a.4, R and ad3: III, 78, a.4, ad2: III, 82. a.5, R: III, 78, a.4, ad2.

13. The ecclesial and communitarian nature of ordained ministry is even more apparent when these oft-quoted words are put in context: 'What I am for you terrifies me; what I am with you consoles me. For you I am a bishop: but with you I am a Christian. The former is a title of duty; the latter, one of grace. The former is a danger; the latter, salvation.' (St Augustine, *Sermon* 340,1.) For the Latin text cf. Migne (Paris, 1865 ed.) PL, 38, 1483.

14. Council of Chalcedon, Canon 6. Cf. Ed. N. Tanner, *Documents of the Ecumenical Councils* (Georgetown, 1992), Vol.1, p.9. Note the nuanced comments on this by E. Schillebeeckx in *Ministry* (New York, 1981), p.153, n.55.

15. In relation to much of what is being discussed here, it is interesting to recall the reflections of St Juliana on Christ as Mother, in the *Showings* (long text), especially in Chapters 57-63. *Juliana of Norwich: Showings*, (New York, 1978), pp.290f.. With reference to my suggestion that in the Paschal Mystery, Christ, as the exem-

plar of redeemed human existence in and through his 'perfect' self-donation to the Father-Mother and to humanity, achieves complete individuation and, in this sense, transcends the limitations of gender, consider the following text from St Juliana: 'The second Person [of the Trinity], who is our Mother, substantially the same beloved person has now become our mother sensually, because we are double by God's creating, that is to say substantial and sensual ... in our Mother Christ we profit and increase, and in mercy he reforms and restores us, and by the power of his Passion, his Death and his Resurrection he unites us to our substance.' *Ibid.* p.294. It is difficult to see how such a Christ could not be 'represented' by a woman disciple! On the writings of the mystics as sources for systematic theology, cf. K. Rahner, 'Faith between Rationality and Emotion', *Theological Investigations* Vol 16 (1983). Since Catholic theology answers not only to academe but to the lived ecclesial faith of the People of God, a bridge must always remain between the language of abstract systematics and that of lived faith, hope and love.'

16. I refer once again (cf. n2) to St Thomas' reflections on the quasi-sacramentality of confession to a layperson: 'But when there is reason for urgency, the penitent should fulfill his own part, by being contrite and confessing to whom he can; and although this person cannot perfect the sacrament (*quamvis sacramentum perficere non possit*), so as to fulfill the part of the priest by giving absolution, yet this defect is supplied by the High Priest (*defectum tamen sacerdotis summus sacerdos supplet*). Nevertheless confession made to a layperson through lack of a priest is quasi-sacramental, although it is not a perfect sacrament (*sacramentalis est quodammodo* [Deferrari translates 'quodammodo' as 'in a measure'], *quamvis non sit sacramentum perfectum...*') ST., Supplementum q.8, a.2, ad 1. I can see no binding theological reason why we cannot follow St Thomas' line of thought and include in contemporary sacramental practice, a rite whereby, in urgent cases, of which there are surely many, people could choose to 'confess' in the manner that brought them the deepest experience of reconciliation and then celebrate this ecclesially and communally, during perhaps Advent and Lent, in a liturgical service in which they would receive sacramental absolution from a presbyter.

17. cf. A. Teetaert, *La Confession aux laiques dans l'Eglise latine depuis le VIIIe jusqu'au XIVe siecle* (Paris, 1926) esp. pp. 44f., pp. 90f., pp. 119f., pp. 260f., and pp. 324f..

18. J. H. Newman, *The Arians of the Fourth Century* (London, Longman Green, 1908) p. 445, Note v.

19. This opinion is developed by Cardinal Ratzinger in his book, *Rapporto sulla Fede*, translated as *The Ratzinger Report* (1985), in which he sought to portray the reception and implementation of the council as characterised by 'dissent', 'self-destruction', 'decadence' and 'heretical deviation'. Needless to say, the book raised a storm of protest. Cf. 'Ratzinger's sad book' in the *Tablet*, 13/7/1985, pp. 723-724. (The author of this review article remained anonymous but his style is not difficult to recognise.) The book is a development of an article published by the cardinal in November 1983 which called for the 'restoration of pre-Vatican II values' (cf. p. 138 above) and was instrumental in the word 'restorationism' becoming a term for the overall thrust of the present, fairly co-ordinated reactionary movements in the church. While Cardinal Ratzinger is Prefect of the C.D.F., the views expressed in these publications cannot be said to represent or commit the Holy See. In an interview with *National Catholic News Service* on 19/8/1985, Pope John Paul II stated that these were simply the personal views of Cardinal Ratzinger.

20. Cf. J.O'Brien, *Theology and the Option for the Poor*, (Collegeville) 1992, esp. pp.78-92.

21. Edinburgh (1900).